A SERVANT OF
MANY MASTERS

A SERVANT OF MANY MASTERS

The Life and Times of

Carlo Goldoni

TIMOTHY HOLME

JUPITER · LONDON

First published in 1976 by
JUPITER BOOKS (LONDON) LIMITED
167 Hermitage Road, London N4

SBN 904041 611

Printed and bound by
R. J. Acford Limited, Chichester, Sussex

FOR MY MOTHER

WHO SHOULD HAVE BEEN

A GOLDONI ACTRESS

BY THE SAME AUTHOR

Mamma Mia
Gondola, Gondolier
The Penguin Italian Reader
Viaggio a Roma

CONTENTS

ILLUSTRATIONS

The line-drawings illustrating the four half-titles pages are taken from the Pasquali edition of Goldoni's works (*Fotografia Ferruzzi*)

Prologue

In that part of Paris which was later to become *les Halles*, not far from the foot of Montmartre, the tubby little old gentleman who spoke French with a marked Italian accent was well known to everybody by sight. He was poor and close on eighty, but he always seemed cheerful and walked with a spring in his step. He took a keen interest in the life of the streets, peering benignly at everybody with his one good eye (for the other was blind) and he seemed particularly fascinated by the young maidservants who fluttered and chirruped about the stalls, doing the morning's shopping.

He had a wife, but she was rarely seen out. It was he who did the shopping, while she stayed at home in the *rue pavée Saint-Sauveur,* and besides she was shy and spoke practically no French at all, although they had been living in France for many years. Just occasionally the old couple would go out for a stroll together when the weather was fine, and on these occasions he did his best to avert his eyes from the maidservants.

There were various theories about the old gentleman's past. Some thought he had once held a high position at court, others that he had been a diplomat. It was said that he gave Italian lessons, and a bookseller had put it about that he was involved in the literary trade.

Nobody, except for a few intimate friends with more than one foot in the grave already, was aware that he was the greatest comic playwright Italy had ever seen, the author of more than 150 plays, and that he had reformed the theatre of his native land, compelling the old *Commedia dell'Arte* to give way to a new comedy of manners. The name Carlo Goldoni, if anybody happened to notice it on a bill or a receipt, meant nothing.

As for Goldoni himself, he was content to be anonymous. It was his way to take life as it came to him, never to be inflamed with anger or inebriated with joy. He had not the slightest fear of death which he regarded as no more than the common tribute to nature, and so he did not resent that other seeming death which had fallen upon him as a playwright more than a decade before.

But while he walked the streets of Paris, he surely must have let his mind wander into the past, as is the way with old gentlemen.

Back to the years, not so long ago, with the French court, teaching Italian to the princesses. Such condescension and affability! He remembered the day when he had so unexpectedly lost his sight, and his pupil, Princess Adelaide, had insisted upon tending him personally, showering him with a thousand attentions.

And that evening of evenings when his play *Le bourru bienfaisant* – thought and penned in his own French whatever the malicious might say – had triumphed at the greatest theatre in the land, the home of his beloved and revered Molière, the *Comédie Française.*

He preferred not to remember the sorrow of his departure from Venice, and to dwell instead on the clamorously Goldonian way he had bid farewell to his countrymen. He had written a play for them called *One of the last evenings of carnival*, and everybody in Venice had known that Anzoletto, the designer for the cloth-makers who was leaving for Paris (no, no, not Paris – it had been Moscow in the play, Moscow) – everybody knew that that same Anzoletto was really Goldoni saying goodbye to his public. '*Bon voyage!*' they had called, 'Come back soon!' Anzoletto had promised to return in two years, but Goldoni was never to see Venice again.

Unhappy memories were always dismissed because they might disturb his usually excellent digestion and sleep. But even he could not put from his mind altogether the echoes of that ferocious, long drawn-out campaign of hatred which, even if he would not admit that it had driven him from Venice, had at least made the call of France seem more tempting. He remembered the baying of the Testicular Academy and, at its head, Carlo Gozzi, the Solitary One, who had never been able to forgive him. For what? In spite of the thousands of words that Gozzi had poured out on the subject, Goldoni had never really known the answer to that. And Baretti, that roaring literary barbarian from Turin whose loathing had been, if anything, even more concentrated and inexplicable than Gozzi's. Then the Abbé Chiari, poor, muddle-headed one-time Jesuit who, if plagiary were indulgence, would have discounted an eternity of Hell-fire.

But he preferred to think of the actresses. Oh, the actresses! Even though some of them had been twice as terrible as Gozzi and Baretti rolled into one. The green-eyed Passalacqua with the dagger pointed at her breast, and Maddalena, the beautiful young Venetian, for whom he had written *La*

Locandiera; Caterina Bresciani with the body full of furious fits and starts, and poor little Baccherini whom death had overtaken so unexpectedly. . . .

So many actresses, but only one Nicoletta – resigned, solicitous, tender and, every so often when things got out of hand, timidly rebellious. He recalled his first sight of her in Genoa almost half a century before. One morning he had spotted a pretty face at a window across the street from his own. That was the sort of opportunity he never missed in those days, though he could scarcely have foreseen that this time the adventure would end in marriage. Nor could she have guessed how that glance from her bedroom window would have uprooted her from her quiet life as the daughter of a Genoese notary and whisked her off on a long and hectic whirl across Europe, from city to city, from catastrophe to triumph, from penury to wealth and back again, as the wife of the Reformer of the Italian stage.

Yet had Nicoletta ever really appreciated his great reform? Had her mind ever gone beyond the home, even if they were homeless? And in that incredible year of the sixteen plays, the challenge that had set the Grand Canal on fire, had she ever seen more than the sleepless nights, the ruined meals, the expenditure on candles?

As Goldoni walked, his mind must have ranged ceaselessly over the events, the plays, the people, the places which had crowded his long life. The Red Priest – what was his name? – Vivaldi, muttering his office, scratching testily through his papers and finally hurling his breviary across the room with a howl of triumph as Goldoni pulled off the impossible feat of producing, there and then, effortlessly, the perfect words for an eight-verse aria.

Those early years with the Imer company when the leading lady was Zanetta Casanova, Giacomo's mother. In his mind's eye he saw her vast figure and raddled old woman's face, thick with make-up, but immediately he substituted the vision with the more pleasing one of a lovely and talented young widow.

Farther and farther back in time he went – every story clearer now as he almost unconsciously moulded and shaped it than when it had taken place – to those first unforgettably heady encounters with the theatre when it had been impossible to distinguish between the excitement of the stage itself and that generated by the actresses upon it. He had first seen real actresses – as opposed to boys in female clothes – when he was fourteen and boarded out in Rimini, studying with the Dominicans. That company, whose arrival had altered the course of his entire life, had been managed by Florindo dei Maccheroni whose pockets were always stuffed with richly seasoned pasta which he ate while he was on the stage. And when these players had left Rimini to sail for Chioggia he had run away with them. Three days of high seas and high life, with the girl who played the parts of the maidservants arousing the strangest feelings in him, and the leading lady's cat falling into the sea and drowning. . . .

And beyond even that to his first play, written when he was a little boy, which had caused such a furore in the family; and then as far back as his mind could reach, to early childhood in Venice, when the Goldonis had been rich for a while, and the canal moved sluggishly below their windows, sometimes glinting in the sun. . . .

So sooner or later, back at home in the *rue pavée Saint-Sauveur*, Carlo Goldoni pulled out a sheet of paper and began to write. 'I was born in Venice in the year 1707, in a fine, large house between the Nomboli bridge and the bridge of the Honest Woman, at the corner of the street of the Hundred Years' Old House, in the parish of St Thomas. . . .'

The 104 Escapades of Harlequin
or
The Ingenuous Adventurer

I

*'It is undeniable that I was born under the influence of a star
of comedy'*
Carlo Goldoni

In Venice the past is never a thing of the past. It mingles so much with the present that it is often difficult to tell the two apart, just as it is sometimes hard to distinguish between Venetians and non-Venetians as they interweave in a narrow *calle*. It is almost as though the grim reaper were not quite so ruthlessly efficient in Venice as he is elsewhere.

This sense of the past existing on equal terms with the present is effectively shattered once you are inside Goldoni's birthplace, for it is got up as a museum, the Museo Ca' Goldoni – all glass cases and hushed voices (although the theatrical library which it also houses is one of the friendliest and least formal in Italy). But the spell of the past still holds good outside, or in the courtyard with its formidable marble staircase leading up to the first-floor front door, or by the iron grating through which you can look out onto a desolate little canal with cabbage-stalks floating by in slow majesty.

Once upon a time the house belonged to a family of jewellers, and it looks it, being of three floors and built in an opulent Venetian-Gothic style. This well suited the Goldoni life-style as it then was, for the family was rich. How exactly the money was made is not known, but it was certainly due to a mixture of shrewd business-sense and a streak of adventurousness which never prevented the male Goldonis from being too particular about a quick trip on the windy side of the law. Both these qualities can be found in Carlo, and they were also in the make-up of his grandfather – another Carlo – who brought the family from

Modena, where it had its origins, to Venice. (Goldoni, in fact, is not a Venetian name, and at the time of writing does not appear once in the Venetian telephone directory.)

Through influential friends – Italian ways change little over the centuries – grandfather Carlo got himself a handsomely paid post as one of the directors of what amounted to the Chamber of Commerce. This enabled him to run not only the town house, but a country villa on the River Sile where – the future most unmistakably casting its shadow – he was able to satisfy his passion for the theatre with a private playhouse, where all the most talented Venetian actors and musicians were only too happy to perform.

When his first wife died, grandfather Carlo, left with a grown son named Giulio, took to himself a widow, and as she was the mother of two grown-up daughters, what could be more convenient than to marry off the elder to Giulio? Her name was Margherita Salvioni and her first-born son, all of eighty years later, was to write of her that she was 'a pretty dark-haired girl' and that 'although she limped slightly, she was nevertheless vivacious and exceedingly likeable'.

The four of them, together with Margherita's unmarried sister, lived in the large house near the Nomboli bridge (this bridge no longer exists, the little *rio* which it spanned having been filled in) and it was there, on 25th February 1707, that Carlo was born.

Both time and place could hardly have been more appropriate. Carnival, which was always to be Goldoni's element, was at its height, and the house, five minutes' walk from the Rialto, was at the very heart of that Venice which Goldoni was to paint in play after play and with which he never went wrong; for, though he wrote more than his fair share of rubbish, when the scene was Venice and the characters were Venetians, he was infallible.

At the moment when he was born, this 'most Italian of Italian cities' had long passed its midday of power and, in the brilliantly lit evening, was toppling to ruin. But the headlong fall was every bit as exhilarating as an upward flight and so much less effort. Every one of the 150,000 inhabitants seemed dedicated exclusively to pleasure. Carnival lasted from Christmas to Shrove Tuesday, and then reigned again from the first Sunday in October till Advent and for fifteen days at the Ascension. There was dancing in all the *campielli* and banquets at the Lido or Mestre (no factories then). Every occasion or none was an excuse for fireworks and regattas on the Grand Canal. There were sixteen theatres as opposed to two in London and three in Paris. From Easter Monday until September on every Sunday and holiday there were the *freschi* (from fresh, alluding to the fresh air) at which brilliantly dressed ladies and gentlemen floated down the Grand Canal in their gondolas – flirting, gossiping and eyeing each other – from the Piazzetta off St Mark's Square to where the railway station is today; and, at a slightly lower social level, there was a regular gondola parade of tarts, delicately known as the *Corso delle Cortigiane* and held in the Rio della Sensa at Sant'Alvise.

Goldoni himself gives a vivid portrait of it all. 'At midnight as at midday you can see food of every possible description displayed for sale in Venice, all the drinking houses are open and delicious meals are prepared in the hotels and restaurants; although society dinners are not very common, people join together with freedom and animosity at little supper parties, snacks and picnics. In summer St Mark's Square and its surroundings are thronged by night as by day, the cafés are always filled with merry crowds of men and women of every type. In the squares and in the streets and on the canals they sing; merchants sing as they sell their wares, workmen sing as they leave their work, gondoliers sing as they wait for their masters. The very essence of the Republic is merriment and of the Venetian language, wit.'

Like pollution today, sex was almost perceptible and tangible in the air. 'There is no place in the world where liberty and licence reign more sovereign,' wrote Président De Brosses. There were, in fact, twice as many whores in Venice as in Paris – a count made at the end of the sixteenth century established the figure at exactly 11,654 – and the very convents, which acted as finishing schools for young ladies, took their duty of instruction to limits that many parents might have considered excessive. 'Venice', wrote one French visitor, 'hasn't got a brothel. It is one.' When a new papal nuncio came to Venice ferocious rivalry broke out among three convents which all wanted the honour of supplying him with a mistress from among their own charges. De Brosses describes the dresses of these girls as showing as much neck and shoulders as those of French actresses. The goings-on in the convents are perhaps less surprising when one remembers that religion itself had been reduced to a decorative, but quite meaningless part of social life; the *cicisbei*, those more or less adulterous gallants who accompanied married ladies, waited at church doors to offer finger-tips, dipped in holy water, to their mistresses emerging from mass. The whole thing was neatly summed up by a catch of the time which said, 'Ala matina una meseta, al dopo disnar una basseta, e ala sera una doneta' – 'a little mass in the morning, a card game of *bassetta* after lunch and a woman in the evening'.

But the supreme Venetian vice, which outdid even sex and reached epidemic proportions, was gambling; the very children learnt their alphabets from cards with aces and knaves on them, and in an effort to contain the mania which was bleeding Venice white, the government, in 1638, authorized Marco Dandolo to open an official gaming house in his palace at San Moisé. It came to be known as the *ridotto* or annex, which is what it literally was. The foyer was reserved for promenading and *conversazioni*, and, leading off it, there were two bars, one for coffee, tea and chocolate, the other for cheese, salame, fruit and wine. Beyond the foyer stretched out the ten silent rooms where the real business of the *ridotto* was conducted. Here, at long lines of tables, Venetians and foreigners played at *bassetta, faraone, biribisso, panfil* and *sette e mezza*. And the banks were held by patricians. The *ridotto* was enlarged, and then another one was opened, and the fever continued to rise until, in 1774, the Republic, in desperation, decided to close down both houses. This made little difference, however, as practically every private house in the Republic ran its own games. Indeed, it was considered essential in high society to have a special apartment near St Mark's Square exclusively for gambling, and these private enterprises sometimes developed into clubs with their own membership list. One noblewoman, Lucrezia Nani, went a step further by hiring two con-men to entice rich foreigners into her private gambling salon.

Clearly in such an atmosphere money-values were likely to have a dream-like quality about them and Venetian ducats and sequins were often no more substantial than fairy-gold. So it is hardly surprising that, what with gambling, entertaining and generally living like a lord, grandfather Goldoni, whom even his grandson describes as 'a good man, but scarcely thrifty', should have run through a great part of the family wealth by the time of his death. There is some confusion about this last event because, while the grandson puts it at 1712, documents suggest that it took place before the boy was even born; facts were never Goldoni's strong point. What is certain, however, is that during Goldoni's early youth, the family **was reduced to comparatively poor circumstances.**

It was characteristically at this point that Carlo's younger brother, Gian Paolo, was born – the first of a series of disastrous entrances which he was to make from time to time throughout the Italian part of Goldoni's life and which invariably heralded trouble. Indeed, with Gian Paolo for a brother, it was lucky for Goldoni that he was by nature pacific and never let himself be unduly put-out – a temperament which he claims was due to the fact that his mother bore him without pain and loved him the more for it, 'and since I did not cry on my first appearance in the light of the world, this gentleness seemed from the beginning to manifest my pacific character which has never changed'. Indeed, he goes on with that disarming smugness which is one of the characteristics of his *Mémoires* to say that he was the joy of the whole family.

But no amount of joy in their first-born could solve the money problems and, as was his habit in moments of crisis, Giulio, the father, slipped discreetly away from the scene. Ostensibly, he went to Rome to study medicine and in fact, after four years, he set up in practice. But recently discovered documents suggest that, rather than a qualified doctor, he was a quack with a charming bedside manner. Even Carlo, who doted on his father as a man, cannot have had a very high opinion of his medical qualifications or skills, for, of the decision to go to Rome, he wrote that 'as he always avoided being a prey to sad thoughts he decided to go to Rome to enjoy himself'. And later, when Giulio was actually tending the sick, he wrote of him that 'having the skill to avoid those illnesses which he didn't understand, he was able to cure his patients'.

However, as Carlo remarks at this point of the story, 'let us return to myself, the hero of this work.'

Great men of the theatre usually display precocious manifestations of the love that is to dominate their later lives, and Goldoni was no exception. There was a puppet theatre in which he delighted at the age of four, and there were orgies of reading in his father's library which consisted mainly of plays. Above all he relished the comedies by Giacinto Andrea Cicognini, one of the pioneers of theatre in Italy who wrote, amongst other things, the scenario for *Il Convitato di Pietra*, the Don Giovanni story, which was to crop up in Goldoni's own career. But the most cherished of these childish manifestations was his own first play which, he says, he wrote when he was eight – though the studious pull him up sharply and say he was eleven – and about which, perhaps fortunately, he was to forget everything. At the time, however, it created quite a stir; his governess found it admirable, his aunt teased him, his mother scolded and embraced him, his tutor affirmed that it showed greater wit and common sense than was usual at his age, and his godfather went so far as to say that it was too good to be original. Legend relates, as only legend would, that an Abbé, having read the work, exclaimed, 'This boy will be our Molière!' It is highly unlikely that this was ever said, but that anybody should have bothered to suggest that it was is symptomatic, for the invidious and specious comparison followed Goldoni all the way to the tomb – and, indeed, beyond, as the plaque outside the house where he is believed to have died shows.

This much-discussed piece of juvenilia – 'childish extravagance', its author called it – had one important effect on his life. It was proudly dispatched to Dr Giulio who was now practising medicine and charming the nobility in Perugia, and he was so impressed by it that he decided to have the boy to live with him.

Carlo's mother was shattered at the prospect and at first refused to hear of it. But eventually and reluctantly she gave way, and Carlo set off for Perugia accompanied by a Venetian Dominican who was on his way to Rome. The first stage of the journey was by boat and it is typical of Carlo that, far from feeling sea-sickness, his appetite was keenly sharpened. The second stage involved a six-day horse-ride across Umbria which, riding not being a Venetian accomplishment, involved him in some embarrassment. He was scared of the animal and couldn't make head or tail of the various bridles and stirrups and reins, but after a little discreet wooing with bread and fruit a working *modus vivendi* was established between the rider and the ridden which got them as far as Perugia.

The figure of Dr Giulio Goldoni appears shadowy across the centuries; he had characteristics in common with both his father and his son, but he lacked the drive of the one and the genius of the other. There was at least a trace of roguery in all the male Goldonis, and Giulio clearly shared it. There was also charm and he certainly had his part of that, too: by the time his son arrived in Perugia, he had so ingratiated himself with the Antinoris, one of the leading noble families of the town, as to be living rent-free in a large house owned by them – admittedly in Carlo's description it was also melancholy – and to have had himself appointed physician to a nearby convent; not a negligible feat in view of his qualifications.

Once settled in Perugia, Carlo's education had to be considered, and it was decided to place him with the Jesuits. What happened on his arrival at their college is interesting because it displays the often rampant inaccuracy of the *Mémoires* – so much more entertaining than the truth – and also because, even if it is not true, it demonstrates a pattern which was to be repeated time and time again in Carlo's life: initial disaster drawing humiliation and ridicule upon him, followed, as surely as dawn follows night, by triumphant success and applause.

Because of an interruption in his schooling and the fact that the academic year was advanced, he was placed in the lowest form, but with the tacit assumption that he was ready to move up and would automatically do so. But no sooner was he questioned in class than it began to appear that he was a bottomless well of ignorance; everything he said was wrong, and his performance was so shatteringly bad that the more charitable assumed he must be ill. Then came the day of the final Latin composition which was to decide promotion or failure. According to Carlo, as soon as he sat down to write, clarity possessed him completely, his pen flew effortlessly over the paper, and he was the first student to hand in. Then, when the results were announced, lo and behold, Goldoni was the first among those to be promoted. *Colpo di scena!* Startled whispers and excited chatter, a public reading of the winning piece, a headlong rush into proud parental arms, congratulations from the reverend father headmaster who had known all along that the talent was there. It is a very Goldonian story. Unfortunately, the pedants, who always hover, vulture-like, over Goldoni's stories, flap in to say that in fact he was failed.

But however things might go scholastically, the theatre was not ignored. Doctor Giulio rigged up a private playhouse and directed Carlo and his companions in amateur productions. Perugia being in the papal states, women were not allowed to appear on the stage, even in amateur theatricals, so Carlo, who by all accounts was a pretty lad, became leading lady. But his father – an expert in theatre like all the male Goldonis – said that the boy would never make an actor. 'And', Goldoni wrote, 'he was not mistaken.'

When Carlo had finished with the Jesuits – he alleges they made the somewhat rash proposal that he should join their order – the family decamped to Rimini. There appear to have been two reasons for this move. One was that Margherita, who had joined them at Perugia with her sister and Gian Paolo, couldn't stand the air. 'Most women', wrote Goldoni later, 'cannot live away from their own town' – a remark which appears a trifle pompous when one thinks of the gypsy existence he was later to impose on his poor wife. The other reason was that the local doctors were ganging up on Giulio, probably not without reason.

The uncharitable attitude of his colleagues, however, did not stop Giulio from deciding that his son should follow in his footsteps, and since philosophy was a prerequisite for medicine, he was put out to the Dominicans where he was bored to death. But more important events were shaping. The rest of the family left Rimini, Margherita and Gian Paolo staying at Chioggia and Giulio taking off immediately for Modena with a rather vague excuse about the family business. This left the fourteen-year-old boy alone in lodgings in Rimini. And then one day a company of players came to town. He was later to describe them as 'a company of bad actors playing woeful comedies', but at the time they were rich manna to the starving. Nor was the joy of it purely aesthetic, for this was the first time Carlo had seen a company with real actresses, and the effect was delightfully exciting, particularly that caused by the girl playing the maidservant; and in fact this was the beginning of a passion for maidservants that was to last him throughout his life. At first he was content to watch from the audience, but then, noticing other youths going backstage, he ventured there himself. He quickly made friends with the actresses, and when they – who were all Venetians – discovered he was a fellow citizen there was an explosion of rapture and he was, in his own words, 'covered with caresses'. He was also invited to dinner by the director of the company.

This strolling actor-manager, who was to play a small but determinant part in Goldoni's life, was known as Florindo dei Maccheroni because of his inordinate passion for that variety of pasta. A contemporary chronicler said that whenever a meal was part of the action of a play he would insist that, instead of make-believe food, there should be served heaped plates of *maccheroni* which he then 'devoured rather than ate'. In the Don Giovanni play – the hardiest of hardy annuals in the *Commedia dell'Arte* repertoire – he went so far as to stuff his pockets with richly seasoned pasta which he would eat 'with complete naturalness in the middle of the stage'.

The actor-managers of the period were often a miserly, ruthless lot, but this one must have taken a great liking to Goldoni, for his behaviour towards the boy was more than generous. Friday was then a day of rest for theatres in Italy, and on one Friday during the Rimini visit, the whole company went out for a frolic in the country, needless to say taking Carlo with them, for he had by now given up even token attendance on the Dominicans. While they were there, Florindo dei Maccheroni announced that the company would be sailing for Chioggia in a week's time. The idea of Rimini without the actors was a desolate one, but on top of that, as Carlo pointed out, his mother was in Chioggia. Florindo immediately invited him to accompany them and this was enthusiastically seconded by the company.

So when the night of departure came, Carlo rolled up two shirts and a night-cap into a bundle, stole out of his lodgings and, arriving at the boat before anybody else, rolled himself up under the prow.

'Where is Master Goldoni?' cried the actors and actresses on arrival. Carlo then jumped out of his hiding-place and the joy of all was, apparently, unconfined.

The *Mémoires* have their defects, due to their author's extreme age when he wrote them, his cavalier treatment of facts and his love of a well-shaped story. But they also contain pages which are supreme for vivacity and comedy, and a truth which goes deeper than facts. One of these is the description of the voyage to Chioggia.

'. . . actors and actresses, a prompter, a stage manager, a watchman, eight servants, four maidservants, two nurses, children of every age, dogs, cats, monkeys, parrots, birds, pigeons, a lamb; this was the very image of Noah's Ark.

'Being enormous, the boat was divided up into sections, each of the women having a curtained-off compartment of her own. They made up a very fine bed for me beside the director, and we were all of us very comfortable.

'Our travelling-manager, who was also cook and cellarman, rang a little bell as the signal for meals. We all ate together in a sort of room set up in the centre of the ship on top of trunks and cases and bales. Coffee, tea, milk, slices of toasted bread, water and wine were laid out on an oval table.

'The leading lady asked for a little soup and, as there was none, flew into a rage. Everybody went to great lengths to calm her down with a nice cup of chocolate. She was the ugliest and the most difficult of them all.

'After this snack, a game of cards was proposed until dinner. I played reasonably well at *tresette*, my mother's favourite game which she had taught me. And in fact we were about to begin one game of *tresette* and one of *picchetto* when everyone was drawn away by a *faraone* table which had been set up on some cases. The bank looked as though it was going to be more for fun than gain as the director of the company wouldn't have permitted otherwise. We played, we laughed, we joked, we played tricks until the bell sounded for dinner and everybody ran.

'They brought us an enormous bowl of *maccheroni* onto which we all threw ourselves, devouring three big plates. Then beef *à la mode*, cold chicken, loin of veal, fruit and an excellent wine. Oh, what a delicious meal! Everything was tasty.

'We sat at table for a good four hours, and various musical instruments were played and there was a lot of singing. The girl who played the maids' parts ravished me with her singing, and watching her closely gave me a most singular feeling. But, alas, there befell an adventure which put a stop to all the delights of society. A cat escaped from its cage, and it was the cat of none other than the leading lady. She called everyone to her aid, and everyone ran after the animal which, as ferocious as its mistress, ran, jumped and hid everywhere. But seeing itself pursued on all sides, it finally climbed up the mast. Madame Clarice was desperate. A sailor climbed up to grab it, but the cat threw itself into the sea and was drowned. Its mistress was distraught with grief; she wanted to kill all the animals that were offered to her as a substitute, and to throw her maid into the tomb of her darling kitten. Everybody was on the maid's side, and the quarrel became general. While it was going on, the director arrived; he laughed and joked and petted the afflicted lady. Finally even she started laughing, and the cat was forgotten. . . .

'The wind was unfavourable and we stayed at sea for three days, enjoying the same delights and pleasures with the same appetite, arriving at Chioggia on the fourth day.'

In essence that ship had contained within her bows all the great loves of Carlo Goldoni's life, and when she finally docked on the fourth day, he was a changed boy.

II

'In youth I easily fell in love and as easily fell out of it.'
Carlo Goldoni

Except for Venice itself, no place had so vital an influence on the life of Carlo Goldoni as Chioggia. If, as he himself says, he studied in two books, the World and the Theatre, it was in Chioggia that he began to apply himself seriously to the first, as an assistant to his father and then as a sort of unpaid magistrate's clerk. The fruit of all this came over forty years later when, on the brink of leaving the lagoon for ever, he thought back to his adolescence and wrote a sprawling, brawling masterpiece called *'Le Baruffe Chiozzotte'* or *'The Chioggia Squabbles'.*

At first sight Chioggia appears to be a poor man's Venice, but closer inspection reveals differences. While Venice is a chaotic jumble, Chioggia is symmetry itself, with one main street and three canals, all parallel and crossed at regular intervals by nine bridges; and although the town is only a few miles from Venice, its people have none of the Venetian grace; even their dialect, which Goldoni describes with scientific accuracy in the preface to *'Le Baruffe'*, is different, lacking the music and being practically incomprehensible to all but Chioggian ears. It is said to be the speech of the first settlers in the lagoon.

Anyone with even a slight aversion to fish would quickly lose his wits in Chioggia, for fish is the *raison d'être* of the little town which is the most important fishing port in Italy. 'What mainly forms its wealth', said Goldoni, 'is the prodigious quantity of fishermen and sailors and their women'. Today when the men are not at sea, you can scarcely see the water in the canals for the brightly painted craft moored in them, hull to hull. There is a large and ugly wholesale market for fish and a retail one, held twice on weekdays and once on Sundays, which is small and old, and crammed with as bewildering a variety of different types of fish as you are ever likely to see.

Substantially unchanged over the two and a half centuries intervening, this was the town at which Goldoni arrived with the actors in 1721. You can still see the house he lived in; slightly more elegant than its neighbours, it stands directly opposite the crumbling church of St Francis and almost opposite the headquarters of the Communist Party in Chioggia. By a strange coincidence, before the Goldonis moved in it had been the home of the artist Rosalba Carriera, who with Goldoni was one of the handful of people to represent the essence of Venice in the eighteenth century. And, on the subject of coincidences, just round the corner a couple of hundred yards away stands a house where Eleanora Duse – perhaps the greatest actress ever to play Goldoni – spent part of her childhood.

Carlo must have been nervous of the reception awaiting him, for he begged Florindo dei Maccheroni to intercede for him. This presented no problem as far as Margherita was concerned, and soon tears of rapture were being shed by mother and son; as for Giulio, he was away as usual and would have to be faced later.

The joyful tears, however, were scarcely dry before Carlo was off to the theatre. A local priest, who seems to have had Signora Goldoni up the sleeve of his cassock, obliged her to extract a promise from the boy that he would go no more to see the plays. Perhaps as a result of his brief stay with the Jesuits, Carlo was able to interpret this oath in the most literal sense as a ban on the plays, but not on the players. 'Particularly,' he says, 'I frequented the girl who played the maidservant, and thereafter I have always had a sort of preference for the actresses who played these parts.'

Shortly after this, Giulio arrived, forgave his son and set up shop in Chioggia; and as Carlo was still theoretically destined for medicine, it was decided that he should act as his father's assistant, a job he found highly distasteful – ' taking their pulses, studying their urine, examining their phlegm'. There was consolation, however. 'So long as the actors continued their performances, I felt I had been compensated.'

Nor was drama the only compensation. Doctor Giulio was called to a female patient who was both young and beautiful, 'and suffering from a disease which I dispense myself from mentioning, a trifling illness which did not prevent her from taking part in friendly conversation.' At a certain point, when Dr Giulio was not present, the girl's mother managed to persuade Carlo – not, one imagines, with any great difficulty – to sit on the bed, feel the patient's pulse and examine her thoroughly. When the examination was under way, the accommodating mother slipped out to buy some medicine. 'And I', says Carlo, 'stayed alone with the patient, who was sitting up in bed, with a very pretty pink gown, a bonnet tied under her chin and such a glow in her cheeks as made the doctor fall ill.' It was Giulio who eventually extricated his son from the affair, 'and from then on he only took me with him to visit female patients if they were old'.

Thus the story as he tells it in one of the prefaces to the Pasquali edition of the plays. But a very different account appears in the *Mémoires*. The adventure is approximately the same until the point when the mother is about to leave the two young people alone – in the *Mémoires* she offers to go out for wine, not medicine. But then the story takes a very different turn. As Carlo was putting his hand in his pocket to get some money for the wine, there came a knock at the door. It was his mother's servant. 'He had seen me entering the house of that rabble, and an angel had made him follow me. He whispered a word in my ear, I came to myself and immediately left.' An ending, as sloppily virtuous as Goldoni's own *Pamela*, which fits like a badly made wig.

Since the *Mémoires* contain numerous other incidents where a story, concerning a woman and obviously more or less accurate at the beginning, suddenly swerves off into artificiality or evasiveness, it is worth considering why Goldoni, who in other cases never minded showing himself in a bad light, should have refused to admit that he was gulled by a pretty whore with the pox and her mother. On reflection there seems to be only one possible explanation. The *Mémoires*, unlike the prefaces to the Pasquali edition, were read by his wife, Nicoletta, as he wrote them, if they were not actually dictated to her, and Goldoni, with all his faults, was invariably thoughtful towards her. True, this thoughtfulness did not go so far as to prevent him from enjoying his adventures, but it did prompt him to censor them in the telling.

Shortly after the affair of the young lady and her mother, it was decided in family conference that Carlo was unsuitable for medicine and should try the law instead, and so a noble protector was induced to use his influence to obtain a place at the papal college of Pavia. The place was duly made vacant, but two apparently insurmountable obstacles prevented Carlo from taking it up immediately. All students had to be at least eighteen and to have taken minor orders. Carlo was sixteen, and the Patriarch of Venice inexplicably seemed reluctant to confer any ecclesiastical status upon him. Fortunately, the Bishop of Pavia proved to be more compliant, and Carlo received his tonsure on, of all days, Christmas Day, 1722; it goes without saying that it had no influence whatsoever on his life and was, indeed, never again referred to, except by his mother. The age problem seemed to be more difficult. Carlo's account of its solution is typically cavalier. 'I can only say,' he wrote, 'that I went to bed one evening aged sixteen and woke up the next morning aged eighteen.' The true explanation is more down to earth; his birth certificate was falsified. Those two minor hindrances resolved, the way was now open for him to take up his place at the university.

The aspiring young priest-cum-lawyer spent the greater part of his time chasing women and gambling. Indeed, the members of the university in their brilliant uniforms, decorated with the papal crown and the keys of St Peter,

'Getting ready for the performance' (eighteenth-century Venetian school). The habits of players before curtain-rise haven't changed much over the centuries.

The statue of Carlo Goldoni (Dal Zotto) seeming to stride across St Bartholomew Square, Venice. Genial, benign, smiling – this is how generations of Venetians have seen their own 'papa' Goldoni.

were looked upon by the inhabitants of Pavia in much the same way that the citizens of a town with a military or naval academy consider the officer cadets: that is to say, they were loathed, and probably envied, by the men, and adored, albeit often in secret, by the women.

At the end of the first year, he went home for the holidays and his mother, 'who was pious', was deeply impressed by his priestly dress and received him as if he were one of the twelve apostles, urging him to exhort and reprove his younger brother, Gian Paolo, who as usual was behaving abominably. She, somewhat unrealistically, was hoping Gian Paolo would enter a monastery, while Giulio, who knew his boys, destined him for the army. And before long, in fact, he was in a Dalmatian regiment at the service of the Republic, from which he was to re-erupt disastrously into Carlo's life a little later.

After the high life of Pavia, Chioggia was tedious, and Carlo, in an attempt to alleviate the tedium, asked – of all people – that same priest who had tried to ban him from the theatre if he might borrow some plays to read, and the priest surprisingly came up trumps with a copy of the exceedingly bawdy *Mandragora* by Machiavelli. This Carlo devoured until his father discovered him reading it and made a scene. Margherita did her best to defend her son. 'He can't have meant any harm', Goldoni quotes her as saying 'My boy is good. He often goes to confession and he was already saying the office of the Madonna with me when he was four!' But Giulio nevertheless confiscated the play and returned it in high dudgeon to the priest who, not having read the piece, had only erred in default. But the importance of the story – as Carlo himself insists – lies in the fact that *Mandragora* was the first real comedy of character that he had ever read.

During a short trip towards the end of these holidays, a servant-maid called Antonietta, 'neither old nor young, neither ugly nor beautiful', fell instantly and deeply in love with him and, bursting into his bedroom, attempted – unsuccessfully, Carlo assures us – to rape him. On departure he gave her a tip of one *zecchino* which she kissed and put, choking with tears, into her pocket.

Another romp is hinted at rather obliquely on the occasion of his return to Pavia for the third year. Once again the story starts off realistically enough, recounting how he was picked up by a Venetian lady of easy virtue during the journey and how they shared the same coach together. She, on noticing how people were staring at them, suggested that he should take off his clerical collar – a detail which sounds very authentic. But by the time they arrived at Desenzano on Lake Garda things get very odd indeed. The hotel apparently only had one room vacant, though with two beds. The couple supped, bade each other good-night and climbed into their separate beds, whereupon 'I fell asleep in the twinkling of an eye, as is my custom.' During the night he was awoken by a din and, by the light of the moon, saw his companion in her nightdress holding a burglar at pistol-point. Then, help having been fetched and the burglar having been carried off, Carlo returned peacefully to bed and to sleep. They parted in Milan, 'I well-pleased with her reserve, she perhaps ill-pleased with my continence.' This is according to the *Mémoires*. However, in one of the prefaces to the Pasquali edition he says they were together for five days in Milan and that she later visited him in Pavia. One can almost see the tubby little old man in Paris relishing the distant memory of wanton lakeside delights – to which it is not inconceivable that the burglar was also admitted – and then, perhaps with a sigh, doctoring the story for Nicoletta's eyes.

Back in Pavia trouble was waiting. What exactly set it off is uncertain and Goldoni himself gives two completely different accounts of the initial events. It is probable that the men of Pavia had ganged up on the students, threatening to boycott any woman who received members of the university at her home, and it is certain that some individual girl had left Carlo for another man. So it was that out of pique, and not innocently compelled by bad companions, as he rather priggishly suggests in the *Mémoires*, he set out to revenge himself on Pavian women in general by writing a satire called the *Colossus*. To construct this colossus he took parts of the female body, not overlooking the most intimate, from twelve young ladies of the town's highest society. This satire understandably swept Pavia like a hurricane, and with scarcely less disastrous results, for the offended families would be satisfied with no less than blood. The college was besieged and Carlo arrested to save him from lynching; he was formally expelled and then, when the worst of the fury had somewhat diminished, he was ignominiously smuggled out of town. 'What horror! What remorse! What repentance!' he very properly exclaims. Unfortunately, the satire is lost.

Back to Chioggia again and more parental forgiveness, followed by a move to Udine with Giulio who obviously practised in various cities as long as the going was good. In Udine, predictably enough, there was more trouble with women. Carlo saw and fell in love with a local girl and started following her to church in the hope of being able to tackle her, but before an opportunity presented itself, her maid, Teresa, came to see him and offered to act as go-between. Finally, after he had given her some jewels for her mistress, she announced that the young lady was prepared to show her gratitude on the following Thursday at the house of a washerwoman some way out of town. But when Carlo got to the place of assignation – 'an attic with one filthy bed and a broken chair' – the mistress was nowhere to be seen and it was the maid, one gathers, who took her place – a not uncommon Goldonian situation. Soon afterwards, with the help of a little milliner, he was able to unmask Teresa altogether. She had, of course, never spoken a word of Carlo to her mistress, who, in so far as she was aware of his existence at all, thought – rightly as it turned out – that he was Teresa's lover.

No sooner was that affair over than he toppled into another with the daughter of a coffee-house keeper; or, as he puts it himself, 'to heal myself of one illness, I caught another.' Having duly fallen in love with the girl, he had himself smuggled into her bedroom at night by the maid. Creeping on tip-toes through another bedroom where the girl's mother was apparently asleep, he knocked over a chair. The mother, however, stirring in her pretended sleep, allowed him to get away with this. But when he finally reached the beloved's bed, she changed her tactics. There came a violent battering at the door. Carlo contemplated jumping out of the window, but prudently decided that it was too high. The door and the mother burst, respectively, open and in. There was a violent scene with threats to arouse the whole neighbourhood and denounce the seducer, but when the topic of marriage was introduced the storm subsided almost miraculously. Carlo, in his own words, 'baffled cunning with cunning', declared his willingness to be led to the altar, and then the next day skipped hot-foot to Gorizia with his father.

They stayed in Gorizia with an Italian officer in the Austrian army whose table was almost legendary, a fact that Carlo – a cheerful and enthusiastic glutton – remembered with relish. 'The base [of a roast dish] consisted of a quarter of mutton or kid or breast of veal, with hare or pheasant on top, then partridges, then snipe or thrushes, and the whole pyramid crowned with larks and warblers.' This was preceded by not one, but three soup or pasta dishes, and washed down with a red wine known as the 'baby-maker', 'which gave rise to very merry jokes'.

After a visit to Germany and a return to Chioggia, Carlo set off for Modena, the Goldonis' native town. It was thought that by continuing his legal studies there he might kill two birds with one stone by also avoiding payment of an absence tax, which the Modenese government imposed upon its subjects.

Whatever he may say about it in the *Mémoires*, it seems probable that Carlo had been placing a fairly considerable strain on his virility. This, together with the fact that he did hold minor ecclesiastical orders, however little importance he gave to them, may have accounted for the next crisis. One day in the street he saw a priest being publicly condemned to the stocks for an affair with a woman, and the sight of it so appalled him as to set off a religious crisis – the first and last in his life. He attended every mass, sermon and ceremony that the church offered, and this orgy culminated in the decision to become a friar, which he at once communicated to his father.

For all his oddnesses, Giulio was a sensible father and on this occasion he neatly saved a brand, not so much from, as for the burning. He offered no resistance to the decision, but suggested that Carlo should ratify it at home. Once having got him there, Giulio whistled him off to Venice where the social whirl, visits to the theatre and, it has been suggested, to the stews made him forget all about the religious life. 'I continued to feel pity for the man I had seen in Modena, but I realized it was not necessary to renounce the world in order to avoid such a fate.'

Back in Chioggia, it was time once again to think of the future. Gian Paolo, the younger brother, was already off with the military, but Carlo, by now twenty-one, seemed to be no nearer a career than he had been on his first arrival in Chioggia. 'So many unusual disasters had befallen me, so many unpleasant adventures that I saw no other possibility for me than the theatre which I had always loved and which I would have entered long before if I had been master of my destiny.'

But the theatre was still some way off, and in the meantime Giulio got a job for his son as a clerk – unpaid, but with a variety of perks – in the criminal court of Chioggia. The perks included a place at the table of the twenty-seven-year-old governor, a Venetian patrician named Francesco Bonfadini (Chioggia was not considered important and young patricians were usually sent there to gain experience) and all the delights of society including balls, parties and gambling.

By all accounts, some work was done as well, and Carlo seemed to enjoy the job. 'The law', he wrote, 'has laid down certain formulae for interrogation which must be followed in order that questions should not be fraudulent and human weakness and ignorance should not be taken advantage of. It is necessary to know or divine the inner character of the man one has to examine and, striking the happy medium between humanity and severity, try to discover the truth without violence.'

Not always, however, quite without violence. Often the accused were examined while hanging up in the air by their wrists, and indeed the frontispiece of one volume of the Pasquali edition of the plays shows him questioning a man in such conditions: Carlo is holding his quill pen daintily in the air and gazing at the poor wretch with what seems to be a roguish air. 'One gets accustomed to everything,' he observes in the preface to the same volume.

He also probably witnessed real torture which took place, though under strict control, in the presence of the judge, the chancellor, and a doctor to set dislocated limbs. The more imaginative and gruesome forms of torture had been abandoned the previous century, and examinining authorities were left only with the rack on which people could be stretched for fixed periods of time, checked with a watch and varied according to their condition. Minors, the nobility, doctors and the upper classes in general could be submitted to no more than seven minutes 'without jolting of the arms'. Those of low degree and evil fame could suffer from fifteen minutes to an hour 'with jolting of the arms', while indefinite stretching was reserved only for those guilty of the most abominable deeds.

But such horrors as there were did not seem to upset Carlo who said that of all the jobs he had done, this was 'the finest, the most enjoyable, the most in conformity with my inclination'. And elsewhere he enlarges on the subject. 'What interested me above all was the preliminary examination and the report I had to prepare for the chancellor, for on this summary and this report, the condition, the honour and the life of a man may often depend. True, the accused is defended and the evidence discussed, but the first impression comes from the report.'

The governor's term of office came to an end after sixteen months and in the general administrative shake-up Carlo's immediate superior was posted to Feltre, from where, he promised, he would send for Carlo to take up a paid position. 'Finally I was settled with a job. Until now I had only regarded posts and positions from a distance; now at last, having one that I liked and that was advantageous, I resolved never more to leave it. But man proposes and God disposes.'

While waiting for the call to Feltre, there was time for another adventure in Chioggia. 'Beauty Bartered, or the Scheming Nun' Carlo might have titled a play on the subject if the laws prohibiting the representation of religious on the stage had not been so severe. He appears to have constructed a sort of pipe-line to femininity for himself by cultivating the acquaintance of the nuns of St Francis at whose institute many girls were finishing their education. One of these, Carlo felt, would have done splendidly for him, being lovely, very rich and altogether delightful; too perfect, indeed, for he thought that he didn't stand a chance. The nun in charge of her, however, was more optimistic and whenever he visited the convent she invited the young lady into the parlour so that he might see her. And every day he fell deeper and deeper in love.

It appeared that the young lady had an old and decrepit guardian who, despite the rapid advance of senility, had pretensions on his ward. But there was no need to worry about that, said the nun, undertaking personally to steer the young couple to the altar steps.

In spite of love for the girl, Carlo did not renounce contact with her companions, continuing to converse with them in sign language, his bedroom window being opposite the church of St Francis which formed part of the convent. But the conversation, he assures us, was 'always on grave and modest subjects'. It was from these girls that he learned that his love was to marry her guardian.

Full of indignation, he rushed across the road and demanded to see the two-faced nun who, seeing him trembling with rage, took the bull by the horns so to speak and, before he could get a word in, announced that Miss was indeed going to marry her guardian. What was more, it was she, the nun, who had arranged the match for Carlo's specific benefit. Was he, she asked, in a position to marry the girl immediately? No, he wasn't. Should the young lady await his convenience? No, she shouldn't and couldn't. What then was to be done? If she married a young man, she would be lost to Carlo for ever. But if she were to marry an old man, things would be very different. The nun protested that she knew nothing of the delights and tribulations of the married state, but she understood that a young wife could notably shorten the days of an old husband. 'Thus,' the nun concluded, 'you will be able to possess a lovely widow who will have borne no more than the name of wife, and who will also be considerably richer than she is now.'

At this point the young lady herself appeared behind the grating, and the nun exhorted him to congratulate her on the forthcoming wedding, but he, unable to bear the sight of either of them, turned and stumbled out of the convent.

He didn't have long to brood over it, however, as the call to Feltre came almost immediately and there – O bliss! O poop-poop! – was a company of players. What we know of its members is a clear demonstration of the drawing-room intimacy of eighteenth-century Europe, particularly noticeable in a little world of its own like the theatre where the same characters met and crossed continually. This company was directed by an actor, five years Carlo's senior, called Carlo Veronese. This same Veronese, who had to overcome the handicap of a glass eye, was to precede Carlo at the *Comédie Italienne* in Paris where they would meet over thirty years later and where one of his two daughters, Camilla, would act triumphantly in a Goldoni script. Moreover, one of the actors in Veronese's company was that same Florindo dei Maccheroni who had aided and abetted Carlo's escape to Chioggia. 'Having aged, he now only played the parts of kings in tragedy and noble fathers in comedy.'

Perhaps because Carlo was pleased with his new job he did not become quite so involved with the players as he would have done before. Indeed, he appears to have applied himself diligently, even going so far, in an attempt to ingratiate himself with his superiors, as to dig up a case which his predecessors had been only too anxious to leave buried. This case involved 200 people who had been illegally felling trees which were the property of the Republic. Carlo quickly regretted his busy-bodying when he realized that the wrath of the 200 was likely to fall on the official 'who had awoken the sleeping dogs'. Fortunately the mountain, on whose sides the forest stretched, laboured and gave forth a legal mouse: the Republic was content to ensure the cessation of the felling without punishing the offenders, and so, for the second time in his short life, Carlo narrowly avoided lynching.

A more pleasant assignment fell to him after this. He was sent to conduct the preliminary hearing into a brawl involving fire-arms which had caused several casualties in the country some way outside Feltre. Five other young men and six girls went along for the ride, together with four servants, and they rode through leafy spring countryside, passing villas and gardens, ambling along vine-flanked roads shaded by fig-trees. They spent a comfortable twelve days on the expedition, of which only two hours were taken up with legal business, and never ate twice in the same place or went to bed, at any rate to sleep. Wherever they stopped there were parties, banquets and merriment.

Inevitably Carlo was in love with one of the six girls. Her name was Angela and she was as grave and modest as her married sister, also of the company, was crazy. Poor Angela must have been delicate for she was so exhausted by the expedition that she ran a high temperature for forty days after it.

When they returned to Feltre, some amateur theatricals were got up, and Carlo directed two tragedies by Metastasio and two farces by himself named *The Good Father* and *The Singer*. He alleges that these two pieces were later filched from him by a Venetian lawyer who presented them in the city under his own name.

Apart from the fact that she had a high temperature, rehearsals were torment for the unhappy Angela. She was too shy to take part and anyway her parents wouldn't let her – the same parents had apparently raised no objection to her going off on a lengthy expedition with six young men and no better chaperone than a crazy married sister, but let it pass; the story is moving to a conclusion which is all too patently true and reflects no great credit on our hero. Angela was painfully aware of the intimacy between Carlo and the girls who did take part, and she suffered agonies of jealousy. She loved him deeply, or so he says, and hoped to be his wife, and he loved her 'with all his soul'. But all his devotion did not prevent him from making a somewhat chilly calculation. 'Her sister, having been of a rare beauty, became ugly following her first confinements. This girl had the same features and the same complexion. She had that delicate beauty which so easily fades, and I had seen proof of it; the strain of the journey had changed her incredibly. I was young, and if my wife were to lose her freshness after a little while, I could imagine how much it would make me suffer.' 'To tell the truth,' he adds a little shamefacedly, 'the reasoning is a little cold for a lover.'

Anyway, he abandoned Angela and – although she certainly did not realize it at the time – she was well out of it, for married life with Goldoni would quickly have driven her out of her wits. And, although he omits to mention it, he also abandoned the job at Feltre which had so recently been 'the finest, the most enjoyable, the most in conformity with my inclination'. It is not beyond the bounds of possibility that the delightful expedition into the country with its balls and banquets had been charged to the Serenissima as expenses, and, as a result, it was the job which abandoned him.

Meanwhile papa Giulio, who was still zig-zagging hectically about the north of Italy, had been offered a job at Bagnacavallo, near Ravenna, and Carlo set off to join him there. On the boat from Venice to Ferrara he was fleeced at cards by the son of a Paduan butcher who was 'thin and pale with black hair and hollow eyes'. But worse was to come in Ferrara where they stopped overnight. While Carlo was supping alone in his room, the butcher's son came in and offered him his revenge. Carlo demurred, but the butcher's son insisted and the game began. Before long a difference of opinion arose, and the butcher's boy pulled out a pistol and stole the ten *zecchini* which Carlo had staked on the game. At this point a third young man, an accomplice of the abominable Paduan, burst into the room and threatened to denounce them for illegal gambling unless it was made worth his while not to do so. Carlo paid up.

At Bagnacavallo Giulio became ill, but in spite of the illness he took his son to Faenza 'to procure me new delights' and, probably as a result of the journey, worsened, took to his bed and died. He was only forty-seven. He had been a quack, an adventurer, a bad, not to say a non-existent husband, but he had also been tenaciously devoted to his elder son, and if he had not exactly shielded him from the temptations of the world, he had usually managed to save him in the nick of time from the worst consequences of yielding to them; in a sense he had even sacrificed his life to give pleasure to Carlo. Now he was buried in the church of San Girolamo in Bagnacavallo, and his son would henceforth have to look out for himself.

III

*'Honour is the lawyer's greatest capital. An honest man is held
in greater esteem than a learned one.'*
Carlo Goldoni

A year after Giulio's death, Carlo and his mother and aunt returned to Venice. As always there was the problem of the future. Carlo had studied law – albeit somewhat erratically – in Pavia, Modena and Udine; now was the moment to gather up these fragments of study and piece them together to form a means of livelihood. Unfortunately, though not unusually, there were snags. If he wanted to practise in Venice – as he did – he would have to have a degree from the university of Padua, as the Republic would only accept Paduan lawyers. And this university demanded that its students should frequent courses for four years before taking a degree, and for Carlo, now nearly twenty-five, this was too long.

But of course the Goldonis managed to find a loop-hole. The university of Padua made an exception for 'foreigners' – that is to say anyone who did not come under the jurisdiction of the Republic of Venice; such people could turn up at any time and sit the examination. True, Carlo was every bit a Venetian, having been born within a generous stone's-throw of the Rialto, but – and one can almost see mother, son and aunt apprehensively eyeing the loop-hole to assess whether it was wide enough – the family came from Modena and it might be possible to put Carlo forward as Modenese. And so it turned out to be. No less an authority than the Duke of Modena was persuaded to write a letter asserting that Carlo was his subject, and the problem was solved.

Next came the question of passing the examination which, at first sight, appeared to be child's play, having been reduced over the years to a ceremonial formality. Indeed, it was child's play in the most literal sense of the word. Casanova claimed in his memoirs that he had entered the university of Padua as a law student at the age of twelve and taken his degree at the age of sixteen, with a civil law thesis on wills and a canon law thesis on the rights of Jews to build new synagogues. This claim seemed to be so outrageous that it was long held to be one of Giacomo's taradiddles until, in 1923, somebody ran down the document which proved it.

Nevertheless, a little brushing-up of law could do no harm, and Carlo went for lessons to a genial contemporary and childhood friend called Francesco Radi who had been enrolled in the register of Venetian lawyers three years before. As Radi shared Carlo's inordinate passion for gambling, one may take leave to wonder how much study got done, but as they considered the examination a formality, a certain lack of preparation would not have put them out unduly. And, in fact, as soon as they arrived in Padua they went straight to the bursar's office to pay for the doctorate, a fee which was cheerfully accepted. They then proceeded to make the rounds of the various professors, as was the custom for outsiders, and one may imagine that a consideration was left on the desk of each. But a rude shock was awaiting them when they knocked at the door of a certain Abbé Arrighi, one of the principal luminaries of the university and the author of works on territorial divisions in ancient Rome. This wet blanket had the bad taste to demand an earnest of some knowledge of the law and to express his horror at the bursar's office having accepted the doctorate fee in advance. He brusquely told Radi to wait in the library and then set about questioning Carlo on everything 'jumping from the Justinian Code to the Canons of the Church and from Digests to Pandects'.*

If such rigour had been practised for long, Carlo remarks indignantly, the university would quickly have disintegrated. And, what was worse, Arrighi had the face to express himself dissatisfied with Carlo's answers and to suggest that he should withdraw and study a bit harder before coming back. But Carlo insisted on taking the public examination, saying that he intended either to obtain his doctorate immediately or to abandon the law. Arrighi replied that it was his right to make the attempt, but if he put so much as a foot wrong he would be failed.

The next day Carlo drew by lots the subjects he was to discuss. According to university archives these subjects concerned 'imperfect law' and 'sickness in the clergy' while, according to Goldoni in the *Mémoires*, they were 'bigamy' and 'successions of ownership'. This discrepancy may or may not indicate a certain crafty manipulation of subjects. But he didn't get much time to mug them up, for he and Radi spent the entire night gambling with five young men they had met at supper, and Carlo only staggered away from the table in time to go to the

---

* A lawyer has unkindly pointed out that Digests and Pandects are the same thing.

great hall of the university, where he was to argue before six professors of law, including the captious Arrighi.

At this point the story is all set for a typically Goldonian finale with cheers and flourishes of trumpets. Everything was against our hero, the sleepless night and the antagonism of Arrighi; and then, to make matters worse, when somebody tried to prompt him, there came a sharp admonition and he realized that *all* the professors were disposed against him. But, when everything seemed lost, such a stream of eloquence burst from his lips as to dumbfound all listeners. He swept unerringly along the corridors of the legal mazes, expounding both Greek and Roman law 'and not forgetting to quote the ecclesiastical councils'. 'I brought immortal honour on myself,' he says modestly, adding that he won his doctorate *nemine penitus penitusque discrepante*, or without a single unfavourable vote. Then the public swept into the arena, and he was overwhelmed with compliments and embraces. But, as usual, the hovering vultures of pedantry flap in to show that, according to the records, he obtained his degree *nemine penitus dissentiente*, which indicates that only two-thirds of the votes were favourable. But the achievement is still no small one, and Goldoni's knowledge of law must have been pretty good – a supposition borne out by subsequent events.

Having been fleeced at cards the night before, Goldoni and Radi did not even have the money for their fare back to Venice and Carlo had to hock a diamond ring which had been given him by a girl.

Before being called to the Venetian bar, two years' apprenticeship were required, but once again Goldoni managed to pull a fast one. The functionaries who checked these things were overworked and indifferent and they tended to glance at the years rather than the precise date; thus by starting his apprenticeship in October 1731 and finishing it May 1732, he managed to get away with eight months.

It was also obligatory for Venetian lawyers to reside, or at any rate have their offices, in the same district as the law courts, and so Carlo rented a house in San Paterniano – the same house, by an odd coincidence, that was to be occupied rather over a century later by the only other Venetian lawyer to attain world-fame, the great champion of the city's liberty, Daniele Manin.

Came the day of the ceremonial calling to the bar and Carlo, robed in his toga and weighed down by an enormous wig, entered the palace of justice, flanked by two older lawyers who acted as his sponsors. There followed an hour and a half of 'so much bowing and scraping that my back was broken and my wig became a sort of lion's mane'. When it was all over, he sent a servant to fetch him a gondola, 'not wishing to be seen in the streets so tousled and crumpled', and sank down to wait on a bench.

There followed a curious encounter. With the extraordinarily accurate photographic memory which Goldoni, at close on eighty, could bring to bear on the past, when it suited him to do so, he describes the scene in the *Mémoires*.

While he was waiting on the bench, he was approached by a woman of about thirty. She was not, he says, ill-looking, but his description scarcely bears this out for she was 'plump and white with a squashed nose and cunning eyes', and she was hung about with a quantity of gold. She described herself as 'a daughter of the law courts' and added that she knew all the lawyers so well that people in need of legal aid were constantly applying to her for advice in the choice of their representative. Indeed, she had made the fortunes of some of the best-known lawyers in the city, and was prepared to do as much for Goldoni. The cases she could pass to him, she hinted, might not be entirely straight, but they would be profitable. Carlo refused the offer 'in a resolute and intrepid voice' and then the woman, suddenly changing tone, warned him that what had passed between them was 'not without secrecy' and that he should speak of it to nobody. Then, with an admonition to rectitude, she made off. The woman was obviously an *agente provocatrice*, and her bid to ensnare Carlo represented a sort of lifeless twitch of what had once been a ruthless police state and was now, by comparison, a simpering caricature; even if Carlo had fallen into the trap, the woman's report would probably only have been filed and forgotten.

Having come through temptation unscathed, Carlo sat down at his desk to wait for clients. He spent much of his time, one gathers, speculating about future pickings which could be rich. There were 240 lawyers in Venice at the time and they shared between them a heaving throng of litigants who, for a mere consultation, were prepared to spend a *zecchino* or about five guineas. And, as Carlo pointed out, it was possible to have as many as twenty consultations before you even caught sight of a judge. This meant that a lawyer in the top flight could make a vast annual income. On the other hand, only about ten lawyers could be considered in the top category while about twenty others made up the second. This left 210 to go grubbing about in search of clients, helped by legal touts 'who were prepared to act as hunting dogs on condition that they could share the prey'.

There is reason to suppose, however, that if Carlo had not been beguiled by the theatre he might well have reached the second or even the first legal category. 'But', as he wrote years later when he was in a state of penury, 'since I am not given to saving, I would probably have been like so many others who throw away their profits and, at the end of the year, are in the same position as I am now, and perhaps worse, because, if I haven't got any money, I haven't got any debts either, or at any rate very few.'

An incident towards the beginning of his legal career shows that he must have had considerable ability. An uncle, also a lawyer, passed him a case concerning a miller who had bought a stretch of water only to discover, after purchase, that the owner of the land containing the spring from which his water came, had deviated its course, thus leaving the miller's wheel idle. The importance of the case from Goldoni's point of view, however, lay in the eminence of the lawyer appearing against him. Carlo Giorgio Maria Cordelina was one of the brightest stars in the Venetian legal firmament of the eighteenth century. He was only four years older than Goldoni, whom he was to outlive by one, but he was already acclaimed throughout the city – a sort of young Hailsham of the Republic. Later he was to appear frequently on behalf of Carlo Gozzi and, as an art collector, to become Guardi's patron. His villa at Montecchio Maggiore, still one of the great sights of the Veneto, was hung with paintings by Tiepolo.

On this occasion Cordelina argued to the court for an hour and a half without interruption and Carlo had to get to his feet immediately afterwards, without any pause for preparation. This he did, and spoke for two hours, finally staggering out of the court, 'bathed in a sea of sweat from head to foot'. He was joined a few minutes later by his uncle with news that, not only had he won, but that the opposition had been ordered to pay costs.

But in spite of this flash of glory he remained an unknown beginner, obliged to spend much of his time doodling at his desk. This doodling took the form, at first, of a rather heavy-handedly humourous almanac for the year 1732 'in triplets in the manner of Dante'. But there was also something rather more consonant with the workings of his own destiny. 'In Perugia, in Rimini, in Milan, in Pavia,' he wrote later, 'in the midst of . . . first of all medical and then legal activities, I always managed sometimes to give vent to my passion for the theatre.' What he elsewhere described as 'my violent inclination' was now given its head in the composition of a tragedy to be set to music, entitled *Amalasunta*, whose protagonist was a Queen of the Ostrogoths, murdered by her cousin; not particularly dazzling material, one would have thought, and hardly Carlo's cup of chocolate either, but at the time he was plainly besotted with it. But before going on to the fate of the tragedy – hardly less cruel than that of its protagonist – it is necessary to go a short way back for the start of a somewhat contorted *affaire* in which, once again, Carlo had the worst of it. In itself it is little more than another vivid portrait of life in eighteenth-century Venice, but if it had not been for this little upheaval, Goldoni might indeed have stayed on to become Cordelina's learned and respected friend. 'The Aunt and the Niece', the episode may be called, 'or the Battle of Love and Reason'.

Goldoni's mother had been friendly for some years with two Venetian ladies, and when she returned after the death of Giulio, she picked up the friendship again. The ladies were sisters, one married and one unmarried, living in separate apartments in the same building, and Carlo was soon presented to them.

The spinster was the richer of the two. 'She was not young, but she still had attractive features; at forty she was as fresh as a rose and white as snow, well-coloured with witty, vivacious eyes, an enchanting mouth and a delicate, well-kept complexion. Only her nose – aquiline and somewhat high – spoilt her appearance a little, but it gave her an air of authority when she was on her dignity.'

This lady seems to have been a little choosey, having hitherto refused all offers of marriage although, thanks to her wealth, if not her looks, she had never been short of pretenders. But as soon as she set eyes on Carlo she took a great fancy to him, and he to her. In so far as we may trust the possibly doctored account in the *Mémoires*, neither of them would take the first step of the dance, she for modesty and he for fear of a refusal. So Carlo spoke to his mother. Signora Goldoni must have had a steady eye to the main chance for, discounting without hesitation the aquiline nose and the fifteen years' age difference, she assessed the dowry and decided at once that the lady was an excellent match for her son and consequently offered to act as go-between.

The plot is now developed as deftly and professionally as in one of Goldoni's own plays. The scene having been set and the principal characters introduced, a new group of characters is brought on stage to embroil the situation. From the upstairs flat the married sister arrived for a game of cards, bringing her two daughters with her. The elder of these Carlo dismisses as 'deformed' while the younger was 'ugly, it is true, but not disagreeable'.* She also had a lovely pair of mischievous, black eyes, a Harlequin mask and simple yet provoking ways.

The unmarried sister must have had a job keeping herself under control during the card-playing sessions, for her ugly niece with the Harlequin mask and the mischievous black eyes, who had already put her aunt's aquiline nose out of joint in the past where suitors were concerned, was all too obviously trying to do so again with Carlo. He seems to have handled the situation with some skill for, he says, 'I enjoyed myself with the niece and held on tight to the aunt.' One can imagine the deadly female darts pinging to and fro over the playing cards and the cups of chocolate.

How long Carlo would have been able to maintain this dangerous equilibrium it is impossible to tell for, at this point, another character made his entrance and reshuffled the cast. This was a titled gentleman whom, with sweet and gentle glances, the unmarried sister set about catching in her net. But, in case anybody should nourish any delusions about genuine feelings, Carlo is quick to point out that 'the lady was in love with his title and the gentleman with her fortune'.

Seeing himself thus thrown aside in favour of a title, Carlo felt piqued – a little unreasonably in view of his own behaviour – and he set out to revenge himself by redoubling his court of the niece. So effectively did he do this that he found himself engaged to her at the end of two months. Anything the girl may have lacked in beauty was made up for by the business side of the contract,

---

* Goldoni has an odd tendency to dismiss his women as ugly. If they were indeed, they must have been *jolies laides*, for all the other evidence suggests they were extremely attractive. The most striking example of this occurs later on with the actress, Elisabetta Passalacqua.

which promised Carlo an annual income belonging to his fiancée, the family diamonds and a considerable sum of money promised by an anonymous friend and protector of the household.

Exactly how, it is a little difficult to understand, but in spite of the close vicinity of the two camps, the aunt remained in ignorance of the betrothal, and Carlo continued to 'call on her'.

The situation changed kaleidoscopically once again when the aunt, finally suspicious of the goings-on upstairs and anxious to rid herself once and for all of sister, niece and Carlo, tried to precipitate her own marriage with the titled gentleman. It then became humiliatingly apparent that His Excellency expected to receive half her property on marriage and the other half at her death. Learning this, 'She gave way to the most violent transports of rage, hatred and contempt, sent a formal refusal to her suitor and practically died of grief.'

At this point in the *Mémoires* there occurs one of the unkindest phrases in a work which is otherwise remarkable for its benevolence. 'Those of her household who listened and could not keep silence took the news to her sister and, behold, both the niece and the mother were in transports of delight.'

The unhappy sister now tried to double back on her tracks and return to Carlo, but the next incident, in which the author confesses to perfidy, squashed all hope of that. Carlo wrote a serenade, had it set to music and arranged for it to be sung on the canal beneath the window of his ugly, but not disagreeable love. But of course a serenade under her window was also a serenade under her aunt's window. So it was that one evening while the full cast, except for His Excellency, was enjoying a game of cards, they were interrupted by the sound of music floating up from the water, and they crowded onto the balcony to listen. Apparently both aunt and niece thought the serenade was intended for herself alone, and although the author was officially anonymous, suspicions fell heavily on Goldoni who, neither denying nor confirming, let them fall.

The crunch came the next day when Carlo attended on the aunt. She accused him openly of authorship, but said that as there was more than one woman in the house she would like to be certain that she was the one who had to thank him. He replied that he was not the author; she insisted that he was. He said that even if he were, he would not have dared address the serenade to her. She wanted to know why, realizing, perhaps, even as she asked, that she was making a fatal mistake, for the way was now wide open for Carlo to reply – not without justice – that only great gentlemen were good enough for her. She knew that she was beaten, and one can only hope that she got some consolation from the air of authority which her aquiline nose gave her in such moments.

She salvaged what she could from the wreckage by dusting off a former suitor – humble, but respectable – who lived on the other side of the canal. He seemed willing, and any doubts he may have had were dispelled when she bought him a position of rank – something which was now not only permissible but enthusiastically encouraged in the Republic. Within a week the marriage was settled.

Everything seemed set for a snug ending, the more so since the aunt's future brother-in-law was also on the point of wedlock. This, together with Carlo and his intended, made three marriages which, it was decided, would be celebrated jointly.

Unfortunately, Carlo got cold feet. This may have been partly the result of the manifold and complex rituals preceding a Venetian wedding, which, if you were not head-over-heels in love, must have seemed increasingly like the formalities leading to an execution. The first of these rituals was the signing of the contract, followed by the giving of the engagement ring, a ceremony which was celebrated by a party for friends and relatives with an abundance of food and drink. 'Indeed,' Carlo remarks drily, 'there is no occasion in Venice which is not accompanied by prohibitively expensive refreshments.' The next major ritual was the presentation of a pearl necklace by the groom and his mother to the bride, who would then wear it for the first year of her marriage. But pearls were exceedingly rare in those days and few families could muster up enough money for a necklace, so jewellers ran a highly profitable hire service. The handing-over of the necklace was accompanied by balls, banquets, new clothes for all concerned, 'and, as a consequence, heavy expenses'.

It was as they were coming up for the pearl necklace hurdle that Carlo made a blood-chilling discovery concerning the various benefits that were to accrue to him on marriage. The bride's income which was to be made over to him was a sort of regular grant from the Republic for which she had, indeed, been chosen, but the snag was that she had to wait her turn, which would only come up after four other young ladies had died. The diamonds also were to come to her, but only after her mother had passed to a better world. And as for the anonymous friend and protector who had promised a considerable sum of money, he was away on a journey and would not be back for some while.

Carlo saw himself, as he put it, on the edge of a precipice. 'I thought, I reflected, I underwent the hideous conflict between love and reason, and it was this latter faculty of the soul which overcame the kingdom of the senses.' Or, in other words, he decided to cut loose. But, as the contract had been signed, this was not so easy; the only way out, he decided in conference with his mother, was a midnight flit from Venice. It was not to be the last. He duly made it and discovered, on arrival in Padua, that 'the delights of freedom compensated me for the loss of my love'.

He had lost practically everything, but as he sailed down the Brenta towards Padua, one ineffable consolation rode with him. Stripped he might be of worldly goods, but his real love, his joy, his sweet pride, *Amalasunta*, that tragedy of the Queen of the Ostrogoths to be set to music, snuggled safely in the travelling bag at his feet, promising immortality.

IV

'I was not made to enjoy any good fortune for long. Delights
and rebuffs always followed each other rapidly in my life, and
the day in which I delighted most was always the eve of an
unhappy overthrow.'

Carlo Goldoni

Amalasunta was almost certainly an atrociously bad play, but it dominated
Carlo's thoughts and actions for the next few weeks. With the naivety of which
only perhaps a young artist or a virgin are capable, he thought he would sell it
for a hundred *zecchini* in Milan, so it was for Milan he headed when he escaped
the clutches of his ugly love, following the same course as the *autostrada* does
today – Padua, Vicenza, Verona, Lake Garda, Brescia and Bergamo.

In Vicenza he showed *Amalasunta* to an old Venetian acquaintance who
received it 'very coldly' and suggested, wisely, but for the moment vainly, that
Carlo should try his hand at comedy. Also and predictably at Vicenza he visited
the Palladian theatre with its famous *trompe l'oeil* of perspective, unchanged
today except for the introduction of the mournful little man who repeats the
same desolate and solitary minuet on the stage to demonstrate the perspective,
accompanying it with a set piece in Italian, English, French or German,
according to the nationality of the visitors.

At Desenzano he slept at the same hotel where he had spent the night with
the Venetian lady of easy virtue on his way to Pavia, and he learned that the
wretched burglar who had broken into their room had since been hanged.

In Brescia he gave a reading of *Amalasunta* to a group of local intellectuals
who – mistaken as intellectuals invariably are – applauded it warmly.

Bergamo is traditionally the native town of Harlequin and, although Carlo
looked in vain for traces of him, the shade of that wildest and warmest of the
Italian masks was nevertheless propitious, for the governor of the city turned

out to be Francesco Bonfadini, the young Venetian patrician who had been governor of Chioggia when Carlo was there. (Once again one has a sense of the intimacy of the European stage where the same characters were continually bumping into each other.) Bonfadini gave Carlo an uproarious welcome, and Bonfadini's wife gave him a letter of introduction to the Venetian ambassador in Milan.

Like all the male Goldonis, Carlo was an adventurer, and nowhere in the *Mémoires* is this demonstrated quite so clearly as when he describes his arrival in Milan. 'I lodged at the Inn of the Well, one of the most famous in Milan, because anyone who wishes to make a good showing, if he is not rich, must appear to be so.' And this after he had just scrounged ten *zecchini* off Bonfadini.

Having settled in at the Inn of the Well, he made contact with the Venetian ambassador who asked him to dine. He didn't push his luck there for the moment, however, as he was more concerned with selling *Amalasunta*. To this end he brought into play a Venetian ballerina in Milan whom he had known before. She, at her *conversazione*, introduced him to a certain Caffariello, the leading man of the opera, and to a count who was one of its directors. The count said he would be happy to arrange for a reading of *Amalasunta* at the theatre, but that, in the meantime, he would like to form some idea of what it was like. There followed what was perhaps the most embarrassing scene in Carlo's life.

'A little table with a candle was drawn up, everybody sat down and I began reading with the title – *Amalasunta*. Cafferiello then chanted the name Amalasunta, and it seemed both long and ridiculous to him. Everybody laughed, but I didn't laugh. The ballerina raised her voice and the singing-bird Caffariello was silent. I read out the names of the nine characters, and at a certain point the voice was heard of an elderly eunuch who miaowed away in the choruses like a cat, 'Too many, too many – there are at least two characters too many!' By now I perceived that I was in trouble, and I should like to have stopped reading, but the count silenced the insolent eunuch (who didn't even have the excuse of Caffariello's talent) and, turning to me, said, "It is true, sir, that normally one does not go beyond six or seven characters, but if the work deserves more one is happy to spend the extra money for two more actors. Please be so good as to continue reading."

'I started reading again. "Act one, Scene one. Clodesil and Harpagon." Caffariello interrupted once more to ask the name of the character of the leading singer. "This is it, sir," I said, "Clodesil". "What!" he replied, "Would you open the scene with your leading actor and make him appear amidst all the uproar of people looking for seats? Indeed, sir, you will not have me among your actors. Lord, what patience one needs with these authors!" The count then said, "Let us see if the scene itself is interesting." I started to read the first scene, and while I was doing so, one of the singers drew a sheet of music out of his pocket and went to the spinet where he started rehearsing an aria.'

The ballerina begged his pardon, and the count led him gently off for a private reading of the work, explaining, when they had reached the end, that musical tragedies had to be composed to certain fixed rules; that, for example, the three principal characters must have five arias each, two in the first act, two in the second and one in the third, and that, above all, bravura pieces must not be given to small part players.

Shattered, our hero stumbled out into the night. Back at the hotel the waiter asked him what he would take for supper and he replied that he would not sup, but that he wanted a good fire in his room. It was to the flames of this fire that he consigned *Amalasunta*.

'Everything was finished. I thought no more of my tragedy, but stirring its ashes with the tongs . . . I began to reflect that, whatever disasters had befallen me, I had never before gone without my supper.' A most Goldonian reflection, and no sooner had it been made than he called the waiter, ordered that the table should be laid and then, having 'eaten well and drunk better', went to bed and slept like a baby.

The next morning he philosophically decided to play his second card, the Venetian ambassador, from whom he managed to extract another invitation to dinner, and then an appointment as under-secretary.

It was while he was engaged in the extremely undemanding tasks this job involved that he came across a brilliant eccentric – one of the many to cluster the stage of eighteenth-century Europe – who was to play a vital though indirect part in the shaping of Goldoni's destiny.

Buonafede Vitale, nicknamed The Anonymous, had been both a Jesuit and a university professor of medicine, abandoning both careers for the more entertaining one of itinerant charlatan, selling his own medicines and running a sort of one-man show. The non-stop patter with which he induced the public to buy, however, was no ordinary street barracking; he would speak on the most complex scientific and medical themes, his mind leaping like a mountain goat from subject to subject. He would also answer any questions that the public cared to throw at him. Not surprisingly the square in which he set up his booth was invariably packed both with hoi polloi and the gentry in their carriages. He ended his extraordinary career in Verona where he was called to help out in an epidemic. It is said that he cured all comers with apples and Cyprus wine, and that the grateful municipality nominated him medical officer of health which, if it is true, suggests that the authorities in Verona were a good deal more gullible 200 years ago than they are now. But, overcome either by the honour or by the effort of doling out apples and Cyprus wine, he succumbed himself, 'wept by all', says Goldoni, 'except the doctors'.

The Anonymous had a devouring passion for the theatre, and he maintained a small company of actors who stooged for him during his own star act – catching the money thrown up in knotted handkerchiefs and throwing back the handkerchiefs with remedies wrapped up in them – and then went on to give a perfomance of their own by torchlight.

Carlo, as usual, wanted to meet the actors or, more exactly, the actresses. And so he presented himself to The Anonymous who, thinking him to be a patient, looked him over and prescribed a cup of chocolate which was indeed Goldoni's remedy for all ills throughout his long life. Adventurer recognized adventurer and the two of them got on together famously. Carlo persuaded the Venetian ambassador to use his influence to obtain a contract in Milan for The Anonymous's company, and in return he was given a free stage box for all performances and *carte blanche* behind the scenes.

It was this company which presented Goldoni's first work for the professional theatre. There wasn't time to write a play, he says, and so he composed an intermezzo for two voices, called *The Venetian Gondolier*. It is no masterpiece, but it is interesting in so far as it displays him for the first time aiming, instinctively and accurately, in the general direction of the one target he was never to miss.

While this was being played, together with *Commedia dell'Arte* scenarios, the company started an intensive publicity campaign for their forthcoming production of a play called *Belisarius,* which they represented as being the last word in theatrical perfection. So effective was the campaign that when *Belisarius* opened, the theatre (the largest in Italy until it was burnt down some while after) was packed, with the audience overflowing into the corridors.

But when the curtain went up, there was a sad surprise. The production, says Goldoni, was lamentable, with the blinded hero, Belisarius, being beaten onto the stage by Harlequin, and all the worst lapses of taste of which the *Commedia dell'Arte* was capable. Carlo was profoundly embarrassed because of all the free tickets he had handed out to influential friends, and he sternly upbraided the leading man, Gaetano Casali, who was later to star in some of Goldoni's own plays. Casali – whose prodigious vanity finally resulted in his dying of pique as the result of a bad reception in Florence – listened to Carlo's outraged protests with what one may imagine was a cynical grin; did not Carlo realize that the totally unjustified publicity build-up was what was known in the business as 'a roast'? The public, after all, was accustomed to that sort of treatment. One thing led to another and Casali finally suggested that Goldoni should write a proper play on the subject of the Roman general, Belisarius, as a vehicle for the actor. Carlo promised to do so, and if any single incident may be considered as the grain of seed from which the top-heavy tree of Goldoni's 'collected works' was to spring, it would probably be this.

In fact he wrote the first act in a few days, but other events were brewing which were to thrust *Belisarius* into the background for a while. The Venetian ambassador returned to Venice for a visit, leaving under-secretary Goldoni in charge of various affairs, most particularly asking to be kept informed of the political situation which threatened to engulf Milan in the Polish war of succession.

On 1st February 1733, August II of Saxony and king of Poland had died, leaving two pretenders clamouring for the throne. One was his son, Frederick August, whose claim was backed by Austria and Russia. The other was Stanislao Leszczynski who had the support of Charles XII of Sweden and, being the father-in-law of Louis XV, was also France's obvious candidate. And in fact, in September 1733, Stanislao was elected to the Polish throne, but his rival refused to back down and called in Russian troops to support his claim. So France – with her allies Piedmont and Spain – struck back by declaring war on Austria, Frederick August's other powerful supporter whose army was at the time entrenched in Italy. The French crossed the Alps, joined forces with Carlo Emanuele III of Sardinia, and swept onto the plain of Lombardy. It was this army which was on its way to Milan while Goldoni was in charge of the affairs of the Venetian embassy there.

But neither wars nor rumours of wars could interrupt Carlo's amorous adventures. One day, heedless of any vital despatches that might be piling up on his desk, he went out into the country with a friend, stopping at the then famous Trowel Inn where they ordered a light snack of meat-balls, thrushes and lobster. Strolling in the garden waiting for the snack to be served, Carlo spotted a delightful little face at a first-floor window 'pretending to hide itself behind the curtain'. That pretence should have put him on his guard, but of course it didn't. On making enquiries of the landlord, he learned that the lady had arrived with a man three days before, that the man had gone out the next morning and had not returned since, that the lady appeared to be in distress and that she was, the landlord believed, Venetian.

A pretty Venetian, and in distress to boot! The combination was altogether too much for Carlo who charged up the stairs and knocked at her door. At first she would not open, but when he spoke to her in Venetian dialect and told her of his position with the Venetian ambassador, she received him 'with a flood of tears and in the greatest desolation'.

The friend, who had accompanied Goldoni, was ill-natured enough to laugh uproariously at the whole scene and, later in the interview, to demand loudly and querulously that they should go and eat their food. But Carlo, always pliable as modelling-wax in the hands of a pretty woman, would not be warned. The lady, it seemed, had fallen in love with a young Venetian nobleman, but because of family opposition they had been obliged to elope, aided and indeed accompanied by a friendly uncle of hers. The family had given chase and overtaken them, and the poor uncle had been arrested and hauled off to prison, while the couple had somehow managed to escape and that same night had lodged at the Trowel Inn. But the next morning the young nobleman vanished, and the poor lady had been vainly waiting for him ever since.

Goldoni swallowed this somewhat improbable story whole, or at any rate he tells us he did, and as he took an affectionate farewell of the unhappy young Venetian that evening, he begged to be told her name. At first she was reluctant to give it, but then she whispered into his ear that it was Margherita Biondi. 'I learned later,' he says a little drily, 'that she was neither Margherita, nor Biondi, nor a niece, nor indeed a young lady.'

The following day he rented her a furnished apartment in the town and, as he says he visited her there often and found her more fascinating every day, one need not feel too sorry for him even if he was, once again, the gull in the end. Indeed his delight at the time was such as to provoke that comment in the *Mémoires*, quoted at the head of this chapter, which may well be applied to the rest of his life, if not to the human condition as a whole.

His overthrow in this particular case began one morning when his servant, drawing the curtains open, informed him in what one imagines to be a Jeeves-ian hushed voice that Milan had been overrun during the night by 15,000 troops – that same army formed by France and her allies to overthrow the Austrians, a garrison of whose troops was at present occupying Milan.

Goldoni received the news of the occupation without undue dismay, dressed and went down to the coffee-house in the hope of further information. Reports there were conflicting, but he managed to piece the facts together sufficiently to send a despatch to the ambassador who returned to Milan three days later.

Great political dramas are no more than the sum of their human consequences, and one consequence of the invasion of Milan concerned the future of Carlo's pretty Venetian lady whose apartment was requisitioned by the military. Unwilling to put her up at an inn again, he was obliged to settle her with a Genoese merchant of his acquaintance which meant, unhappily, that he could only visit her in the midst of the merchant's large and turbulent family.

The war didn't unduly upset the routine of civilized existence. There was a background hum of cannon-fire as the troops laid siege to the castle of Milan without the walls and every so often a badly-aimed shell 'came to visit us in the city'. But that was about the worst of it, and life would have continued happily for Carlo had the ambassador not been ordered by the Venetian government to withdraw to his residence at Crema for the duration. Goldoni, promoted from under to private secretary, was to accompany him, and so, before leaving, he bade farewell to his mistress who was desolate and in tears, but bucked up somewhat when he paid over a sum of money for her keep to the Genoese merchant and another sum into her own hands.

The Venetian lady's uncle had been imprisoned in Crema, so as soon as they arrived there Carlo went to the prison to try and use his influence and good offices to get the poor man out, only to find that earlier efforts, made from Milan and, of course, at the niece's insistence, had already been successful in procuring his release and that he had left for Milan, presumably crossing with Carlo on the road. Further enquiries revealed that the uncle had somehow tracked down his niece to the home of the Genoese merchant and made off with her. So that was the end of that, or so it seemed.

At Crema Carlo was engaged in making summaries of the despatches which were pouring in to the ambassador from Milan and Turin and Brescia and other cities where troops and supplies were eddying and flowing. Then, on the occasion of a three-day armistice in the siege of Pizzighettone – where the Franco-Sard army was besieging the Austrians within firing distance of Crema – he was sent along there as a sort of amateur spy. 'It is impossible', he wrote, 'to describe adequately the exquisite scene of a camp of battle during an armistice; it is the most riotous party, the most brilliant scene you can possibly imagine. A bridge, thrown over the breach, opens the way between besiegers and besieged; everywhere you can see tables laid for banquets, officers exchanging presents. Indoors and out of doors, in tents or huts and under pergolas, they give balls and banquets and concerts. On foot, on horseback and in carriages the people from all about pour in. Food and drink arrive from all corners and there is abundance in the twinkling of an eye. Charlatans and tumblers are everywhere. In a word, it is all a delightful fair-ground, and a vastly entertaining concourse of humanity.'

In the midst of all these pleasures, he managed to get his little bit of spying done, and he reported back to the ambassador that the military would shortly be moving away in the direction of Parma and Piacenza. This turned out to be true, which greatly diminished the pressure of despatches and allowed time for the completion of *Belisarius*.

Once again everything seemed set for calm and prosperity, an infallible sign that trouble was looming. It arrived first in the shape of his brother, the abominable Gian Paolo who, for the temporary lack of anyone else to sponge on, thought he might as well try Carlo. And Carlo, most unwisely, obtained for him the post which he had himself previously held. But Gian Paolo was not cut out for work and, to make matters worse, he and the ambassador didn't get on together. 'If one had a hot head,' Goldoni wrote, 'the other had a boiling one,' and before long Gian Paolo was off in a huff. Unfortunately, his memory lingered on and things were never quite the same again between Carlo and the ambassador, into whose confidence, moreover, a 'hypocritical Dominican' was already worming his way. The smallest misunderstanding would now be enough to break off the once happy relationship. And the smallest misunderstanding was not slow in appearing.

One day there arrived in Goldoni's room a thin little man, none too well dressed, with a limp and a very shifty-looking countenance. This visitor turned out to be the Venetian lady's uncle who, not to make so fine a point of it as Goldoni himself does, was out pimping for his niece and announced that the lady, being newly arrived in Crema, was expecting Goldoni at the White Hart Inn. Carlo, who had to copy a confidential document for the ambassador, said that he would come that evening as soon as he had finished it. At this point the story is plainly doctored for Nicoletta's eyes, for he says that he spent the night at the White Hart playing cards. But whatever he was playing made little difference to the ambassador who concluded that he was divulging the contents of the secret document – not to foreign powers which he probably wouldn't have minded in the least, but to a rival within the Venetian Republic which was really serious. The scene the next morning was a painful one. Carlo even lost his temper, which was very unlike him. The ambassador threatened to have him arrested, and Carlo took refuge with the Bishop of Crema who managed to patch up the worst of the quarrel, but it was plain that the job could no longer go on, and so once again our hero packed his bags and set off – this time for Modena where his mother was living.

His first stop on the journey was at Parma where he lodged at the Cock Inn and was all but swallowed up by the brimstone tide of war. His reporting of the events is masterly although he gets the date wrong – the battle of Parma was in 1734 – and his account deserves a place in any anthology of war correspondents' despatches.

'In the morning I was awoken by a terrifying uproar. I jumped out of bed, opened the window of my room and saw the square full of people running in all directions, bumping into each other, weeping, shouting, despairing. Some women were carrying children in their arms and others were dragging them along. Here men were hauling boxes and baskets and coffers and bundles, there old people were falling to the ground, the sick were fleeing in night-shirts, carriages were overturned and horses were bolting. "Whatever is afoot?", I wondered, "Can this be the end of the world?" [It is typical of Goldoni that he should have kept his cool even in such apocalyptic circumstances.] I put my long coat over my night-shirt, went downstairs, ran along the corridors, went into the kitchen, asked, insisted, but nobody would answer. The landlord had collected all his silverware together, and his wife, who was much dishevelled, held a case of jewels in her hand and other things in her apron; I tried to say something, but she slammed the door in my face and ran off. "What's happening?" I asked everybody I met. Finally at the gate of the stables I saw my coachman and ran up to him, and in fact he was able to satisfy my curiousity. "Sir," he said, "The whole city is in terror, and not without reason. The Austrians are at the gates, and if they come in they will surely sack everything. Everybody is taking refuge in the churches and putting their goods under the protection of God". "Do you think," said I, "that the soldiers will take God into account under such circumstances. And anyway, are all the Austrians Catholics?"

'But even as I was talking with him, there was a dramatic change of scene. There were shouts of joy and bells ringing and explosions of fireworks. All the people poured out of the churches with their goods, searching for friends and relatives, meeting and hugging each other. What could be the motive for such a sudden change?'

The motive was that a spy, who had been playing a double game with the Austrians and the allied troops, had warned the latter the night before that a party of the Austrian forces would try to take Parma the next morning. But before he had a chance to inform the enemy of the counter-move that was being prepared, the allied commander, who was suspicious, had him smartly hanged. So it was that just as the Austrians were about to fall on Parma, the allied troops arrived and engaged them.

'Everybody ran to the walls of the city, and I ran with them,' said Goldoni. 'It would be impossible to see a battle from closer to, and indeed the gun-smoke often prevented us from making out objects clearly. Firing continued for nine hours, and when night separated the two armies, what was left of the Austrian forces fled and scattered in the mountains of Reggio, and the allies remained masters of the field.'

The next day he saw the bodies of the Austrian commander and the Prince of Wirtenberg being brought into Parma on stretchers to be embalmed and sent home. 'But on the day after that there was an infinitely horrible and more disgusting spectacle – that of the 25,000 dead they had stripped the night before, naked and piled in heaps. You could see legs, arms, heads and blood everywhere.' This was a far cry indeed from the 'delightful fairground' and the 'vastly entertaining concourse of humanity' he had seen at Crema, or rather it was the other side of the same coin, though Goldoni, who was not given to metaphysical speculation, does not compare the two events.

The inhabitants of Parma were understandably concerned about the effect of so many putrefying carcasses on the good local air, but the Venetians, who never missed a trick, were quick to realize that Parma was unhealthily near the territory of the Serenissima, and so they sent along enough lime to deal with the problem.

The curtain having come down on that scene, Carlo wanted to go on to Modena, but his coachman refused to take him because, he said, the ravages of war had made the roads unpassable. And so Goldoni shared a coach to Brescia with a young priest who was devoted to the theatre, which made him a sitting duck for a private reading of *Belisarius*. And in fact, as soon as they stopped for a meal, Carlo set out on Act One, Scene One, between mouthfuls. Unfortunately, the coachman insisted on leaving before they had even reached the end of the first act, but undeterred by this, the author continued the reading in the coach, bumps and all. Even he, though, had to admit defeat when they were held up by bandits. Five of them with bristling moustaches and sabres ordered the two passengers to get out. One demanded Carlo's purse which he handed over 'without being asked twice', a second ripped away his watch and a third, going through his pockets, relieved him of a tortoise-shell snuff-box. The other two stripped the young priest bare of his possessions, and then all five threw themselves onto the luggage. The coachman, as soon as he saw his coach unloaded, whipped the horses off at a gallop, and Carlo, at the same time, leapt a ditch and took to his heels across a field, thanking providence that the bandits had been content with his money and his chattels, and had left him the manuscript of *Belisarius*. The young priest must have gathered up his skirts and galloped off in the opposite direction, for we hear no more of him.

As always, Goldoni adapted himself cheerfully to his circumstances. Falling in with a band of peasants, he was only too grateful to share their meal with them, and would have gone on to pass the night in their company if they had not suggested he might be more comfortable with the local parish priest. Conducted thither, he was received with open arms, and his short stay there gave rise to one of the most delightful little scenes in the *Mémoires*, described with such alchemy that you feel as though you were present.

'As soon as I awoke the next morning, they brought me a good cup of chocolate; and then, as the weather was good, I went for a walk until midday which was the hour for lunch. I was delighted to see the parish priest again, and we dined with two other priests of the parish. After we had eaten I prepared myself to give them a reading of my *Belisarius*. My host asked permission to bring in his old maid and his bailiff; and as for me I should have been happy if the whole village had been present.

'My reading was greatly relished by all. The three priests, who were far from dense, noted all the most interesting and lively passages, while the peasants demonstrated clearly with their applause that my work was within the range of everybody and could please the ignorant as much as the learned.' Thus satisfied, he set off for Brescia the next morning accompanied by one of his host's servants.

In Brescia one is struck once again with the extraordinary intimacy of Goldoni's world for, rounding a corner on his way to see if he could extract some money from the governor, who should come limping round the corner but the uncle of his Venetian beauty. Human nature, as Goldoni knew better than most, is unpredictable, and the uncle – rogue and pimp that he was – had no sooner heard of Carlo's misadventures than he insisted on succouring him, and invited him forthwith to the house where he and the niece were lodging. Goldoni, perhaps a trifle pompously, refused, and the little man 'jumped round my neck, begged me, embraced me, recalled his many obligations to me and his gratitude, then took me by the hand and dragged me with him'. Back at their lodgings the niece was overjoyed to see him, and the uncle limped hastily off to give some money on Carlo's behalf to the servant of the parish priest.

When the couple were alone, the girl finally recounted the truth of her circumstances which was indeed already fairly obvious. The man was not her uncle, and had been systematically – and, one must admit successfully – pimping for her for some while. The main trouble, however, was that 'what she earned with repugnance, he spent in profusion'. Now she wished to break from him, and she asked Goldoni's advice about how she might do so. He says, and judging by his generosity on other occasions, there is no reason to doubt him, that he would have bought her freedom himself if he had the money. As it was, he could only suggest that she got her family to help her.

The uncle returned and, obviously considering Carlo now as one of the family, announced somewhat coarsely that as they had no customers that evening the three of them would dine together. The events of that night are obscured for Nicoletta's benefit, but one has an impression that the old man in Paris tried, in describing them, to tip the wink to his readers. He was shown into a room with a large, curtained bed – the young lady's reception room, said the uncle with a leer, adding that Carlo might occupy it that night alone or in company, as he wished. But then, just as one can imagine Nicoletta's brows were beginning to contract, Goldoni quickly adds that the place filled him with horror and that he was only dissuaded from leaving the house at once when they showed him a chaste single room. He makes no bones, however, about the less compromising fact that the three of them dined together in great high spirits and that the 'uncle' lent him six *zecchini*, refusing even to take a receipt. The next morning, after they had breakfasted together, Goldoni left for Verona. Years later, he says, he came across the lady, happily married in Venice, while her pimp finished up in the galleys.

Today the Roman arena in Verona is principally famous for the opera season which is held in it every summer, although it is also used for gymkhanas and other events including an alarming brass band competition which reaches its climax when all the 100-odd competing bands blast their heads off in deafening unison; and it has even been the setting for one of those hearty international television games in which people thrash about in artificial lakes in an effort to retain their balance on two floating pumpkins (the smugger Veronese grinned like so many Cheshire cats when it poured with rain throughout the event). When Goldoni arrived in 1734, it was used for an equally catholic range of entertainments including a sort of bull-fight (recent attempts to bring the bull-fight back to the arena finally came to nothing after enough political in-fighting, denials, counter-denials and accusations to serve an entire general election). And there were also theatrical performances for which an improvised theatre was set up on trestles. So it was that, on coming out of his hotel the morning after his arrival, Carlo saw a playbill advertising *Harlequin Dumb with Terror*. He went that evening and, although the programme had been changed, he was delighted to find that the leading man was that same Gaetano Casali who had asked Goldoni to write his version of *Belisarius*. Through Casali he met the rest of the company – on tour from its permanent base in Venice – and its actor-manager, the Genoese Giuseppe Imer. Imer invited him to lunch the next day and, after an uproarious meal with the whole company, Carlo read them his *Belisarius*. The reading was a triumph, and before an audience not of benevolent country priests and peasants, but of tough professionals. Imer announced that he would produce the play and, as an earnest of future benevolence, invited its author to be his guest for the rest of the stay in Verona.

Carlo had been received into his kingdom at last. With fanfares.

OPERE DI CARLO GOLDONI

Sentit enim vim quisque suam quam
possit abusi.
Lucr Liber V. vers 1032

The Lawyer Beguiled

or

The Scales and the Masks

V

'Remember that you actors are held in hatred by God the blessed, but tolerated by princes for the entertainment of the people who take a delight in your iniquity.'

Nicolò Maria Tiepolo, Venetian inquisitor

In the aviary of eighteenth-century Venice, the players were the sparrows – cheeky, grubby and irrepressible. They were both the delight and the despair of those who came in touch with them. Goldoni, thanks to his almost phenomenal serenity, usually managed to keep his head, though the effort required was often Herculean and not always sucessful. As for poor Carlo Gozzi – aristocrat, amateur man of letters, and later one of Goldoni's fiercest opponents – they plainly drove him out of his wits; it is true that from the serene vantage point of his memoirs he tries hard to show how unruffled he was by them, but the exasperation rising to frenzy jangles through like an alarm bell.

Probably no other playwright, with the possible exception of Jean Anouilh, has ever been so obsessed with actors and actresses as was Carlo Goldoni. They swarmed and clattered through his life; he wrote plays not only for them, but about them, delighting in the play within the play, the mask which becomes the face and the face which becomes the mask.

These players were still blessedly disreputable; no Venetian Sir Henry Irving had strutted onto their scene to atrophy them with respectability. Giving permission for the annual opening of the theatres in Venice, the inquisitor quoted above warned them, 'The doors of the theatre are opening this evening, but not the doors of the brothel. You actors easily lose your heads, but remember that the magistrate will be watching you with vigilance. So off you go and behave like Christians even if you are only actors.' Another inquisitor sternly forbade the use of obscenities 'which you are always putting in'. The theatre was enjoyed, but not very highly considered; Carlo Gozzi's collaboration with the Sacchi company, as will be seen, was heavily paternalistic, like a randy clergyman appointing himself chaplain to a bawdy-house.

The players often led hard, rough, but on the whole cheerful lives. One writer spoke of their 'precariousness, their wandering from inn to inn, their prodigal ease alternating with cramped misery', but he added that they were distinguished by 'a gaiety and a carefree quality that seemed to derive from the radiance of the sky, the mildness of the climate and the general vivacity of our land'. The carefree quality they would certainly have needed for, out of their often miserable earnings, they had to find, not only their own costumes, but travelling expenses as well – and the Venetian companies were on tour for six months of the year.

When Goldoni started to write for them, they already had a tradition of at least two centuries of theatrical craftsmanship stretching behind them, of companies in which each member had a specific and unchangeable part to play – the *primo amoroso* or leading man, usually played by the manager of the company; the leading lady; the supporting 'straight' male and female roles descending strictly in order of importance; the maidservant, and the traditional masks – in Venice the four principal masks were Pantaloon and the Doctor, Harlequin and Brighella. These actors had a multitude of skills, including fencing and dancing and miming and tumbling, and in fact most of the actors in the Medebac company, for which Goldoni wrote many of his greatest plays, were tumblers by origin, including the leading lady.

Not all the players, however, were born into the business, and vocations for the theatre, like the good seed, seemed to fall on all sorts of ground. There was a Genoese lawyer who suddenly turned actor. He stayed on the boards for some while with distinction, and then returned to the law where he found that his theatrical experience helped him to manage 'even the most complicated situations in favour of his clients'. Another actor was described as 'a Veronese gentleman, learned in Latin and Greek'. Cesare D'Arbes – one of the great Pantaloons of his age and a Goldoni actor – started life as a mirror-maker. Other actors had been soldiers, tailors, doctors and even barbers. But perhaps the strangest destiny of all, if we may anticipate a few years, was that of a young Venetian copyist named Giovanni Simoni who found himself entrusted with the copying of plays by Goldoni. The effect was so drastic that he laid down his pens for good and took to the stage where, because of the singular origins of his vocation, he became known as Goldoncino, the little Goldoni. He married and started his own company where, said a chronicler of the time, he was particularly good in 'affected or exaggerated parts'.

So then it was a mixed bag of people for whom Goldoni wrote and for whom he created his characters. 'All my plays I have written for people I knew, with the characters of the actors who would represent them before my eyes, and this, I believe, has greatly contributed to the success of my compositions; indeed

'The sooth-sayer' (Pietro Longhi). The side-shows of characters like this made it seem as though Venice were imitating Goldoni.

Rosaura, loving and beloved, and Harlequin, the most famous of them all.

Florindo, the lover, with his Bergamask servant, Brighella, who is traditionally shrewd and cunning.

'A stroll in the square' (Pietro Longhi). The mask – part fashion, part titillation – is omnipresent in Goldoni's plays.

so accustomed did I become to this rule that, having found the subject of a play, I did not first draw the characters to then find the actors, but rather I began by examining the actors in order to imagine the characters they would play.'

It wasn't quite as smooth sailing as he makes it sound, though, and Goldoni's career is littered with hysterical scenes. 'Apollo save a poet from being reduced to paid writing for actors!' exclaimed his colleague and enemy, Carlo Gozzi; 'No galley-slave is more prisoner than he, no porter carries a weight such as he bears, and no ass has to put up with more prodding and insults.'

Gozzi, of course, was driven to distraction by them, and his chilly, aristocratic heart was subjugated and tormented by an actress, Teodora Ricci. It is the memory of her, one suspects, that makes his memoirs seethe with such violent judgements of the profession. 'Of all mortals the most difficult to understand are actors and actresses . . . Audacity is their main attribute . . . You can believe with your eyes shut that the principal idol adored by the players is venal gain. They look on courtesy, civilized living, Christianity as so many means towards their own profit, and if this idol is touched, however justly and reasonably, all shreds of grace drop from them. One hint of gain and they will throw their benefactors and the reputation of the whole world to the winds . . . Unmasked, they laugh in your face with unspeakable boldness, as though to say, "You are indeed stupid if you flatter yourself you have discovered something new" . . . The present is the only time contemplated by the players'.

And as the present was their time, so love was their element. 'We mortals have no other happiness than to make love until the hour of our death,' Gozzi's Teodora told him. And elsewhere Gozzi says, 'He deludes himself who believes he can deal with actresses without making love to them. They are soaked in love. Love is their principal guide from the age of five or six.'*

Nor was this love always disinterested. One writer describes how, particularly in Naples, the leading ladies, the maid-servants and the comediennes did little to contribute towards the good name of the profession. 'Practically all the women in the theatre', he said, 'came under the law which relegated whores to certain districts of the city, so that in order to act they were obliged to obtain special dispensations. And the actors were no better, often living on the shoulders of their wives whom they forced into prostitution.'

Goldoni gives a wonderfully vivid portrait of two actresses in a third-rate touring company in *La Locandiera* (*The Mistress of the Inn*). 'Making love with you actresses, to tell the truth,' says the Count D'Albafiorita to one of them, 'gives me little pleasure. One moment you're here and the next you're gone.' The reply could hardly be more real. 'Isn't it better like that, sir?' says Ortensia, 'In that way friendships don't drag on for ever, and men don't ruin themselves.' Fundamentally they don't care much about anything, but while the going is

---

* Gozzi's account of the almost monastic moral code reigning in the Sacchi company is another matter and will be gone into in its place. See page 148.

good they solicit gifts, guzzle, clown and make casual love; then, characteristically without a goodbye, they are off – to some other inn, one imagines, where they will set up another set of relationships as permanent as the scenery against which they act. When Eleanora Duse gave her famous instruction that Goldoni should always be played 'with lace cuffs', she can hardly have been thinking of these two, for they are bawdy, strident gipsies.

Their predatory nature is reflected by Carlo Gozzi who says that 'many actresses made a regular habit of ensnaring their lovers and gently fleecing them of everything they possessed. To obtain fortune they did not bother whether the way was clear or muddy.'

Goldoni's pair, like the gipsies they are, spatter their conversation liberally with slang, and the definition of two of the words they use gives a fair idea of the things that went on. *Micheggiare* means using blandishments to put someone in a position where he felt bound to give money, and a *gonzo* was a foolish lover who, flattering himself that he is loved in return – and thus weakened – behaves with such liberality as to ruin himself. 'The powder of the dressing-rooms', said the Abbé Chiari (who makes his entrance later in this story), 'is like gunpowder; it stains, scorches, burns, breaks and kills.'

Vice is easier to write about than virtue, and one tends to forget that, like everywhere else, there was good as well as bad in the little world of the Italian theatre in the eighteenth century. It takes Goldoni to sum up the situation fairly. 'For twenty years now,' he wrote in a letter, 'led by my genius, I have had to do with practically all the players on our stage. Among these I have come across lewd women and profligate men with the same passions, the same vices that I have seen in ordinary people in many more respectable places. But I have also seen men of such honesty, women of such high moral conduct that would put the most retiring to shame. Nor can this justice that I render to many virtuous actors and actresses be ascribed to partiality. Anyone who does not believe me has only to ask and he will surely find that if the theatre is not exactly a school of the most austere virtues, nor is it the place of scandal that it has, too unjustly, been called.' And even Gozzi admitted that 'it is easier to find a good wife in the theatre than in many private families.'

If the actresses made good wives, they hardly made literate ones. Gozzi says that all their education lay in the ability to read and write 'more or less correctly' and that some couldn't even do that. 'They had their parts read over to them by a friend or relative until they were sketched upon their memory.' And Teodora Ricci showed 'such boredom and disgust' at Gozzi's attempts to educate her that he had to limit them to running over her part with her – and superficially at that.

But whatever their cultural defects may have been, their standards of acting were, to judge by all accounts, high. One writer says that they were unequalled in the improvisations of the *Commedia dell'Arte* and 'much sought after and applauded abroad'. Even in Naples where the conditions were so miserable, he adds condescendingly and illogically, there were the most brilliant Pulcinellas (Pulcinella was one of the Italian masks). When Cesare D'Arbes died, his obituary notice said there would never be another Pantaloon like him. And Antonio Sacchi, though a tyrannous and dirty old man, was unquestionably what we should call a great actor.

To put these actors and their lives into greater relief it is useful to look at the material they had to work on before Goldoni gave them scripts with dialogue which had to be learned by heart. *Commedia dell'Arte* productions were based on scenarios, within the rough framework of which the actors would ad lib. One writer said that these scenarios suffered from the worst of all defects 'total lack of vitality', and adds, 'They are mummified before they are born.' At the time of Goldoni's birth there were rather less than 300 of them, going the rounds of the theatres rather as dirty jokes go the rounds of schools. And indeed they were little more than protracted dirty jokes, liberally dotted with angelical or diabolical intervention. 'The public revelled in indecent jests,' said Carlo Gozzi, who, although the most formidable champion of the *Comedia dell'Arte* (as will be seen), nevertheless disapproved of all bawdry that was not his own. 'And if the lips that spoke the jests,' he goes on, 'were young, female and pretty, then the jests seemed the more savoury.'

One of the most fascinating and freakish of all Goldoni's plays is *Il Teatro Comico*. It has no plot whatsoever and might be sub-titled 'A morning in the life of a theatrical company'. It is, in fact, Goldoni's way of presenting his theatrical reform to the public, but for us it has the far greater value of being the most vivid and detailed picture of actors at work that has ever been passed down the centuries. The members of the company come and go, they rehearse scenes from a new play, they grumble and quarrel and put forward their points of view; a starving author tries to sell his atrocious masterpieces; the prompter complains to no avail; the actor-manager lectures everybody about how to do their jobs. Then finally at the end of the morning – and the play – they all go off to lunch.

Il Teatro Comico not only looks forward to the Goldoni reform, but backwards to the *Commedia dell'Arte*. Apart from bawdry, comic violence was the great stand-by of the *Commedia*, and whenever the action showed signs of flagging it could always be whipped up again by Harlequin hitting somebody over the head with a bladder or a sausage. 'And while Pantaloon is in the house, what shall the Doctor say?' the actor-manager asks the aspiring author. 'While Pantaloon is in the house,' the author replies, 'the Doctor . . . the Doctor can say whatever he likes. And in the meantime – yes, listen – in the meantime Harlequin, the Doctor's servant, comes up slowly from behind and beats his master.' To which the actor-manager very properly replies 'Ouch! From bad to worse!'

This *Commedia dell'Arte* with its violence and its vulgarity and its charm as well sprang from the sacred representations of the church in the middle ages. Then slowly the actors began to desert their origins and develop into the mimes and masks and jugglers and tumblers of the *Commedia*. It is not underrating

Goldoni or the actors of his theatre to say that these tumblers were often superb craftsmen and artists. The most inventive member of the company would think up a story which he and his companions would then improvise in words and gestures. And if the result didn't please a clamorous fairground public they were out of business.

At the beginning the action, which had to be fast and furious, dominated over the words, but with the passing of time the dialogue gained its own importance, partly because the public always liked dirty jokes and partly because, Italy being continually under foreign domination, the *Commedia* was a wonderful vehicle for patriotic innuendo - a sort of bawdy, theatrical version of *Finlandia*.

The actors toured the country very much as they do today, and stopped at the same places. The sixteenth-century writer and jurist, Tommaso Garzoni, has left a description of the arrival of a *Commedia dell'Arte* company in town. 'As they enter a town the sound of a drum immediately spreads the news that such-and-such a company of players has arrived, and the leading lady, dressed as a man, sword in hand, goes the rounds of the town and invites the people to a comedy, a tragedy or a pastoral in some large house or the pilgrim's inn where the groundlings, ever curious by nature and desirous of new things, hasten to fill the room. One passes into a hall with an improvised stage bearing charcoal-painted scenery of the worst taste in this world. There is an overture which sounds as though it were played by asses and bumble-bees, a prologue recited in the tones of Friar Stoppino [a *Commedia dell'Arte* figure], action as vile as can be imagined and intermezzos as horrible as a thousand gibbets.'

The action usually centred around the stereotyped intrigues of a couple of lovers whose very names were limited, the women being almost invariably Flaminia, Isabella, Ortensia, Beatrice or Rosaura and the men Lelio, Leandro, Florindo, Ottavio or Orazio - a custom continued by Goldoni. But the lovers were little more than an excuse. All the life (and the immortality) of the *Commedia dell'Arte* productions came from the masks - Pantalone (Pantaloon), Arlecchino (Harlequin), Colombina (Columbine), Pulcinella (Punch), Scaramuccia (Scaramouche), Fracassa (Capitaine Fracasse) and many others. It was them that the public flocked to see.*

The *Commedia dell'Arte* flourished between the sixteenth and the eighteenth centuries. It was as Italian as spaghetti. It had its virtues and its

---

* The history of all the masks would require a book to itself. They came from different parts of Italy, and their characteristics depended upon their place of origin and varied according to the actor behind the mask. They travelled across seas and continents, many of them like Punch and Harlequin taking up permanent residence abroad. The origins and history of the four great Venetian masks - Pantaloon, the Doctor, Harlequin and Brighella - are discussed in Chapter Seven.

defects, and it was only when the latter began to overwhelm the former that there was need for a reformer who appeared – very much willy nilly – in the person of Carlo Goldoni. But for two centuries it kept the whole of Europe in a roar, and there were *Commedia dell'Arte* companies in permanent service at the courts of France, Austria, Bavaria, Saxony and Poland.

The Goldonian scenarios were written with a certain minimum of elegance and they read today rather like short stories. But the scenarios by Goldoni's predecessors, those going the rounds when he started writing, were a very different matter indeed, a mixture of slang and shorthand which is often very hard to disentangle. Here are some extracts from one called *La Trapolaria (The Swindles)*. It was written by a bizarre genius named Giovanni Battista della Porta, a Neapolitan, also credited with the discovery of the telescope, and in his day – he lived from 1535 to about 1615 – famous for studies on magic, cryptography, physiognomy, palmistry, agriculture, etymology, mnemonics, fortification and geometry; such was the climate of the age. *The Swindles* was based very approximately on a comedy by Plautus, as many of the *Commedia* scenarios were based on Latin plays. The plot, as public taste required, was of almost nightmare intricacy, but a simplified version of the main outline is more than enough as a background to some extracts from the scenario.

At the centre of the plot is Policinella's slave-girl, Turchetta, who is loved by a young man named Fedelindo (whom she loves in return) and also by a handsome Spanish captain whose intentions, unlike those of Fedelindo, one is given to understand, are strictly dishonourable. The main thread of the action concerns the various attempts by Fedelindo and the Captain to buy Turchetta from Policinella. Fedelindo is helped by the Harlequin-type servant, Coviello, while the Captain uses his servant, Pasquariello. A courtesan named Isabella is introduced at a certain point and Coviello tries to palm her off on the Captain in place of Turchetta. The ending, of course, is happy, and Turchetta and Fedelindo are finally united.

Here, without any introduction or instructions for the actors, is how the scenario begins. 'Captain speaks of his love for the slave-girl and wishes to buy her and knocks. Policinella, his funny business indoors, and then comes out. Captain believes him a servant of the house, asks him for Policinella; he [Policinella] tells him to speak. Captain says he wants Policinella; he [Policinella] uses gag: *Try knocking again*. Finally understanding. Agree about price of the slave-girl, and that he [the Captain] will send servant with sign [of recognition], speaking in [Policinella's] ear. Turchetta at window has seen all, is sorry not to have understood what sign is, and enters [the house]. Policinella enters [the house]. Captain off.'*

* I have tried to translate as literally as possible to give the impression of the breathless shorthand which is all the actors had to go on. Anything added for the sake of clarity is in brackets.

Shortly after this comes a scene between the two lovers, Turchetta and Fedelindo. They both know they are to be separated; she because she has overheard the scene between the Captain and Policinella, and he because he has just been sent to Barcelona by his father. She is crying when they meet, and there is 'misunderstanding scene' between them. When she hears that he is to go to Barcelona she faints. 'Coviello [Fedelindo's servant] sees slave-girl fainted and runs for water with gags: fresh water or flower water, from cistern or fountain? Hot or cold? Finally falls with jug and pretends to use it as chamber-pot. Turchetta regains consciousness. Coviello [says] that his urine is balm. Turchetta reveals that she has been sold [to the Captain]. Fedelindo faints. Coviello with urine, raises price of urine. Then hearing of the lovers' misadventures pretends to faint. They call for water, he for wine.'

If the action was turbulent on the stage, it was no less so in the audience. Everywhere in Venice – as Goldoni himself pointed out – there was music, and the theatres were perhaps the only places where it couldn't be heard, such was the uproar made by the audience, shouting at each other across the stalls or from box to box. The wife of a Venetian ambassador in Paris wrote home to a friend saying, 'The theatres here are very different from ours. Just imagine that people go to them in order to be silent and listen . . .'

In *Il Teatro Comico* the actors complain about the noise in the audience. 'To tell the truth,' says one of them, 'it's a great trial for us players to have to act against the din of the audience. We shout ourselves hoarse in order to be heard, and often that's not enough.' A more easy-going actress replies, 'One must be patient with the public. And when they whistle and crow like cocks? Young people enjoying themselves – you just have to be patient.' A third actor complains of the people who deliberately start yawning in order to ruin a play, and a colleague reminds him that a popular catch of the audience runs, 'My dear good sir, don't try to be funny – I do what I want 'cos I've paid my money!'

The prompter laments about the people who pour up from the pit and stalls on to the stage and is reminded that the reason they do so is to avoid being spat upon by the people in the boxes, where cheerful supper parties and gambling sessions were held during the play. And as the theatres were very dimly lit, the boxes were also ideal places for love-making. Président De Brosses, who missed nothing in Venice, records this scene. 'To my great surprise I saw a young man and a very beautiful young woman going into a box together; there they listened to an act or two, chattering away together with great vivacity, after which they withdrew themselves from the view of the stage and the audience, closing the green taffeta curtains which shut off the front of the box.'

To face that sort of competition, the actors had to be good indeed.

VI

'Yes, my dear reader, I got married, and this is how it came about'.

Carlo Goldoni

The Imer company, with which Goldoni was to collaborate on and off for the next ten years of his life, was a cut above the companies of The Anonymous and Florindo dei Maccheroni from which he had received all his direct experience of the theatre so far. If they were of the level of the third- to fourth-rate little troupes that used to hack their way round the provinces of Britain, the Imer team was more comparable to a first-rate repertory company.

Giuseppe Imer, its actor-manager, was from Genoa, and, like all businessmen from that city, he was a shrewd, hard dealer. Physically he was short and heavily built with small eyes and a little squashed nose and a head planted aggressively on his shoulders without any intervening neck. A theatrical chronicler of the day described him as 'an excellent actor, a tolerable musician and poet' and added that he was famous in the parts of lovers, but Goldoni says that he was ridiculous in serious parts which, given his appearance, is more likely.

As was usually the way in these companies, the actor-manager's family was actively involved. His wife, Paolina, who the same chronicler described as his downfall, was the 'third lady', a position she can hardly have relished. One of the daughters, Teresa, sang in the musical intermezzi and the second daughter, Marianna, also acted. With three female members of his family in the company, the atmosphere must have been fairly tense, for Imer tumbled his actresses whenever he had the chance, and his mistress at the time Carlo joined the company was Zanetta Casanova, Giacomo's mother. Goldoni describes her as a beautiful and talented young widow while another writer with a more recognisable smack of truth said that she was 'more than forty, with a colossal figure and an old woman's face in spite of all the make-up.' In spite of this, he added, she played the leading-lady parts which must have been galling for Signora Imer. And, as if that wasn't enough to disturb the peace of the household and the company, she was also rampantly unfaithful to Imer.

Carlo's first job in the troupe was to knock together a musical intermezzo for Imer – who had a good voice and revelled in it – Zanetta Casanova and Teresa Imer. It was always Goldoni's system when pressed for material to exploit any situation that happened to be around. So now, with some audacity for a new boy, he took the subject of Imer's love life, put it into verse and titled it *The Ward*. Imer immediately realized that he was being parodied, but he must have appreciated the humour of it, for he laughed, applauded, and sent the work off to Venice to be set to music.

In the meantime preparations were going ahead for the production of *Belisarius*, and Gaetano Casali, who took over from Imer as leading man for this play, was so delighted with the work that he gave six *zecchini* to Carlo who, characteristically, remembered his debt to the limping 'uncle' of his Venetian mistress and sent the money straight off to him. 'This', he explains, 'is my system. I have always tried to avoid baseness, but I have never been proud; when I have been able I have helped all those who have had need of me, and I have received such help as I needed without embarrassment, and asked for it without blushing.'

It was now the end of September and the theatrical season was due to open in Venice, so the company packed up and trundled out of Verona. Carlo was a little anxious about the lady with the aquiline nose and her niece, but his mother was able to assure him that they, having heard of his association with a theatrical company, now felt nothing but contempt for him.

Back in Venice after two years of wanderings, Carlo was introduced by Imer to the patrician, Grimani, who was the owner of the San Samuele theatre where the company acted. Grimani was affable and promised Goldoni further work at the San Giovanni Grisostomo theatre in Venice which was also his property, and so it was in a favourable and optimistic atmosphere that the final rehearsals went ahead for *Belisarius* and *The Ward*. Indeed, Carlo was so buoyed up that he threw off a tragedy called *Rosamund* and, more to the point, another musical intermezzo called *The Scapegrace* which was based upon the tumblers in St Mark's Square whose ways he had been observing.

On 24th November 1734 *Belisarius* opened at the San Samuele theatre and was an immediate smash hit. 'The play was listened to with a silence which was extraordinary, indeed almost entirely unheard of in Italian theatres. The audience, accustomed to uproar, broke its banks during the intervals and with cries of joy, applause and gesturings from the stalls and pit to the boxes acclaimed the author and the actors. At the final curtain all these signs of approval were redoubled, and the cast was deeply moved. Some wept and some laughed, but it was the same joy that produced the different effects.' The play was repeated every night for the rest of the autumn season until 14th December which was considered a very long run indeed.

Some half a century later, in the *Mémoires*, Goldoni admits that he was extremely lucky, 'particularly when one thinks that my composition did not have the merit that was attributed to it'. Another critic puts it somewhat more strongly. 'The characters', he says, 'are ridiculous, the plot clumsy and puerile, and the verses horrible'. The whole, he adds 'is a theatrical monster'. But some of Goldoni's old love for the play lingered on, for he indignantly refutes Imer's suggestion that it was the intermezzo, *The Ward*, which kept *Belisarius* going, asserting that it was the other way round.

After Christmas they put on *Rosamund*, but it tottered alarmingly after its triumphant predecessor, even when supported by the intermezzo, *The Scapegrace*. Finally after eight performances it had to be taken off and replaced by *Belisarius* which ran on until the end of carnival.

This was also the end of the theatrical season, but during the two weeks of celebration for the Ascension, Grimani wanted to put on a musical spectacle at his San Giovanni Grisostomo theatre and so, true to his promise, he offered Goldoni the job of adapting an existing script of *The Patient Grissel* story which was to be set to music by none other than Vivaldi, 'called the red priest because of his hair and better known by that nickname than by his own name', says Goldoni, adding rather patronizingly that he was 'an excellent violinist and a tolerable composer'. The description of the meeting between the two of them is one of the richest passages in the *Mémoires*.

'I found him', says Goldoni, 'surrounded by music and with his breviary in his hand. He got up and crossed himself enormously, putting his breviary aside and paying me the normal courtesy. "What gives me the pleasure of seeing you, sir?" "His Excellency Grimani has given me the job of making such changes as you think fit in the opera for the forthcoming celebrations. So I have come to learn your plans." "Ah ha, so you, sir, have been given the job of adapting *The Patient Grissel*? So Master Lalli is no longer entrusted with the entertainments of Master Grimani?" "Master Lalli, who is much advanced in years, will continue to enjoy the profits of such works as I do not handle, and I shall have the honour of setting out on a new employment, which will give me nothing but pleasure, under the orders of Master Vivaldi." At this point the Abbé Vivaldi took up his breviary again and, without answering me, crossed himself once more. "Sir," I said, "I should not wish to distract you from your religious duties. Allow me to return at another moment." "I know very well, my dear Master Goldoni, that you have talent for poetry; I have seen your *Belisarius* which gave me much pleasure. But this is a very different matter. One may write a tragedy, even an epic poem if you wish, without being able to write a single verse to be set to music." "Will you be so good as to show me the script?" I asked. "Yes, indeed, most gladly . . . Now where the devil has this Patient Grissel gone and hidden herself? *Deus in adjutorium meum intende. Domine . . . Domine . . . Domine . . .* It was here just now. *Domine ad adjuvandum . . .* Ah! Here it is! Now look, sir, at this scene between Walter and Grissel – a most interesting and moving scene. The author has put a sad aria at the end, but Mademoiselle Giraud doesn't like melancholy songs; she wants an expressive piece with some movement to it, an aria which expresses passion in various ways with short words and throbbing sighs, with action and vitality. I don't know if you follow me?" "Yes sir, I follow you perfectly, but I have had the honour of hearing Mademoiselle Giraud sing, and I know that her voice is not strong enough . . ." "What, sir, do you insult a pupil of mine? She is excellent and can sing everything." "Yes sir, you are right. Only let me have the script and leave it to me." "No sir, I cannot do that. I need it and the work is wanted urgently." "Well then, if the work is wanted urgently, lend it to me for a moment and I will give you satisfaction immediately." "Here and now?" "Yes sir, here and now."

'Making fun of me, the Abbé handed over the drama together with pen and ink, took up his breviary again and, walking up and down, recited hymns and psalms. I glanced through the scene, which was already known to me, and went over in my mind the Maestro's specifications, and in less than quarter of an hour I had thrown down an aria of eight verses divided in two parts. I called the priest and showed him my work. Vivaldi read it, frowned, read it again and then with a howl of joy threw his breviary onto the ground and called for Mademoiselle Giraud. She came. "Ah!" said he, "Here is a rare man, an excellent poet! Read this aria. This is the gentleman who wrote it—here—without moving, in less than a quarter of an hour!" Then, turning to me, he continued, "Ah sir, I beg your pardon!" Then he embraced me and protested that he would never again use any other poet than me.'

When Goldoni had finished his work on *The Patient Grissel*, the Imer company was on tour in Padua where he joined them to find that there had been various important changes, two of which affected him personally. Zanetta Casanova had walked out, having had a better offer from the court at Dresden, and her place had been taken by Antonia Ferramonti who was young, pretty and talented. And an actress called Elisabetta Passalacqua had taken over the maids' parts. Both these women were to leave their mark on Goldoni, though in very different ways.

First it was the turn of Antonia Ferramonti with whom Carlo fell head over heels in love. A husband was also involved, being towed about by la Ferramonti although he was not a member of the company. But like many theatrical husbands of the time he appears to have been complaisant, and a cordial friendship was struck up between him and Goldoni who, in his own words, had set about 'making a real actress of the girl'. Understandably this aroused violent squalls of jealousy among the other women in the company, the most difficult of whom was a tough old war-horse called Adriana Bastona who, in spite of her fifty years 'which jewellery and make-up could not hide', had a very sweet voice and an excellent stage presence which was only marred by a tendency, sternly noted by one critic, to play for laughs in the serious scenes. She, above all, bayed for revenge on Antonia Ferramonti and all too tragically she was to have it.

In the meantime the affair went its way and the company shifted from Padua to Udine, Carlo refusing a lift from Imer and riding instead with Antonia and her amiable husband. As soon as they arrived in Udine – and in spite of Antonia – Carlo briefly and most imprudently renewed his acquaintance with the daughter of the coffee-house keeper. By now she was married, but as soon as she heard that Carlo was in town she wrote him 'a very astute letter'. His report of the encounter is somewhat enigmatic. 'I went to see her at an hour agreed upon and found her much changed. Our meeting did not last too long, and, as I had no desire to sacrifice my new inclinations, I saw her once again and then no more.' It seems probable that the young lady, now safely in the port of matrimony, conceded what her mother's guile had previously compelled her to withold.

Also in Udine Carlo produced a piece for the opening of the following season in Venice which caused all the banked-up jealousy in the company to overflow, for the part written for Antonia Ferramonti was bigger and better than that for Adriana Bastona. La Bastona egged on the others against Carlo and the unfortunate girl, and their hatred seemed to act like a spell of black magic. Antonia, who was pregnant, suddenly began to suffer from grave complications. A midwife was called in and then a specialist, and it was decided to try a Cæsarian operation. But the child was born dead and the mother quickly followed it.

Unable to bear Bastona's grisly triumph, Carlo fled to Venice where he was tenderly welcomed by his mother to whom he recounted his adventures, concealing, however, those he felt might shock her. 'I made her laugh, weep and tremble. That day we dined with various relatives and she was dying with eagerness to tell them the stories I had told her, but she kept on getting mixed up and only succeeded in arousing their curiosity, so I was obliged to start telling them all again. The merriment of the table went to my head, and so I recounted all the things I had previously kept silent with my mother. "Ah, you villain!" she said every so often, "you didn't tell me this or that or the other!" I spent the day very happily obliging my old uncles and aunts, who never laughed normally, to laugh then at my expense. Maybe I'm better at talking than I am at writing.' The scene and its conclusion are typically Goldonian.

September came round again and the company returned to Venice where they opened with the piece that Goldoni had written for them in Udine. It was tolerably successful, but Imer was not pleased with Elisabetta Passalacqua. 'Her voice was false, her manner of delivery monotonous and her features were distorted by a grimace,' says Carlo who later on describes her as 'thin, with green eyes, and a great deal of make-up covering her pale, yellowish skin'. This unusually cruel portrait may have been painted for Nicoletta's benefit, for all other sources indicated that la Passalacqua was a vivacious and attractive woman, while the events immediately following the company's return to Venice show that she was unmistakably pleasing to men. She came of a theatrical family and had been taught the trade by her father. A contemporary says that she was a brilliant dancer, musician and fencer.

Imer, however, to shore up whatever weakness he felt she constituted, hired a delightful eighteen-year-old girl to sing an intermezzo, accompanied on the violin by her sixty-year-old husband, thus arousing the jealousy of Passalacqua who, already having tried unsuccessfully to get her hooks into Carlo at Udine, now made an all-out effort to conquer him. She sent him a note inviting him to her house - an invitation which, he said, politeness forbade him to refuse. She received him in unequivocally erotic *déshabille* and sat herself next to him on a sofa, telling him 'the most flattering and gallant things in the world'. Carlo, on his part, bore the siege with 'heroic continence'. Passalacqua tried every trick that she knew, finally bursting into tears and saying that she was a poor, weak, defenceless woman who would be lost without his protection. These arguments, he confessed, moved him somewhat and he agreed to give her his assistance. She then changed her tone completely and, in the sunniest of manners, suggested a ride out on the lagoon by gondola. 'I refused, she laughed and insisted, taking me by the arm and pulling me. How could I not follow her?' How indeed? Once in the cosy intimacy of the gondola cabin, when the gondolier had closed the curtain which cut off the passengers from the rest of the world, one imagines that la Passalacqua's advances met with no further resistance. Nor can the gondolier have been in much doubt as to what was going on in his craft for when, after some while, Carlo popped his head out through the curtain and asked the hour, the man replied, 'Faith, sir, I do not know the hour, but it is the lover's hour if I am not mistaken', after which he rowed them home singing all the way the twenty-sixth strophe of 'Jerusalem Delivered'. The couple then had an intimate supper-party at la Passalacqua's home and when Carlo finally tottered out into the night, the actress was able to congratulate herself on total victory. And in fact, the next morning, Goldoni set to work on an intermezzo for her.

But it soon became clear that Elisabetta's alley-cat instincts were stronger than any desire she may have had to keep her author enmeshed. One of the principal actors of the company was Antonio Vitalba, described by Goldoni as 'a handsome man, an excellent actor, a great chaser of women and a supreme libertine'. Another writer said he was the idol of Venice and 'the most vivacious actor ever seen on the stage', whose talent was only sullied by a tendency to 'revert to Harlequin' and play for laughs when he shouldn't. This Vitalba was also la Passalacqua's lover, and as soon as Goldoni discovered that he was working in shifts with one of the leading actors, either from pique or fastidiousness, he broke off the affair. Passalacqua wrote him a pathetic letter to which he replied in self-righteous wrath. She wrote him again, imploring him to go and see her 'once, for the last time; as she had something of vital importance to tell him. He hesitated, then went.

'I found her lying on the sofa with her head on a pillow. I greeted her and she did not reply. The blood rose to my face; I was blinded and maddened with anger, and I gave free vent to all my resentment, not sparing her any of the reproof she deserved. The actress remained silent, but now and then she wiped her eyes; I, fearing those treacherous tears, made to leave. 'Go, by all means,' she said with a trembling voice, 'Go. My decision is already made. In a few seconds you will have news of me.' These ambiguous words did nothing to stop me and I continued walking towards the door. But turning to say goodbye I saw her with her arm raised and a dagger in her hand, its point to her breast. The sight appalled me. I lost my head, ran, threw myself at her feet, tore the dagger from her hand, dried her tears, forgave her everything, promised her everything and stayed with her. We supped together and . . . there we were, back at the beginning again.' But a couple of days later he heard that she and Vitalba had been supping intimately together, laughing uproariously at the story of Goldoni and the dagger.

Carlo took his revenge in the only way he knew — he bundled the whole episode up into a play and obliged Vitalba and Passalacqua to play out their infamy in public. The subject he took was the Don Giovanni story, such a hardy annual in the *Commedia dell' Atre* that the actors believed the original author must have made a pact with the devil to keep it going so long. Goldoni dressed it up in his own verses and introduced a shepherd and shepherdess called Carino and Elisa, near enough Carlino, the diminutive of Carlo, and Elisabetta, to be instantly recognizable. Vitalba, of course, was Don Giovanni. Elisa's speeches were taken from Elisabetta's mouth, and even the episode of the dagger was included.

Not surprisingly La Passalacqua took umbrage and stormed off to both Imer and Grimani saying that she refused to play the part. They, forewarned by Carlo, stood firm and insisted that the only alternative was for her to leave the company. Any humiliation was better than that, and she set about learning her lines immediately and played the part perfectly'. This triumphant, probably contemptuous portrayal of her own perfidy is much in character, for Elisabetta Passalacqua was a woman of spirit as she was to show when darkness overtook her. Some years later, while simulating a flight at the Santa Cecilia theatre in Palermo, she fell and received injuries from which she was never to recover. But she refused to give up and go into retirement; instead she went on doggedly hacking in fifth-rate companies although, as a chronicler unkindly says, 'her talent was lost and she was neglected by the actors'. She finally died in misery at Finale di Modena in 1760 when Carlo was still at the height of his fame.

Playgoers were accustomed to the Don Giovanni story being presented as the most vulgar of cheap farces and, unaware of the reform that Goldoni had up his sleeve for them, were a little baffled at the relatively serious treatment he gave the tired old story. But fortunately, enough of them were aware of the Passalacqua–Vitalba–Goldoni affair to make the play run on its scandal value, and in fact it kept on until the closure of the theatres at the end of carnival.

The company then went on tour to Genoa, and Imer asked Goldoni to accompany them because of more changes in the cast list. This time, there being no Antonia Ferramonti to ride with, Carlo travelled in Imer's coach and then stayed with him in a house near the theatre.

One morning, soon after their arrival, he spotted a pretty face at one of the windows of the house opposite. He winged a tender, albeit silent message across the intervening street. Did the pretty face acknowledge receipt? One could not be entirely sure. Anyway, it vanished instantly, to appear no more. Carlo made inquiries and discovered that the house opposite was owned by a certain Agostino Conio, a Genoese notary who, in spite of the fairly substantial pickings of his trade, was handicapped by having a very large family. He also learned that Conio was one of the notaries for the Bank of St George in Genoa, a useful detail because Imer had an account there, and Carlo was therefore able to go along with one of Imer's bills of exchange and sum up the father of the pretty face at his leisure.

Conio made a good impression immediately. He explained to Carlo that the bill of exchange was not payable at the bank, but that any broker or indeed merchant in the city would change it for him. Carlo apologized for his ignorance and said that he was a stranger who happened to be staying nearby. The conversation got amicably underway and, as it was closing-time, Conio suggested they should continue it while walking home. Things continued to go swimmingly and he then invited Carlo for a cup of coffee. 'I accepted,' wrote Goldoni, 'because in Italy people drink as many as ten cups of coffee a day' – a phenomenon which is as true today as it was then.

At this point Conio revealed that he had seen Carlo with the actors and he asked what part he played, which suggests that his instant geniality might have been motivated by a desire for an introduction into the wild and wicked world of the theatre. Carlo's reply shows all too clearly in what consideration the players were held. He was not, he said, offended at the question because anyone else might have been deceived by appearances, but he was in fact the author. Conio apologized.

Things could hardly gave gone more smoothly, for the notary was a great theatre-goer and had had occasion to admire Goldoni's plays. So the two men began to exchange visits and Carlo came to know the pretty face at the window which belonged to one of Conio's daughters, Nicoletta, in whom, day by day, he found new grace and merit. So much so, indeed, that at the end of a month he asked for her hand.

Conio gave guarded approval, but reserved final consent until information about Carlo should come from the Genoese consul in Venice. Fortunately this official came up trumps and a month later, a dowry having been agreed on, the wedding went forward to the disgruntlement of Imer who was obliged to do without Goldoni for the rest of the tour.

Nicoletta is a shadowy figure, always there in the background, though usually just out of sight, uncomplaining, forgiving, always ready to pack up at a moment's notice, though she would probably have often preferred to stay where they were. Most writers on the subject have tended to be a little sorry for Nicoletta, and many of the Italians refer to her somewhat witheringly as *'la buona Nicoletta'*. Indro Montanelli, as is his wont, puts it more strongly. 'Once again the good Lord showed himself to have a weakness for the shiftless,' he wrote, 'by making him bump into the only woman who could make a wife for a husband such as he. Nicoletta Conio was not only pretty and in possession of a fair-sized dowry, but she also showed understanding, patience and devotion when it was necessary (and God knows it was necessary often enough) to put up with the infidelity of a lay-about like him.'*

But one may wonder whether Nicoletta was quite so badly off after all. Not only did she have adventures and excitements such as few girls dare dream of, but she kept her husband at her side until the very end, and after fifty years he was able to write of her, 'She was and always has been my only consolation' and elsewhere, 'I married a wise, pretty and honest girl who made up for all the wrongs I had suffered at the hands of women, and reconciled me to the sex. [She is] the delight of my life.'

The fullest portrait of Nicoletta, however, was written by Goldoni after they had been married for many years. It is contained in the introductory letter with which he dedicates a comedy to his father-in-law. 'You could not', he wrote, 'have given me a greater treasure than your exemplary daughter and my most loving wife. She has always been such a good companion that in all the many years we have been together I have never for an instant – either from domestic quarrels or inflamed temper – regretted having married her. She has borne with tranquillity the blows of fate, content with little and wishing only for peace which she always promoted and guarded.'

She was also an excellent housewife and a devoted mother to the two children that were later dumped on them by Carlo's benighted brother. But – perhaps more important than all these qualities for the wife of a playwright – she was the perfect audience for the first reading of his plays. 'I have seen her laughing and crying,' he said, 'and her laughter and tears have always corresponded exactly with the reactions of the audience in the theatre.' Furthermore, he went on, she always knew when to speak and when to be silent, she was able to cheer him up in moments of depression, and altogether their

---

* This is translated from *Italia nell'ottocento* by Indro Montanelli and Roberto Gervaso, just one volume of Montanelli's brilliant and highly individual history of his native land.

marriage was as delightful after many years as it had been at the outset. A wife could hardly ask for a more loving tribute than that.

But whatever other views may be held about Goldoni's marriage, the couple were unquestionably blissful when they left the church together. 'I was', says Carlo with feeling if not undue originality, 'the happiest of men.' And, as always with him, this state of euphoria was the infallible sign of trouble. In fact, no sooner had they withdrawn to their room, than Carlo was struck down by a raging temperature accompanying an attack of smallpox. So poor Nicoletta had to spend the entire first night of the honeymoon weeping and nursing her husband. 'Poor' is the other adjective most frequently applied to Nicoletta by Italian writers although of course, on this occasion, nobody would deny its aptness. Fortunately, the attack was not a serious one, and Carlo emerged from it, in his own words, no uglier than he had been before.

VII

'One cannot become a master all at once!'
Carlo Goldoni

The smallpox was unfortunately timed, but quickly forgotten, for Goldoni says that he was so taken up with the first year of his marriage that he did not have time to produce a comedy - an admission he was never to make again. He did, however, manage to knock together two tragedies from existing material and these kept the players going.

There were more changes in the Imer company - and they were to have even more importance in Goldoni's life than the previous lot. Bastona, the old war-horse, at last gave way in favour of her daughter, Marta, which must have been a great relief for all. Poor Passalacqua was sacked: 'I felt no rancour,' said Goldoni, 'but I was better off without her.' And two new actors came into the company. One was Francesco Gollinetti, a Pantaloon of some standing, but also skilful at working without a mask. The other was the famous Harlequin, Antonio Sacchi. Sacchi, a year older than Goldoni, had been born in Vienna, the son of an actor who was working at the court there. As a child, Antonio learned every aspect of the business from his father and was a thorough-going professional, in addition to which, judging by all accounts, he was an actor of genius. 'Our century', wrote Goldoni, 'produced three great actors at almost exactly the same time: Garrick in England, Préville in France and Sacchi in Italy.' And he added with some bitterness, 'Dukes and Peers walked at the funeral of the first, the second is heaped with rewards and honours. But the third, for all his fame, will not finish his career in opulence.' The prophecy was accurate. More than half a century after joining the Imer company, Sacchi - by then a lecherous old tyrant – died destitute while crossing from Genoa to Marseilles. He was buried at sea. But when he joined up with Imer he was still young and riding magnificently towards the long zenith of his career. Nor was he only great in himself, for he was also to produce greatness in Goldoni: it is no exaggeration to say that it was the genius of them both that produced *The Servant of Two Masters*, the first unalloyed Goldoni masterpiece. This is so true that, as you read it today, by some strange alchemy, you can still see Antonio Sacchi acting. (To be accurate, the original script was a *Commedia dell'Arte* scenario, but when Goldoni came to write out the play in full for publication, he deviated little, if at all, from the original, unscripted production. So it is true to say that the text we have today is imbued with Sacchi's performance.)

These various changes in the company occurred arbitrarily, depending on the whims of Giuseppe Imer, but when they had all been made, they seemed to form part of one indivisible miracle, for it was now the perfect vehicle to start the famous Goldoni reform of the Italian theatre. 'This was the moment to attempt that reform I had had in mind for so long, to mould plays of character which are the only source of true comedy. It was with these plays that the great Molière began his career and arrived at that perfection which had previously only been reached by the ancients and never before touched by modern writers.'

Thus Goldoni in the *Mémoires*. But one may take leave to doubt whether it was quite so clear-cut as all that. Goldoni always followed the sweet scent of success, and it is far more probable that, observing the members of this new Imer company, he thought that the public would *enjoy* comedies of character, based on the personalities of these actors. The experiment came off – not invariably, but often enough – and little by little Goldoni adopted the idea that he was, in fact, creating a reform. Then finally, looking back on it all as an old man, about fifty years after it started, he convinced himself that the whole thing had been a mighty crusade, consciously and from the beginning.

Whatever his intentions, however, he did make a revolution in the Italian theatre, every bit as vital as that of Ibsen and Shaw. From where we stand it is a little difficult to see it in perspective for there is something appealing about masks and we have been, and still are, satiated with realism. In Italy in the eighteenth century, it was the other way about and, of course, the entertainments that were given with masks had nothing intellectual or experimental about them; they were far more akin to the shows given by those fifth-rate variety companies that used to droop about the provinces. Sometimes if the actors were good – as with Sacchi – the sad embers of the *Commedia dell'Arte* would be blown for an instant into flame, but more often they produced only smoke, and murky, acrid smoke at that.

'Comedy in our theatre had been so corrupt for more than a century,' Goldoni wrote in a preface, 'that it had made itself an abominable object of contempt to the nations beyond the Alps.' (Not strictly true, as the *Commedia dell'Arte* triumphed in Paris for many years.) The actors, Goldoni went on, were aware of this bleak situation and did their best to warm it into life by introducing all sorts of novelties, spectacular scenic effects and transformation scenes. But these things only cost money and the public continued to stay away in large numbers. Then the actors tried musical intermezzi – 'and I was one of the first to contribute,' says Goldoni – but as they weren't musicians the public quickly realized that the art of comedy is different to the art of music.

The solution, as Goldoni found out, lay in plays which would – in the words of a colleague – hold a mirror up to nature. And so, if one were to sum up the Goldoni reform in a sentence, one might say that, over a period of some years, he transformed a decaying actors' theatre into a living writers' one. He threw the old scenarios out of the window – although as he never shut it very firmly on them, they kept on fluttering back. He started writing his dialogue down and making his actors, often with great reluctance, learn it by heart. He eschewed bawdry, rhetoric and forced lines or situations, and he embraced naturalism with all his heart.

It was a gradual process. He began tentatively by putting sections of plays on paper and leaving the rest to improvisation, and his wary – or hesitant – progress was often interrupted by temporary withdrawals. And even if he did consciously see himself as a reformer, or perhaps a Reformer, he didn't like to rush things. When the leading man in *Il Teatro Comico* asks the manager why they don't get rid of the masks altogether, the manager replies, 'It would be the worst thing we could possibly do – the time isn't ripe. The great secret in everything is never to take the world head on. Before, the public went to the theatre just to laugh and didn't want to see anything except the masks on the stage; if there was a scene for serious characters, they got bored immediately. Now they're getting accustomed to the more realistic bits, they listen to them gladly, they enjoy the language, they appreciate the niceties of plot and the moral. Indeed, they've learned how to laugh at the humour of the realistic scenes, but they still want to see the masks, and it would be wrong to take them away altogether . . . '

And in fact, far from killing the masks, Goldoni did more than anybody else to immortalize them, except for their original, anonymous creators. As the dead-weight caricatures they had become, time would have swallowed them, but as creatures of flesh and blood it would bear them down the centuries.

Goldoni speaks of 'the four masks' which is a sweeping over-simplification because the Italian theatre was rife with masks. There were, however, four principal masks in the Venetian theatre, and these four were the descendants of two, great archetypal ancestors – *il Magnifico* and Zanni, his servant. The original *Magnifico* was, as his title suggests, a great man, and one of his original names was Piantaleone: literally 'Plant the Lion', suggesting the standard-bearer of the lion of St Mark. This was transformed into Pantalone or Pantaloon, whose full name was Pantalone de' Bisognosi. The other fruit of *il Magnifico's* loins was the Doctor who represented the Bolognese branch of the family and usually, though not necessarily, practised law. When Goldoni came along these were two dirty and foolish old men, and he invested them with dignity. Pantaloon, above all, he transformed into a solid, honourable Venetian merchant, usually a widower with a daughter to wed. In *Il Cavaliere e la Dama (The Knight and the Lady)*, he defends the honour of his class when a patrician calls him 'a vile merchant and a vulgar fellow'. 'If you realized what the word "merchant" meant,' he says, 'you wouldn't talk like that. Buying and selling is of great utility to the world, and it is indispensable for trading among nations. When a man buys and sells honestly, as I do, you don't call him a vulgar fellow. Far more vulgar is the man who, just because he's inherited a title and a bit of land, idles his days away and thinks it's his right to trample over everybody and live by bullying.' He is a conservative, an upholder of the great old values of the Republic, he likes his comforts and his little ways, he only eats 'good stuff', but it has to be 'stuff that I know and that won't do me any harm'.

From the birth of the masks there were two Zannis, the servants, working together like Laurel and Hardy and with characters no less opposed. The first was a wily, cunning rogue and he evolved at the beginning of the seventeenth century into Brighella (the very origin of his new name, *brigare*, means to intrigue). He dressed with some elegance, spoke with distinction and was traditionally skilful with musical instruments. In Goldoni's hands his skill at intrigue was directed more at serving his master's interests than his own.

The second Zanni – foolish, clumsy and the slave of an ever-clamorous belly – became the most famous of all the masks, Harlequin. And since the actor who effected the transformation from second Zanni came from Bergamo, Harlequin has ever since been considered to be a citizen of Bergamo. Goldoni changed Harlequin from a vulgar pimp into a peace-loving fool. His voracious appetite and unfailing capacity to make things go wrong remained, but he was stripped of pornography.

The different characteristics of Brighella and Harlequin are highlighted in the play within the play of *Il Teatro Comico* when the two of them are bidding for the hand of Columbine. Brighella says that a woman is better off married to a wise man and Harlequin insists that she is better off married to a fool. 'I'll marry whichever of you convinces me,' says Columbine.

Brighella: As a wise man I'll work and sweat so that you'll never be short of food.
Columbine: That's not a bad capital.
Harlequin: As a fool who can't do anything, I'll allow kind friends to bring food and drink into the house.
Columbine: That's not a bad idea either.
Brighella: As a wise man who knows how to protect his honour, I'll make you respected by everybody.
Columbine: I like that.

Harlequin: As a fool – and a man of peace, too – I'll make you loved
by everybody.
Columbine: And I don't dislike that.
Brighella: As a wise man, I'll run the house perfectly.
Columbine: Good.
Harlequin: As a fool, I'll let you run it.
Columbine: Better.
Brighella: If you feel like enjoying yourself, I'll take you out wherever
you want to go.
Columbine: Very good.
Harlequin: If you want to go out, I'll let you go out wherever you like
by yourself.
Columbine: Excellent.

Columbine's final decision is extremely feminine. 'Now that I've heard both your arguments,' she says, 'I've decided that Brighella is too strict and Harlequin is too lax. So let's do this – go and mix yourselves up together nicely and make one sane man out of two fools. And then I'll marry you both.'

Goldoni's transformation of the masks, although it certainly included the suppression of vulgarity, was a great deal more than mere goody-goody bowdlerization. What he did was to make them human and credible so that they could co-exist with the other characters, rather in the same way as Walt Disney, in some of his later films, made cartoon characters mix with real actors.

Reactions to the Goldoni reform as it slowly evolved were mixed. Packed houses proved indisputably that the public was in favour of it. 'I didn't think that the Italians liked comedies of character,' says the would-be author in *Il Teatro Comico*. 'On the contrary,' replies one of the actors, 'Italy is now packing out the theatres only for this sort of comedy, and what's more the public's taste has so much improved in such a short time that even the groundlings can make the most shrewd criticisms about the characters or the defects of a play.'

Not all the actors were quite so happy with the new style, however, particularly the older ones who were now obliged to forego the improvisation at which they had become skilled and set to work learning their lines. Their point of view is summed up by the actor who plays Pantaloon in *Il Teatro Comico*. 'Joking aside and down to facts,' he says, 'these comedies of character have turned our whole craft upside-down. A poor actor who's learned his trade with the *Commedia dell'Arte* and got accustomed to improvising more or less well, now has to study and say what he's learned by heart. To save his self-respect he has to rack his poor brains out, and there he is, trembling whenever there's a new play to be done, terrified either that he won't know his lines well enough or that he won't be able to play the character as it ought to be played.' The actor-manager agrees that the new style needs more hard work and attention, but adds that it also gives more satisfaction: 'When', he asks

Pantaloon, 'have you ever had applause such as you've had in some of the Goldoni plays?' 'True enough,' replies the poor actor, 'I'm delighted, but it still makes me tremble all over.'

So in 1738, at the age of thirty-one, Goldoni had a company of actors who could help him deliver what had been unconsciously gestated in his mind. 'Now, I said to myself, I am well off and I can allow my imagination free play. I have worked on rancid material for long enough. Now I have actors who promise well, and I must create for them, I must invent. But first, in order to get the best out of them, I must study them. Each one has his natural character, and if the author can give the actor a character which resembles his own, then success is sure.'

Goldoni's first choice for putting his theory into practice fell on the Pantaloon of the company, Francesco Gollinetti. 'I watched him closely on the stage; I observed him even better at table, in conversation, out walking, and he seemed to me to be just the sort of actor I was looking for. So I composed a comedy, based on him, with the title of *Momolo Cortesan*.' In fact, only Gollinetti's part was written out and the rest was left to improvisation, but, when Goldoni started to publish his plays, he filled in the whole script and gave it the title – more comprehensible to non-Venetian ears – of *L'Uomo di Mondo (The Man of the World)*. It opened during carnival with Imer and Antonio Sacchi in the cast.

At this point came one of those disastrous adventures which regularly punctuated his life. The Genoese consul in Venice died and Nicoletta's father, who had some pull, obtained the post for his son-in-law. Between dispatches Carlo threw off enough of the old-style scenarios to keep the actors going, but he was largely caught up with politics, and one has the impression that the glory of his new position went to his head. He moved into a new house near St Mark's Square, furnished it lavishly, established a large household and kept magnificent table for all comers. The giddy pace was kept up for some months, but came to an abrupt halt when he learned that the position of consul was unpaid, a detail Nicoletta's father had somehow overlooked. Unfortunately, Carlo was unable to resign immediately as he was involved in an affair of some delicacy. A Genoese functionary had absconded with public funds and valuables belonging to the state of Genoa and had taken refuge in Venice. The Genoese – as notorious as the Scots for their attachment to money – bombarded Carlo with demands that he should either get the property back or at least obtain the arrest of the malefactor. Somehow Carlo succeeded in restoring the money and valuables to their rightful owners, but the affair had an obscure though plainly disastrous epilogue. The valuables had included two gold boxes, studded with diamonds, which Carlo was asked to sell on behalf of the Genoese. He unwisely entrusted them to a shady broker who promptly hocked them with a Jew and fled, thoughtfully leaving behind the pawn ticket. Carlo, being responsible, was obliged to redeem them and, as he was already at a low financial ebb, a good part of Nicoletta's dowry went over the counter of the pawn-shop. The details remain vague, but there were whispers in Venice that Carlo's own conduct in the affair wasn't all that it should have been. He indignantly and rather pathetically denies any jiggery-pokery, adding, 'I have a nephew who bears my name, and if I have nothing else to leave him, he can at least enjoy the reputation of the uncle who acted as a father to him.'

To make matters worse, the Goldoni family income which he received regularly from the ducal bank of Modena was frozen by the Duke of Modena, who needed money to pay his troops. And as if that wasn't enough, Gian Paolo, Carlo's profligate brother, also feeling the draught from the Modena freeze, decided to warm himself at the fireside of his brother and sister-in-law, and neither Carlo nor Nicoletta were bold or resolute enough to turn him out.

In the midst of all these tribulations, however, Goldoni was able to make a perceptible move forward with his reform. Looking round the company once more for inspiration, his old fondness for those actresses who played the maidservants led him to choose Anna Baccherini, 'a pretty and cheerful Florentine girl, most vivacious, with a plump little figure, a clear complexion and black eyes'. The old man in Paris half a century later seems to be deliberately tantalizing his readers with his description of their relationship. 'She was married and so was I. So we joined together in warm friendship, each having need of the other; I worked for her glory and she dissipated my ill-humour.'

Anna Baccherini was longing to show off her talent – and her femininity – in a role in which she could appear in a series of different guises, so Goldoni wrote for her *La Donna di Garbo (The Well-mannered Lady)*, the first of his plays to be written out in full and the first which can be considered a real comedy of manners. The company – particularly, of course, la Baccherini – were enchanted with the play when he read it out to them, but unfortunately the season in Venice was too far advanced to put on a new play, and so they decided to do it in Genoa where the actors were to spend the spring. Goldoni planned to join them there and kill two birds with one stone by watching his own first night and at the same time, if possible, coaxing the Genoese authorities into giving him a salary; but a series of 'singular disasters' intervened and prevented him from seeing *The Well-mannered Lady* until four years later.

While waiting in Venice for the Genoese to approve a substitute so that he would be able to leave, he was plainly eaten up with desire to rejoin la Baccherini. Then, when approval had been given and he was ready to leave, the actress's brother came and showed him a newly arrived letter with the news that Anna had died suddenly. She was twenty-three years old. This was the second time that death had intervened in a love affair of Goldoni's to complete the triangle – or, rather, the quadrangle if one is to include the husbands. 'My wife saw me afflicted and was reasonable enough to associate herself with my sentiments': really, there are moments when one cannot help wondering whether those Italian writers who keep on harping about Nicoletta's 'poor-ness' are all that wide of the mark.

In the midst of his grief he managed to throw off an opera libretto for the feast of the Ascension and then, when the ink of the libretto and the tears for Anna were scarcely dry, Gian Paolo, who was still hovering about in a sinister way, moved in to deal a blow which was to cause yet another headlong retreat from Venice for the Goldonis.

He announced one day that he had just made the acquaintance of a military captain, a most astonishing man with contacts at all the courts of Europe, involved in deals that would take your breath away. This great man was at the moment in Venice recruiting an army, 2,000 strong, for a foreign power; though woe if the Venetian authorities should hear of it for such recruitment was illegal in the Republic. And in this army Gian Paolo was to command a company and Carlo was to be nothing less than judge advocate for the entire force.

Looking back on the story one cannot help thinking that Goldoni behaved in a manner that was altogether too credulous for someone who, allowing for all the good nature in the world, was nevertheless a lawyer. But this is hindsight wisdom, and one should remember that in eighteenth-century Europe, where fortunes ebbed and flowed with bewildering casualness, there was nothing all that improbable about the suggestion and, in Carlo's reduced circumstances, it must have seemed a very attractive one. As for the illegal aspect of it, the prospect of a brief foray onto the windy side of the law never put off any Goldoni worth his salt.

Carlo, however, was a little surprised to hear that Gian Paolo had, on his own initiative, invited the captain to dinner. 'The captain then is a friend of yours?' he asked and, being told that he was, went on understandably to ask how he could be a friend when, according to Gian Paolo, they had only just met. 'We soldiers are not courtiers,' Gian Paolo replied loftily. 'We recognize each other on sight; honour and glory forge the links between us.' Most appropriately chosen words in view of what was to happen.

At this point Nicoletta came in and begged them to stop arguing as dinner was ready. Gian Paolo accused her of impatience and she replied that it was not she who was impatient, but his mother who was living with them. 'My mother! My mother!' muttered Gian Paolo, who was not going to allow sentiment to stand between him and a fortune, 'Let her dine by herself and then go off to bed!' Even Carlo's equanimity might have been shattered at this point if a knocking at the door had not announced the arrival of their guest. High words were swallowed, there were 'a thousand compliments, a thousand excuses' and off they went to table.

Of all the many meals in history at which one might burn to have been present, this surely cannot be the least tantalizing. Gian Paolo smooth, watching for points; Carlo benign and courteous, but a little doubtful; their mother hungry and probably irritable at being put out of her ways; Nicoletta subdued, alarmed, out of her depth. And the captain? He, Goldoni tells us, was polite, honeyed, full of attentions with a pale, long face, an aquiline nose and little, round greenish eyes, 'very gallant and full of attention for the ladies', speaking of morality and a thousand delightful things, recounting witty anecdotes 'without, however, letting these anecdotes prevent him from dining extremely well'.

After coffee and abundant liqueurs, which Carlo had to produce for the captain at Gian Paolo's request, the three men withdrew to the study. Here the captain produced impeccable documents, demonstrating that he was indeed commissioned to recruit an army and that he was to be its colonel-in-chief with full powers to nominate all other officers and functionaries.

At this point the captain had a small request to make. His mission was a delicate one, being illegal in Venice, and he feared that he was already being spied upon; if, however, he could come and stay with Goldoni he would feel entirely protected. Poor Carlo tried to get out of it by saying that his poor house was not comfortable enough for such a guest, but Gian Paolo intervened perfidiously to offer his room, which the captain graciously accepted.

He stayed for three days and exercised his charm so effectively that any remaining suspicions his host may have had were deadened. The captain was then ready for the *coup de grâce*. First he insinuated the news that he had a bill of exchange on some German bankers in Venice for 6,000 ducats which, although perfectly good, was not for the moment payable because the letter of advice had been temporarily delayed. Then on the morning of the fourth day he arrived back in the house distraught with anxiety. He had to pay a considerable-sized debt, and if it was not paid immediately the whole business would be blown sky-high. The captain must have been a master of his trade, for Carlo was deeply moved and, egged on by Gian Paolo, put together all the money he could lay his hands on and presented it to his guest who promptly disappeared.

The scenes were frightful and Gian Paolo set out to scour Venice, announcing that he would kill the captain if he laid hands on him. (But was Gian Paolo the captain's accomplice? Goldoni doesn't even hint at the possibility of such infamy and nor, oddly enough, has anybody else. But the enterprise does not appear by any means to be beyond the range of Gian Paolo's skill.) Because of the criminal nature of the captain's mission, aided and abetted by the Goldonis, there was no possibility of legal recourse. Indeed, there was nothing whatsoever that could be done except to get out of Venice as quickly as possible.

VIII

'I am sometimes tempted to consider myself a phenomenon.'
Carlo Goldoni

Carlo's capacity for attracting disaster was only equalled by the alacrity with which he recovered from it. He left Venice by night, broken and desolate, only – as always – sustained by the tender solicitude of Nicoletta. Then he dropped off to sleep in the coach and woke up in the morning a new man. Life was off once again to a fresh start.

In the *Mémoires* he claims that as soon as he reached Bologna he bundled the whole adventure up into a play called *The Impostor*, but recent research has determined that the play was written ten years after the event. Whatever its date, however, it clearly demonstrates Carlo's ability to use events in real life as grist for his theatrical mill. In *The Impostor* he cheerfully mocks the captain, Gian Paolo and himself.

Now, having sold three other plays he happened to have with him to an impresario in Bologna – thus partially restoring the family fortunes – he wanted to go to Modena to have another go at unfreezing his income there. However, hearing that Modena was in chaos and that the Duke was campaigning with his army, he allowed himself to be persuaded by a wandering Pantaloon, Antonio Ferramonti – the widower of the enchanting Antonia who had so tragically died in childbirth – to go with him to a company of players in Rimini.

Nicoletta, who had been hoping to visit her family in Genoa, agreed to the change of plans – with a little sigh, one may imagine, almost entirely stifled – and they set off for Rimini where their plans were to be upset by another war of succession, this time that of the Austrian empire. On 20th

October 1740 the Emperor, Charles VI had died, leaving his daughter Maria Teresa, on the throne. But her right to it was contended by Charles Albert, the Elector of Bavaria, who was married to Amalia, youngest daughter of the Emperor Joseph I who had preceded Charles VI. So on 31st July 1741 Charles Albert launched his forces against the army of Maria Teresa. He was backed with massive French aid, though France only entered the war officially in 1744. His other allies were Spain, Saxony and Poland. This time, too, much of the battle was fought in Italy, and once again the Goldonis were briefly caught upon its tide. Having arrived within sight of the fortifications of Rimini they were arrested by the Spaniards, who were occupying the city at that moment, and, of all lucky chances, hauled off (because of Carlo's origins) to the court of the Duke of Modena, temporarily set up with the Spaniards in Rimini. This, Carlo felt, was the most fortunate opportunity to discuss the question of his income with the person best equipped to deal with it and, having many friends at court, he was immediately granted audience. The Duke was cordiality itself and graciously inquired what Carlo was doing in those parts, but at the mention of the words 'ducal bank' and 'income in arrears' he deftly changed the subject. 'I realized', said Goldoni, 'that there was nothing to hope for in that quarter.'

So he turned to the players. Ferramonti, who had also been set at liberty, had already spoken of him to the manager, and the whole company was there to receive him. As usual Carlo's eyes went straight to the actresses. 'The leading lady', he said, 'was an excellent actress, but exceedingly advanced in years. The second lady was a stupid and ill-mannered beauty. The Columbine was a fresh, pretty, dark-haired girl, far advanced in pregnancy. She, by the way, was quickly to become my intimate friend. She played the parts of the maidservants which was the main thing.'

Before Carlo had been in Rimini long, who should turn up but Gian Paolo ('My brother, my delightful brother') with two shady Venetian friends. The three of them had a project, which they put to the commanding officer in the city, for conscripting a new regiment in which, of course, Carlo was to be judge advocate. This enchanting prospect, however, had to be foregone for after a couple of days the army struck its tents and marched off, mercifully carrying Gian Paolo and his friends in its wake.

This departure left Rimini open to the Austrians, and for Carlo, who was a Modenese subject and the consul of Genoa in Venice, this could have meant trouble as both Modena and Genoa were aligned against the Austrians. So once again Nicoletta had to pack their trunks and they set sail in a boat, the hire of which they shared with some merchants. As if things hadn't been tough enough for her already, poor Nicoletta was so sea-sick that she spat blood. They landed at Cattolica, left their luggage to be sent on after them and set off on a peasant's cart for Pesaro where they arrived 'tired, shaken, without acquaintances and without lodgings'.

Pesaro, being momentarily a city of refuge from the tide of war, was in a state of upheaval and there wasn't a room to be had anywhere. But as usual Carlo fell on his feet, or more strictly onto the floor of an attic which he managed to rent. Having slept in it for one night, however, he and Nicoletta had to face another catastrophe in the shape of news that Austrian hussars had arrived at Cattolica and swooped away with all their luggage.

At this point one can only admire Goldoni's courage and determination, for he calmly decided to make his way across land torn by war and infested with brigands to the headquarters of the Austrians – of whom he had every reason to be wary – where he would demand his possessions back. Transport was virtually non-existent, and he got a coach; the coachmen were all in hiding, and he managed to find one. And so the next morning, having breakfasted serenely and well, they set off for Cattolica. They had gone less than half-way when Signora Goldoni was forced by an urgent call of nature to dismount. Carlo, perhaps with bandits in mind, accompanied her to a secluded spot and, while they were there, the reluctant coachman whipped up the horses and galloped off back to Pesaro, leaving them stranded.

The countryside was deserted, its inhabitants barred and bolted in their homes for fear of marauding armies. Nicoletta was in tears. Then Carlo, hardly a religious man in the normal way, raised his eyes to heaven and felt a surge of inspiration. ' "Courage!" I said, "My dear companion, courage! We're only six miles from Cattolica. We're young and healthy and we can easily walk that far. It's not worth going back now, and we should only blame ourselves if we did." '

And so they set off to walk. After about an hour they came to a stream, too wide to jump and too deep for Nicoletta to ford, spanned only by a rotting and broken bridge. 'I didn't lose my head. I went down on one knee, my wife put her arms around my neck, I got up laughing and crossed the river with ineffable joy, saying as I went *Omnia bona mea mecum porto."* ' There was another stream, dealt with in the same way, and then a river which was too much even for ineffable joy to cope with. Fortunately, however, by following its course they met a fishing boat whose owners took them to the other bank. And so they reached an Austrian advanced post, where a sergeant of hussars had Carlo and Nicoletta taken under escort to the headquarters of the colonel commanding that regiment.

'You are Signor Goldoni?' asked the colonel, having examined Carlo's passport. With some trepidation in view of his connections with Modena and Genoa, Carlo admitted that he was. 'The author of *Belisarius?* The author of *Momolo Cortesan?*' The colonel was a fan, and so, yet another Goldoni story, having come through tears and travail, arrives at the unfailing happy ending: the luggage was restored, Nicoletta wept with joy, the colonel embraced Carlo. And so back to the players at Rimini where the Austrians had taken over from the Spaniards.

Carlo was unquestionably a sort of Italian Vicar of Bray which explains the fact that now, instead of taking up the delicate point of relationships with hostile powers, the Austrian commander, Field-Marshal Lobkowitz, asked him to write a serenade to celebrate the wedding of the sister of the Empress Maria Teresa. This was successfully presented in the theatre at Rimini and Carlo was handsomely paid for it, but the pickings from this work did not stop there. The composer who had set it to music was a Neapolitan who, in the great Neapolitan tradition, did not miss a single trick. On his suggestion they went round by carriage calling on every officer in and around Rimini, distributing handsomely bound copies of the serenade which, of course, no officer could refuse or ungenerously recompense for fear that his patriotism might be called into question. And so author and composer returned, loaded with loot which, as Carlo primly put it, they divided beween them 'modestly and tranquilly'.

At this point the Genoese Republic informed him that another Venetian was anxious to take over the consulate – without payment, of course – and this gave Carlo the chance to withdraw thankfully yet gracefully, and devote his undivided attention to the social delights of Rimini which, after the austerity of the Spanish occupation, were many and varied. One of these delights, the Columbine of the players, must have put a considerable strain on Nicoletta's tolerance. Goldoni says that she refused to call on the actress, which is more than understandable, but that she did not forbid him to do so, which was more than generous. 'She just didn't like that actress, and there is no accounting for tastes,' remarks Goldoni with that just perceptible taste of pomposity which runs like a thin vein throughout the *Mémoires.*

Fortunately, Nicoletta did not have to bear this particular trial for long as the Rimini party was swiftly coming to an end. First of all the players had to pack up and go because the Austrians preferred opera for their carnival entertainment. Then the army itself, after a spectacular general review of the 40,000 troops stationed throughout Romagna, moved off along the Adriatic towards the south in lumbering pursuit of the Spaniards. The Goldonis, too, left Rimini.

It would seem that the criticisms of Carlo's use of the Italian language, which would soon swell into a savage downpour, had already begun to patter around him, for he now headed for Florence, traditionally the fountain-head of purest Italian. They went on to Siena and then toured round Tuscany in general before arriving in Pisa where Carlo intended to stay for a couple of days and in fact remained for three years.

Arcady was much in fashion at the time, and amateur poets with comfortable incomes would meet in surroundings as rustic as was consonant with comfort to recite their verses. Carlo happened on one of these gatherings in a Pisan garden one day and, having gate-crashed it, recited a sonnet of his own invention. Predictably, this was received with delighted applause. 'I don't know if the session would otherwise have gone on much longer,' says Carlo modestly, 'but everybody rose to their feet and crowded about me.'

The old Goldoni charm worked its magic on the Arcadians and they showered him with invitations. The chairman of the meeting – if anything so esoteric may be chaired – was one of the legal luminaries of Pisa, and it was he who persuaded Carlo to stay on in the town as a lawyer. The facility with which he allowed himself to be persuaded is yet another proof that Goldoni's crusading zeal as the reformer of the Italian theatre was only a result of hindsight vision.

The Pisans promised him clients, and they kept their word, for before long he was working day and night and had more cases on his hands, both civil and criminal, than he could deal with. The stay in Pisa is the longest consecutive period of time in which he practised law, and it is dense with pleadings; but even when it was at its height, he was never quite the complete lawyer, as he shows with the system he evolved for lightening his work-load and, at the same time, making his clients happy 'by demonstrating the harm they were doing by going to law and arranging for them to settle out of court'.

And the smell of grease-paint still lingered in his nostrils, for when a company of players came to Pisa he could not resist giving them a play. It was a shabby sort of company, he says, and not at all to be trusted with one of his new comedies of character, and so he gave them a *Commedia dell'Arte* scenario, *The 104 Catastrophes (which all befell in the same night)*. But either script or actors or both must have been sadly lacking, for the single performance was a sorry flop, and Goldoni says that he overheard someone at a café on the Arno the next morning saying, 'God defend me from toothache and the 104 catastrophes!' Disappointed, and perhaps piqued by this failure, he swore off the theatre for good and plunged yet deeper into the law.

In one of the cases that fell to him at this period he resorted to a stratagem which, though less sensational perhaps, was more unequivocally on the windy side of the law than anything devised by Perry Mason. The only son of a respectable family had broken into the home of the family living immediately below his and stolen a sum of money, and as his crime was aggravated by breaking and entering he would assuredly be condemned to the living death of the galleys. The case was a sad one because the boy was young and had two marriageable sisters whose prospects would hardly have improved with a brother in the hulks. Goldoni's action was as effective as it was outrageous. He simply changed the lock of the lower apartment so that the key of the upper one would open it, and as a result he was able to argue that the youth had absent-mindedly opened the wrong door and then, seeing the money lying there, had given way to temptation. This, of course, enormously lessened the gravity of the case. Goldoni opened his plea by quoting the twenty-fifth psalm, 'Remember not the sins of my youth, nor my transgressions' (which must have sounded good in the ears of the Almighty after all that lock-switching) and then went on to pull out all the stops, legal and emotional, he could lay his hands on. The trick, coupled with the plea, worked and the boy got off with three months in prison. 'The family were delighted with me,' says Goldoni, 'and the judge himself offered me his congratulations.' One wonders what the judge's reaction would have been if he had known the whole story.

Then one day a letter arrived from Venice which was the direct cause of the first authentic Goldoni masterpiece. The letter was from the great Harlequin, Antonio Sacchi, who asked Goldoni to write a play for him and even enclosed the rough plot outline that he wanted. At first Carlo hesitated; legal activities were taking up practically every waking hour of his life. But before long the pull of the theatre became too strong and, continuing to work in the courts by day, he dedicated his nights to *The Servant of Two Masters*.

Not only is the play a pure joy from beginning to end, but it is also a perfectly constructed half-way house between the *Commedia dell'Arte* and the new comedy of character containing, it could be argued, the best of both worlds. Truffaldino, the Harlequin character, is greedy and cheerfully muddle-headed, but the light of pure truth shines in the touching pride he shows at being able to serve two masters at the same time, although the feat involves hard work and kicks. 'So you managed to serve two masters at the same time?' Florindo, the hero asks him at the end. 'Yes, sir', says Truffaldino, 'I've been clever enough to do just that. I took on the job without thinking, but I wanted to see if I was capable of it. True, it didn't last long, but at least I have the glory that nobody found me out . . . ' He is a sort of archetype of all those Italian waiters who even today face a packed restaurant, not as a piece of drudgery, but as a challenge to their skill. Pantaloon is closer, perhaps, to the doddering old fool of the *Commedia dell'Arte* than to the solid-headed Venetian merchant, but he is clearly evolving. Only Florindo and Beatrice, sighing and protesting their passion, are totally lacking in life, but this hardly matters; indeed, they set off the whirl and brilliance of Truffaldino to even greater advantage. And as you read or watch the play, the ghost of Sacchi seems to take on substance and dart about and tumble before your eyes, drunk with life.

The Servant of Two Masters was understandably an immediate success, and Sacchi, who always had a sharp eye to the main chance, sent Goldoni 'a present' together with a request for another play. It is another indication of how haphazard the 'reform' was in its early days that this play, *The Son of Harlequin, Lost and Refound*, was merely one of the old-type scenarios.

Work on these two scripts had temporarily snatched him from the lyrical fellowship of the Arcadians, but as soon as it was finished he rejoined them and was formally enrolled as one of their number under the high-sounding pseudonym of Polisseno Tegeio. It was all a bit ridiculous, but Carlo did not allow himself to be tempted into high-mindedness by it, and one suspects that he went to meetings more for chocolate and gossip than for culture.

There is some record of legal actions – other than the key-switching episode – in which Goldoni was involved at the time. In one case his client was a peasant and, as he points out, 'the peasants of Tuscany live well, go to law continually and pay excellently'. The villainous prior of an abbey was trying to dispossess this peasant of certain lands in favour of a little widow who was under the prior's protection. Although the lands were the property of the abbey, Goldoni won his case by arguing the general principal of a peasant's right to security on the renting of land which he farmed himself. On another occasion he tried to get a court order for the daughter of a rich family to be temporarily enclosed in a convent because, in defiance of a written promise to marry one man, she was trying to marry another. In the end the young lady took the matter into her own hands by eloping with her second lover and, as she was very rich, the matter was eventually settled out of court.

In the last century Goldoni's own rough copy of a defence, now in the museum at Pisa, was run to earth in the archives of a firm of lawyers in the town. This is particularly interesting because it is the only document that shows Goldoni at work as a lawyer first hand. He was defending two brothers accused of aiding and abetting military desertion in that they had bought clothes and arms from two deserters. As the two soldiers had indisputably deserted and as the clothes and arms had, equally indisputably, been found at the home of the brothers, Carlo had his work cut out for him. 'Thou sawest till that a stone was cut out without hands, which smote the image upon his feet that were of iron and clay,' he began, quoting the book of Daniel and mistakenly attributing the verse to the twelfth instead of the second chapter. The quotation leaves one a little perplexed until one realizes that Carlo is comparing the prosecution case to the statue of Nebuchadnezzar's dream. 'At first sight,' he went on, 'the evidence for the prosecution seemed most weighty and such as to put in desperation the poor, unhappy brothers . . . But I hope, with the help of God, to see it thrown down with the same ease with which the proud and mighty statue of Nebuchadnezzar was thrown down and destroyed by a little stone.'

Page after page, the words roll ponderously on, but slowly Goldoni's argument becomes clear: his clients had received the deserters in good faith, believing them to be legally demobilized and therefore fully entitled to sell superfluous clothing. But if the brothers had confessed that the soldiers had told them they were deserters? It still did not inculpate his clients because, even assuming the confession were true, the brothers still could not be accused of aiding and abetting in desertion. Desertion, in fact, could be divided into three distinct stages – before, during and after – and the accusation concerned the first two. By the time the deserters reached the village where the brothers lived, the act of desertion was already fully accomplished and so his clients could not be accused of aiding and abetting it. The outcome of the case is not known, but the conduct of the defence shows that Carlo was as wily as the best of them.

When he was at the height of his Pisan fame he received a snub without which the Italian theatre would probably have been deprived of its greatest playwright. An old lawyer in the town died. During his life he had acquired a large number of regular, solid clients – the sort that provide a steady income without too much hard work – and, as was the custom in Pisa, on his death they

'Carnival scene' (Gianbattista Tiepolo). The swirl and brio that Goldoni caught in so many plays.

'During the performance' (style of Pietro Longhi). The comedy is played out in the audience as well.

were divided up among his colleagues, but this gathering of legal vultures was strictly for Pisans and Goldoni, as a Venetian, was excluded. Somewhat unreasonably, as he was still only a newcomer in Pisa, he took umbrage and before his naturally cheerful disposition had had a chance to reassert itself, he received yet another embassy from the glinting, wicked world of the theatre.

While he was in his office one day, meditating on his supposed wrongs, there entered a very tall man, 'as fat as he was tall, who walked across the room with an Indian cane in his hand and a round, English-style hat on his head'. He introduced himself as Cesare D'Arbes, the Pantaloon of a company playing at that moment in Livorno. This D'Arbes, who had started life as a mirror-maker, was to become one of the most famous names of the Italian theatre, but at this point he was still comparatively unknown and, almost certainly impelled by Sacchi's success in *The Servant of Two Masters*, he had come to persuade Goldoni to write a play for him. He had bet the manager of his company, he said, a hundred ducats that he would succeed and, to prove his liberality, he filled Goldoni's snuff-box with gold ducats. There is something Dickensian about the character of D'Arbes. When Carlo tried to refuse the money, he was waved loftily aside. ' "Come, come, come!" said D'Arbes, "Pray don't take offence. Look upon this as a small account for the paper to write upon." I insisted on returning the money. He continued to gesticulate and pay me compliments. Then he rose, walked backwards, opened the door and went out.'

Goldoni wrote him a play called *Tonin Bella Grazia (The Well-mannered Tonin)*, based on a *Commedia dell'Arte* plot suggested by D'Arbes, and when it was finished he delivered it himself. Livorno, it is true, is not far from Pisa, but the personal delivery is nonetheless significant: when he wrote for Sacchi he sent the plays to Venice, now it almost seemed as though he were deliberately courting temptation.

And certainly there was no lack of it in Livorno. D'Arbes immediately introduced him to the manager of the company and the two men rushed him off for one of those endless, uproarious theatrical meals of which Goldoni's life is so full. This company and its manager were both remarkable. Girolamo Medebac had been born in Rome in 1706, a year before Goldoni. He came of a theatrical family and from infancy on all the world was indeed a stage for him and all the men and women merely players; he knew of no other existence. Like most actor-managers he was mean, a trait Goldoni highlights at the very opening of *Il Teatro Comico*, which he wrote for the Medebac company. At the beginning of the play, in fact, the curtain is only pulled up a little way, and the manager wants it pulled down again because, he says, there's no need to raise the curtain just to rehearse the third act of a play. But the leading man wants it up. 'If you lower the curtain,' he says, 'we shan't be able to see a thing and so you'll have to light the lamps to rehearse by.' 'Come to think of it,' says the manager, 'we'd better raise the curtain.' Then he shouts into the wings, 'Pull it up! I don't want to spend money on lamps.' 'Long live economy!' says the leading man.

In 1738 Medebac had arrived in Venice and attached himself in more ways than one to a company of tumblers and tight-rope walkers which was then extremely popular in the Republic. This company was run by a man called Gasparo Raffi whose daughter, Teodora, Medebac shortly married. Goldoni, who must have seen these tumblers on many occasions without realizing how much his own destiny was to be entangled with theirs, says that Teodora 'danced passably well on the tight-rope, but with supreme grace on the ground'. Another contemporary says that she had 'an expression that shone with grace, a very gentle and clear voice together with all other imaginable gifts a young actress could wish for'. Unhappily for Medebac and Goldoni all this sweetness was soon to turn very sour indeed.

Before Medebac arrived there must have been some kind of silent fermentation of desire in this company of tumblers – almost all of whom were inter-married – for what later came to be called legitimate theatre. Medebac spotted it, decided to exploit it and immediately set about teaching the tumblers and tight-rope walkers to act. There was a fascinating period of transition when they tumbled by day in an improvised theatre in St Mark's Square and acted by night in the theatre at San Moisè which Medebec hired for them. But little by little the acting took over from the tumbling and before long they were a full-time, trained company of players with Medebac as leading man and his wife, Teodora, as leading lady. And to judge by all accounts they were extremely good; all they needed was a playwright to set them off. And all Goldoni needed, since he and Imer had silently drifted apart during the Pisan years, was a company of skilled actors. So the convivial meal at Livorno – with Teodora, whose expression still shone with grace, as hostess – was also a moment of destiny for both of them.

From the beginning the relationship was cordial, and Medebac immediately took off the *Commedia dell'Arte* piece he had billed for that evening and substituted it with a Goldoni script. Carlo watched from a box and was so struck with Teodora's performance that he said she was 'an actress to be esteemed above all others that I know'. The next night they put on *The Well-mannered Lady*, which had been written for poor Anna Baccherini who was prevented from playing it by death. Now, four years later, Carlo saw it for the first time, with Teodora Medebac in Anna's part, but, not being one for undue speculation or weeping over the past, his huge enjoyment was in no way marred by Anna's ghost.

A couple of days later Medebac proposed that Goldoni should become the company's permanent playwright. It was when writing of this fateful occasion that Carlo made the remark about his own phenomenal qualities, quoted at the head of this chapter, going on to say, 'I abandoned myself heedlessly to the comic muse and was swept away by it. Three or four times I have let more profitable chances go to fall into the old snare of the theatre.'

Attractive though the prospect was, though, Goldoni did prevaricate slightly, saying that he must first have the agreement of Nicoletta who was visiting her family in Genoa, although he knew that, unselfish as she was, she would never have attempted to stop him. And in fact she gave her free consent as soon as he asked for it. Goldoni then signed a contract which bound him exclusively, for the first time in his life, to the world of the theatre. He was almost exactly forty years old.

The Venetian Squabbles
or
The Reformer at Bay

IX

Placida: *The author who provides us with plays has written sixteen this year—all new, all plays of character, all written out word for word.*
Eugenio: *Sixteen plays in a year! It seems impossible.*
Orazio: *But he did it just the same. He gave his word that he would, and he kept it.*

from *Il Teatro Comico*

Before taking up his new life and starting on a course of fourteen years' literary hard labour, Goldoni was given six months' pause, ostensibly to clear up his affairs in Pisa. This interval may be profitably spent in an attempt to assess the character of our leading man which, as he enters on the threshold of early middle age, may be considered to be fully formed.

There is no shortage of portraits of Goldoni, but like the ruddy-faced bust on Shakespeare's tomb, they don't give away a great deal. He was obviously plump, probably even as a little boy, and both the drawings by Lorenzo Tiepolo and the portraits by Alessandro Longhi bear witness to self-indulgence; this was a man who liked sweet things and could write 'Long live chocolate and he who invented it' and say of some sweets that they had 'as many flavours as the manna in the desert'. Carlo Gozzi, indeed called him 'il cioccolataio'. But the portraits don't tell us a great deal more than this; nor would it have been playing the game of eighteenth-century Venice if they had.

Then, of course, there is the famous statue near the Rialto bridge which at first sight appears to be the very quintessence of Goldoni. There he is on his plinth, striding through the heart of Venice, smiling down with benignity and affection on the swirling humanity beneath him, observing its little vices and fusing them into comedy with the genial fire of his art. This in short is 'Papa' Goldoni who takes his place snugly on the shelf alongside the Swan of Avon and Father Christmas. This is Goldoni's image as created by his hagiographers. Like all images it is based on a certain amount of truth, and for more than a century and a half nobody even dreamed of doubting it – in public at any rate. Italy is a country where images have always been *de rigueur* for public figures and indeed, like evening dress, there is not even all that much difference between one image and another; Manzoni and Goldoni have both been firmly enshrouded in the same sort of harmless sanctity.

Rather over half a century after Frank Harris's wild attempt to turn Shakespeare into a human being, the Italian journalist and historian, Indro Montanelli, made a similar, though more reliable bid to de-mythify Goldoni. It is to be found in *Italia nell'ottocento*, his volume dealing with the eighteenth century in Italy, written in collaboration with Roberto Gervaso, and it is compelling, racy and almost entirely plausible, though one feels that one or two virtues may have been hastily swept under the carpet so that they won't confuse the reader. Of Gian Paolo they say that he resembled Carlo 'in every detail except for the talent', and of Carlo's return to the theatre after the Pisan interlude, 'it was the same old Goldoni with his conventional and woolly texts, his ample concessions to the most vulgar and licentious tastes of the groundlings, his endings patched together any old how without caring overmuch about plausibility, just so long as they got him out of a difficulty and the public home to bed somehow.' And later, 'Let it be faced once and for all, the man's character was not equal to his talent, indeed he would happily have sacrificed his talent for success and money if the public, threatening to withhold both, had not forced him to become Goldoni.' And again, 'What Goldoni lacked to reach true greatness was precisely a conscience; on this point Baretti, Gozzi and his other critics were perfectly right. In fact he never had any problems, not even of syntax, though he handled it none too well. The only thing that interested him was success . . . He was neither a reformer nor an accuser, but simply an amused – and often an amusing – chronicler . . . On the human level, in spite of his many vices, or perhaps even because of them, he was a likeable character. Like all the Italian intellectuals of the eighteenth century, deprived of any national culture in which they could set themselves, without an audience capable of understanding them on which they could exercise their apostolate, he too was a courtier-adventurer, though among the more amiable and innocent.'

Perhaps the most striking trait of Goldoni's character, which sounds with the reassuring tranquillity of an Alpine cow-bell through all his vicissitudes, is his equanimity. His life was storm-tossed from beginning to end, but his soul was always at peace with itself; even the great eschatological sword of Damocles which hangs over the whole of humanity never bothered him for an instant. 'My character is in complete harmony with my body,' he wrote, 'and as I fear neither cold nor heat, so I don't let myself be inflamed with anger or inebriated with joy.'

If Carlo Goldoni had not had such a character, he could never have borne the gruelling strain of the next fourteen years. There was no telling how many new plays would be performed each year, but as a season lasted for four months and even the most triumphant smash-hit never ran for more than one, it was obvious that several plays at least were needed. Sometimes a play would come off after a couple of nights and Goldoni would have to fill the breach with another, probably still unfinished a few hours before its *première* – so little wonder if the endings were a trifle forced at times. 'You will say write less and write better,' said Goldoni in a letter to a Florentine publisher in 1758, 'but the writer who writes little in Italy eats little.' Inevitably, therefore, Goldoni came to throw off plays with the speed of an Italian village barber shaving beards on a Sunday morning. Of course it was in his nature to write like this, and the only question posterity may care to ask itself, faced with masterpieces like *La Locandiera, I Rusteghi* and *Le Baruffe Chiozzotte*, is whether he would have done any better if he had been given more time. On average he took about ten days to a fortnight to write a play – although he could do it in well under a week and when, in Paris, he was given two months, he was incapable of stringing the work out.

Nor did he refuse any form of literary hack-work, dashing off countless poetic tributes on the occasions of weddings, funerals and the takings of veils. In 1757, with *La Locandiera* already behind him, he celebrated the escape of Louis XV from an assassination bid at Versailles with a Te Deum which was sung at the court of Parma. But the abject depths to which he cheerfully sank in the writing of occasional verse may be illustrated by this poem to Babiole, a poodle belonging to the French ambassadress.

> Babiole casts into the shade
> The most beautiful of bitches
> As the tiny stars
> Outshine the sun in beauty.
>
> Faithful to her mistress,
> Faithful to her lord,
> She also bears respect and love
> For their most worthy children.
>
> Oh happy land of France
> Let me sing the praises
> Of the lovable little bitch
> Who found her birth in thee.
>
> Long live sweet Babiole
> To entertain Madame
> Who caresses and loves thee
> And finds all her joy in thee.

In April 1748 Goldoni left Pisa and the comparatively peaceful existence of a provincial lawyer to plunge once more, as Medebac's hired hack, into the hectic, infuriating, through-the-looking-glass world of the theatre. In the same month a preliminary peace treaty was signed between France, England and Holland with the adherence of Austria and Sardinia. This treaty marked the end of the war of the Austrian succession and also heralded a new age for Europe which was to last until the outbreak of the First World War, but understandably enough all this meant for Goldoni was the unfreezing of the family money in the Modena bank. 'The war was over,' he writes in the *Mémoires,* 'The Infante don Philip was in possession of the Duchies of Parma, Piacenza and Guastella; the Duke of Modena had returned to his residence and the ducal bank was proposing settlements with its creditors. I felt very pleased to be on the brink of once again being able to look after my own interests.'

And to complete his contentment there was the six months' sabbatical before he was due to start work for Medebac. He decided to return to Venice by easy stages, first of all revisiting Florence where he witnessed one of the more eccentric manifestations of the Arcadians. A boy of about ten, known as the Great Sibyl, was presented to the assembly of the elect, one of whom would ask a question which the boy had to answer, on behalf of the oracle, in one word. 'These answers given by a schoolboy who doesn't even have time to reflect were mostly lacking in common sense,' says Goldoni with some understatement, 'but near the platform there is an academician who, rising from his seat, maintains that the Great Sibyl has answered most excellently and proposes to interpret the answer there and then.' The illustration Goldoni gives of this performance is as ridiculous as anything in his plays and even more demonstrative than they of the bottomless well of human gullibility. 'Why do women cry more often and more easily than men?' was the question, to which the answer came back, majestic in its bare absurdity, 'Straw'. An abbé of about forty, 'well-nourished and with a gracious and sonorous voice', spent three-quarters of an hour – so Goldoni alleges – interpreting this. First of all, having examined the fruits of the earth one by one, he concluded that straw was the most fragile of them all. 'From straw he passed to women and, with no less celerity than clarity, he developed an anatomical essay on the human body. He described in detail the source of tears in both sexes, demonstrated the delicacy of texture of the one and the resistance of the other, and concluded – to the honour of the ladies present – by attributing to weakness the female qualities of sensitivity, and being very careful not to mention feigned tears.'

The Medebac company were playing in Mantua when the Goldonis arrived there, and Medebac found them lodgings with a retired actress called Madame Balletti who, of all happy coincidences, had formerly played the parts of maidservants. The only snag so far as Goldoni was concerned was that she was eighty-five years old, though she still showed signs of her former beauty 'and flashes of the vivacity and capriciousness of her spirit'. But in spite of

Madame Balletti, Goldoni was much pulled down by the marshy air of Mantua and had to spend the better part of his month's stay there in bed. Nevertheless he managed to knock together a couple of plays for Medebac, and he had a third ready for delivery when they met again in Modena a few weeks later. Considering that the period covered by their contract had not yet started and that Goldoni was still on holiday, this was not bad going.

Finally, after five years of wandering, Goldoni returned to Venice, and he and Nicoletta went to stay with his mother in lodgings she had taken near St Mark's Square. One of the first questions they asked each other concerned the whereabouts of Gian Paolo. But neither was able to enlighten the other. 'She believed him dead and wept for him. I, knowing him a little better, was sure that one day or another he would be back to live at my expense. Nor was I wrong.'

Medebac had hired the Sant' Angelo theatre and it was here that Goldoni started this new phase of his life. And, as usual, he started it badly.

It was decided to stage *Tonin Bella Grazia*, the play he had written for D'Arbes in Pisa, and so it was immediately put into rehearsal. When actors giggle over a script in the early stages of rehearsal, it is a sure sign of disaster. So it was with the ill-fated *Tonin*. 'The actors laughed like lunatics and so did I. We thought this was a sure sign that the audience would laugh too. But this same audience, which is normally said to have no head at all, had one so well screwed-on and resolute from the very first performance that I was obliged to take off the play there and then.'

This flop was partially redeemed by the two plays that followed it – both starring D'Arbes. The first, *L'Uomo Prudente* (*The Man of Prudence*), had been written while Goldoni was still in Pisa and, taking its inspiration from a celebrated criminal case of the period, made great play of some arsenic which is slipped into Pantaloon's soup by his second wife, Beatrice, and which, fortunately, is lapped up by Rosaura's little dog before Pantaloon can get to it. In the second play, *I Due Gemelli Veneziani* (*The Venetian Twins*), Goldoni exploited what he considered to be the dual personality of D'Arbes by making him play both the twins, one quick-witted and the other simple-minded. 'The resemblance between the two twins could not have been more perfect,' said Goldoni, 'since the same person was playing both of them, but since the names were different the plot was more difficult for an actor to handle, and more delightful for the audience.' Once again poison was woven into the plot, and Goldoni confessed that he was wrong to use it in two plays running 'particularly since I knew as well as anybody else that it was not a good device in comedy'. Nevertheless, if we are to believe him, the play was praised to the stars.

Indeed success must have begun to attend on the company for the nipping and snarling of the jealous which was eventually to drive Goldoni out of Venice now began. For the moment, however, it was the company in general rather than Goldoni in particular which came in for criticism. Making capital out of the actors' origins, the critics dismissed them scoffingly as 'a troupe of tumblers'. But, as Goldoni rightly points out, 'did this company which had become so skilful and of such unwavering integrity deserve to be reproved for its previous activities?' The proof of the pudding, after all, was in the eating, and this proof – at least as far as public opinion was concerned – was not long in being demonstrated. Goldoni's next comedy, *La Vedova Scaltra* (*The Artful Widow*) was a smash hit, running for an almost unprecedented thirty nights in the 1748–9 season and then being brought back to open the following one.

Probably the cheers went to his head for, nearly forty years later, Goldoni displayed an almost schoolgirlish rapture about this piece. 'The beginning of my reformation', he said, 'could not have been more brilliant.' In fact the comedy reads feebly, and it must have been the virtuosity of Teodora Medebac which made this relatively poor *asti spumante* seem like vintage champagne. As the widow, Rosaura, who has to decide between four lovers – a Frenchman, an Englishman, a Spaniard and an Italian – she was able to do a sort of Peter Ustinov act switching, with the aid of masks, from nationality to nationality as she tries to embroil her suitors. (The Italian gets Rosaura in the end, *faute,* one imagines, *de mieux,* in much the same way as it is always an Italian who gets the papacy in the end.) This play also demonstrates clearly for the first time the lack, not merely of perception, but of bare conscientiousness which Goldoni displays in the portrayal of foreigners. His French, English and Spanish courtiers are blatant caricatures, and so little did he care about it that the best name he could manage for the Englishman was Milord Runebif. Sloppy Italianization of English words is a national defect, and there is in this name – as there probably was in Goldoni's mind – a faint echo of that oddly-sounding 'rosbif' or even 'rosbi' which is how the majority of Italian shops deal with roast beef. This feeble caricaturing is even more apparent in the later *Pamela* which, for its sins, is entirely set in England. Baretti was not slow in castigating this culpable ignorance of Goldoni's. 'In one of his plays,' he says, 'he makes a Londoner hint at the canals of London, imagining London to be such a town as Venice; and makes another Englishman talk of a most dreadful and unfrequented forest within twenty miles of London, where an outlawed Scottish lord hid himself in a mountainous cave for many years.' Much of what Baretti wrote about Goldoni was vicious or deliberately wrong-headed, but on this point one is bound to admit that he is right.

But the Venetians cared no more than Goldoni about such piffling matters as authenticity and they flocked to see *La Vedova Scaltra.* Their enthusiastic approval was the direct cause of the first of those literary battles which raged around Goldoni and were eventually to merge into an uninterrupted war. When *La Vedova Scaltra* opened the 1749–50 season, the rival San Samuele theatre hit back with a parody called *La Scuola delle Vedove* (*The School for Widows*). 'If my reader be curious to know who was the author of *The School for Widows,*' says Goldoni of the episode, 'I cannot satisfy him. I will never be persuaded to name the people who tried to harm me.' But the name was pulled to the surface in spite of him by a scholar fishing in the archives of the State inquisition: it was the Abbé Pietro Chiari.

This dapper, pompous little Jesuit, born in Brescia in 1711, five years after Goldoni, was a barefaced plagiarist with a severe form of literary diarrhoea. He had already turned out forty-odd romances which were no more than a remastication of stories from other countries, without any embellishment, and had also been responsible, amongst other things, for a twelve-volume essay entitled *Entertainments for the human spirit concerning the things of this world past, present and possibly to come.* Any hopes concerning a sense of humour that might be aroused by the use of the word 'possibly' should be dashed at once, for Chiari was utterly humourless. Like Goldoni, he gave himself airs as a theatrical reformer, but even if one is to dismiss Goldoni's reforming zeal as an invention of his old age, and put him on a level with Chiari as a literary adventurer, one is still bound to admit that the Abbé did not have the smallest grain of Carlo's talent.

Goldoni, as has been seen, was almost unnaturally restrained in his handling of Chiari; the unkindest remark he made was in a private letter in which he admitted that when in a muddle he was wont to say 'My head's like Chiari.' But Giuseppe Baretti had no such reticence. Having mercilessly slashed Goldoni, he went on to say, 'And of the Abbot Pietro Chiari I have nothing else to say, but that he is, if possible, still worse than Goldoni in every particular.' And of the conflict that now began with *La Vedova Scaltra* and Chiari's parody of it, he wrote, 'These two strange mortals were both in the same year accidentally engaged to compose comedies for two different stages in Venice. It is not to be conceived how prodigiously popular they both became after having exhibited two or three of their phantastical and absurd compositions, and how quickly they brought show, and noise, and nonsense into vogue: the like has never been seen in any country.'

Part of this prodigious popularity they owed to each other, for it was above all the squabble itself that attracted the public, and this became doubly true a little later on when Carlo Gozzi appeared on the scene. But for the moment the centre of the action was *La Scuola delle Vedove* which Goldoni watched one night, hidden in a box in the San Samuele theatre. But, as he points out, it was not so much a parody of his own play as a copy of it, the only variation being in the dialogue which was packed with insults about Goldoni and the Medebac players. One actor would recite a piece from *La Vedova Scaltra* and another would reply 'Rubbish, rubbish!' It was as childish as that, but apparently it was almost as great a popular success as the original *Vedova* had been.

Goldoni under attack was unpredictable. He was capable of almost pathetic non-resistance, but he also had teeth, and on this occasion he used them. In Chiari's piece he had noticed certain rude remarks concerning foreigners and, knowing that the Venetian Republic was extremely touchy on this point – foreigners were always sacrosanct because one never knew when they might come in useful – he held up the offending passages for all to see in a pamphlet entitled *Apologetic prologue to the crafty widow*.

Things change little in Italy and, then as now, if you wanted to get on it was necessary to know somebody in politics. Medebac knew just such a man who obligingly 'protected' the company. This protector, on hearing of Goldoni's pamphlet, became seriously alarmed and went so far as to visit the author advising him not to publish lest he should become embroiled with the state police who, although relatively harmless by now, still evoked visions of the dreadful Council of Ten and secret garrotting by night.

Goldoni's reply was a plucky one under the circumstances. The pamphlet, he said, was already being printed, but the government, who knew where the printers were to be found, was at liberty to suppress the work if it wished; if it did so, however, Goldoni would have it printed outside Venetian territory. The tubby and genial author taking on such an unexpectedly David-like attitude must have impressed the protector for he withdrew after a respectful handshake, and the next day Goldoni distributed 3,000 copies of the pamphlet throughout Venice. Not only was it magnificient publicity, but it also went straight to its target. *The School for Widows* was ordered to be taken off and – a more far-reaching result which Goldoni cannot have foreseen – a law was passed introducing theatrical censorship into Venice for the first time. And, what must have infuriated Chiari more than anything else, *La Vedova Scaltra* swept triumphantly on, her box-office takings increased out of all proportion by the row.

Two other events had taken place between the original production of *La Vedova* in the 1748-9 season and the appearance of Chiari's parody. First of all Goldoni and Medebac renewed their contract for a further four years, stipulating that Goldoni should receive 450 Venetian ducats a year in exchange for an annual output of eight plays and two libretti as well as carpentry work on old plays, attendance at rehearsals and summer tours on the mainland. The second event was the creation of *La Putta Onorata* (*The Girl of Honour*). Far more than the cardboard *Vedova Scaltra,* this enchanting play represents the most important landmark in Goldoni's work after *Il Servitore di due Padroni*. For the first time in a fully written script he shows the people of Venice, including the gondoliers, about their everyday lives. This is the forerunner of the great dialect plays, and it is also the first piece of writing in which it is possible to analyse the Goldoni magic. This magic does not lie in the plots – which in the best plays are almost non-existent – or even in the dialogue or characters, both of which vary enormously in quality, but rather in the capacity to carry the spectator into eighteenth-century Venice. He seems to show you a perfectly constructed doll's house and then, having shrunk you to its dimensions and led you inside, he convinces you that its reality is more sharp by far than the one you have come from. The action may be, indeed usually is, no more than a storm in a doll's house tea-cup, but the reality of it holds you spell-bound. Nor is it ever photographically frozen, but liquid and warm.

When Goldoni is not being dubbed the Molière of Italy, he is often being attacked for lacking Molière's bite, but this criticism misses the point altogether, for the alchemy of Goldoni does not lie in the ability to chasten vice with laughter – although he thought it did – but rather in a unique capacity for spiriting you into his world. Certainly Goldoni could not have written *Tartuffe*, but then neither could Molière have written *I Rusteghi*.

There is another curious phenomenon in *La Putta Onorata* which has its roots deep in Goldoni's art and character. Bettina, the play's heroine, is the most outrageous goody-goody, every bit as irritating as Lucia in *I Promessi Sposi* who has drawn upon her head the contempt of generations of Italian schoolgirls; and yet, by some strange process, Bettina draws the sympathy every bit as much as a rollicking old whore like Doll Tearsheet. This is partly because she is completely real from her very first utterance – *'O caro sto sol!'* which only *means* 'Oh this dear sun!' but the warm, earthy language is irresistible – and partly because, although she won't let him touch the tip of her elbow or speak a word to her unchaperoned, she is obviously head-over-heels in love with her Pasqualino. *'Caro quel muso! caro quel pepolo! Co lo vedo, se me missia tuto el sangue che gh'o in te le vene.'* 'Oh, what a sweet little snout he's got! Oh, what a sweet little shorty he is! When I see him my blood gets all mixed up in my veins!'

Finally *La Putta Onorata* is notable for being the first play to show gondoliers as they were (and indeed are) and to reproduce on stage, lock stock and barrel, that now traditional ritual known as the gondoliers' quarrel. Goldoni, who could be shrewd as well as ingenious, had a very good reason for putting gondoliers into the play. 'I wished to be reconciled', he said, 'to this class of domestics who were deserving of some attention, and who were discontented with me. The gondoliers at Venice are allowed a place in the theatre when the pit is not full; but as they could not enter at my comedies, they were forced to wait for their masters in the streets, or in their gondolas. I had heard them myself distinguish me with very droll and comical epithets; and, having procured them a few places in the corner of the house, they were quite delighted to see themselves brought onto the stage, and I became their friend.'

Goldoni was always trying to jump onto his own band-waggons and, as a result, usually falling flat on his face in the dust. *La Putta Onorata* was a success and so he wrote a sequel called *La Buona Moglie* (*The Good Wife*). But poor Bettina, having successfully held off the advances of the randy marquis and steered her Pasqualino to the altar in the first play, enters upon the second a tired, lifeless version of herself. She suffers doggedly and cradles her baby while Pasqualino dissipates her dowry. It was said that an erring Venetian husband of the time was shamed back to conjugal fidelity by this play. 'If the story is true,' Goldoni comments common-sensically, 'then the young man must have been well-disposed to mend his ways before going to the play.'

The joy felt by Goldoni and Medebac as a result of the defeat of Chiari was soon quenched by two douches of unpleasantly cold water. Goldoni would apparently have been happy to rest on his laurels for that season, but Medebac wanted to present a new play and so he persuaded his author to dust off a piece that was lying unfinished on the bench, called *L'Erede Fortunata* (*The Fortunate Heir*). This was a resounding flop, and on its heels came the news that D'Arbes, the leading male attraction of the company, was off to join the court of the King of Poland. The season was nearing its end and box-holders started cancelling their boxes for the following one, which was about as near the kiss of death as a theatre could get. Something drastic had to be done or Goldoni and Medebac would find themselves cut off from the goose which had so far been laying such satisfactory golden eggs.

What was in fact done has become so encrusted with legend, so drenched with hyperbole, that it is difficult to consider it objectively. For the last night of the season the author customarily wrote an epilogue in which the leading lady would prettily thank the public for their favour in the past and invite their patronage in the future. On this occasion Goldoni baited Teodora Medebac's line for her with the promise that he would stage sixteen brand new plays during the coming season. To read some of the comments that have been written on this gesture one would think that Goldoni had offered to bring about a second redemption of mankind. In fact the dare was almost certainly a publicity stunt excogitated by Medebac; and if one remembers that from season's end to season's end Goldoni had a full year to go and that he was capable of producing a play in a week, then in theory he should have been able to produce fifty-two new plays. What is really astonishing about the affair is the surprisingly high amount of first-class Goldoni which is to be found in the plays.

The trick worked; indeed it was perfectly calculated to generate that delightful, artificial excitement which the Venetians of the period so much enjoyed. Nothing of supreme importance was really at stake, and yet they could work themselves up into believing that everything was. The Goldoni *affaire* was as much a part of the life of Venice in 1750–1 as was the Dreyfus *affaire* in France a century and a half later. One subject dominated all conversation in *caffès* and drawing rooms; even convents were split asunder by it, father was divided against son and husband against wife. Would Goldoni do it? The grinding of teeth at the San Samuele theatre must have been audible all the way from Mestre.*

During the summer months Goldoni not only had to make a start on his sixteen plays, but to tour with the company and help Medebac with the recruitment and training of a substitute for D'Arbes. In this quest they were lucky, finding in Vicenza a soldier-turned-Pantaloon called Antonio Matteuzzi,

---

*Characteristically, Chiari did attempt to steal Goldoni's thunder a little later by offering to write twenty plays in a year, but by then the novelty was exhausted and nobody even noticed whether he succeeded or not.

nicknamed Collalto or long-neck. He must have been good, for a chronicler of the time said that when he played the twin brothers in *I Due Gemelli Veneziani* he merely changed his wig when he switched from one twin to the other 'and yet many refused to believe it was the same person'. Later he went to the *Comédie italienne* in Paris where he was described as 'the real prop of the company which was now too near its decadence'. 'Collalto', said the chronicler, 'earned a lot and spent a lot because he liked doing things in a big way.' So, what with the fervour aroused by Goldoni's self-dare and this excellent substitute for D'Arbes, the future looked promising for Medebac.

For the five out-of-season months Goldoni toured with the company in Bologna, Mantua and Milan, trained Collalto in the new, maskless style of acting, and made a start on the forty-eight acts which he had promised the public.

While they were in Milan he stayed at Castellazzo in the villa of a patron of his, Count Giuseppe Arconati Visconti, to whom, in a tone of obsequiousness which would not have been too fulsome for an Elizabethan courtier writing of his queen, he had dedicated *La Putta Onorata*. In this dedication he describes the villa where he now stayed. 'The vastness of the edifice, the richness of its furnishings, the expanse of the great garden in which one can see the most beautiful greens in Italy diversely laid out and distinguished one from another; the great number of fountains and ornamental plays of water, arranged with art and supplied by machinery with water from under the ground, and maintained at enormous expense; the deer park, the enclosure for wild beasts, the orchard of finest apples; the library, rich in the choicest books; the Mathematics room, in which one may see all the most choice apparatus for study and experiment in the mechanical Philosophy; the collection of celebrated ancient marble statues, among which one may admire a colossal and magnificent statue of Pompey, which your great ancestor brought at immense expense from the Campidoglio in Rome ...' All the immense expense must have been very impressive, and it was in these surroundings that Goldoni put the finishing touches to the first seven of his sixteen plays.

Then at the end of September 1750 he travelled with the company back to Venice where, on 5th October, the new season began and gratifyingly large audiences began to pack out the Sant' Angelo theatre to see if and how Goldoni would keep his word. They opened with *Il Teatro Comico,* that fascinating non-play in which Goldoni outlines his challenge to the public, formally introduces his reform and, almost incidentally, gives an exceptionally vivid portrait of a company of actors at work in the eighteenth century.

An interesting point arises apropos of this play. In the second scene the leading lady announces the titles of all sixteen of the plays, including those which he had not written and at least one - *I Pettegolezzi delle Donne* (*Yack, Yack, Yack!* or more literally *The Gossip of the Women*) - which, on his own admission in the *Mémoires,* had not yet *even been conceived.* Could

jiggery-pokery have been afoot? Or did he select titles before even knowing
what the plays were to be about?

The rest of the sixteen plays may be likened to an enormous rag-bag
containing material of every imaginable sort – something old and something
new, more than something borrowed, though nothing really blue. The ideas of
at least five of the plays are confessedly borrowed – two from Molière, one from
Rousseau, one from Corneille and one – *Pamela Nubile* – lifted lock stock and
barrel from Samuel Richardson. One of the sixteen, *L'Avventuriero Onorato*
(*The Honourable Adventurer*), is a self-portrait with a protagonist who has been
lawyer, magistrate's clerk, consul, playwright and unscrupulous womanizer.
Seven of them were written and first performed after the famous dare but before
the company came back to Venice; the other nine were written and
performed – or so we are to believe – during the 1750-1 season. Two of them
were based on actresses in the Medebac company. *La Finta Ammalata* (*The
Woman Sick for Subterfuge*) was none other than Teodora Medebac who 'was
often ill, often thought herself ill and sometimes suffered from no more than
self-induced hypochondria'. On these occasions, says Goldoni, the only cure
was to entrust a good part to one of the junior actresses and then the patient was
immediately cured. La Medebac immediately realized that she was being
lampooned 'but seeing that the part was a magnificent one took it on gladly and
played it to perfection'. The other play based on a Medebac actress was *La
Donna Volubile* (*The Fickle Woman*). 'We had an actress in the company who
was the most capricious woman in the world,' says Goldoni. 'I did no more than
paint her portrait, and Madame Medebac, who knew the original, although a
good-natured woman, was only too pleased to make fun of her companion.'
Only two of the series flopped completely, and this was one of them.

Looking back on the enterprise, Medebac and Goldoni were fortunate that
there were as few as two failures; played before any other audiences in any other
time or place, there would probably have been several other collapses. And in a
sense it was not the plays themselves that succeeded so much as the great dare
which had such an irresistible fascination; *la toute Venise* felt itself to be
involved and so *la toute Venise* had to be there.

Then there was the abominable *Pamela* which, says Goldoni, the public
found delightful and which above all 'bore away the crown'. An English
audience would be put off before the curtain even went up by the names of the
characters – Milord Bonfil, Miledi Daure, il Cavaliere Ernold, Milord Artur
and Milord Curbrech; indeed Pamela, which even Goldoni could hardly have
mistaken or corrupted, is the only possible name in the whole cast-list with the
possible exceptions of the majordomo, Monsieur Longman, and a servant
improbably named Isaaco. But the names are merely a faint symptom of the real
complaint. The play has all the faults of Richardson's original – it is ridiculous,
boring, morally repulsive and impossibly far-fetched – but if the novel is
redeemed by its authenticity, Goldoni's play is damned the blacker for lack of

authenticity as a result of transplantation. What then allowed it to triumph? One can only assume that the sentimentality which was oozing across Europe – as Maurice Rowdon happily put it – bore *Pamela* on its treacly tide.

And so, play by play, the season went on and the excitement mounted. It was all rather like a well-designed thriller with surprises and *colpi di scena* dotted about here and there so that the reader's interest should not wain. Even the two flops, occurred at the right psychological moment to create tension. The first one – *Il Giocatore* (*The Gambler*) – came immediately before the ten days' Christmas break so that the anti-Goldonians had time to put about the story that he was finished, while the pro-Goldonians could enjoy a delicious period of suspense, holding their collective breath only to let it out again in a delighted gasp as their hero bounded back in top form immediately after Christmas. The second flop, *La Donna Volubile,* came at an even more dramatic moment, the penultimate of the series, so that an effect was created not unlike that of the single rolling drum in the circus which preludes the last and most daring high-wire feat. Could Goldoni do it?

It was the last Sunday but one of carnival and he had not yet written a word of the sixteenth play, nor even conceived an idea for it. So he had less than a fortnight to think up an idea, write it as a play, rehearse and present it. That Sunday he strolled into St Mark's Square, he says, to distract his mind and see if one of the maskers or the quacks could suggest an idea. 'Under the clock archway I saw a man who immediately struck my attention and gave me the idea I was looking for. He was an old Armenian, badly dressed, filthy and with a long beard, who went about the streets of Venice selling the dried fruit of his country, which he called Abagigi. That was all I needed to make me return happily home. I went back, shut myself up immediately in my little study and imagined a comedy of the streets of Venice entitled *I Pettegolezzi delle Donne.'* The play breathes authenticity and is arguably the best of the series.

It was staged on the Tuesday before Good Friday and it closed both carnival and the theatrical season. The theatre was crammed and more than 300 people were turned away – an enormous number in proportion to the theatre-going public. 'The throng on that day was so extraordinary that the price of boxes was tripled and then quadrupled,' says Goldoni, and one can imagine Medebac rubbing his hands as he did the tripling and the quadrupling. 'The applause was so thunderous that people passing near the theatre were uncertain whether it was due to satisfaction or a general uprising.

'I sat peacefully in my box surrounded by my friends who were weeping with joy. Then all at once a crowd of people came to find me. They forced me to go out and then carried me, or rather dragged me in spite of myself to the Ridotto. They led me from room to room where I was overwhelmed with compliments which I would gladly have avoided if I could.

'Too tired to put up with so much fuss, and on the other hand not realizing to what the enthusiasm was due in that moment, I was sorry that that particular play should be placed above so many others which I esteemed more highly.

'Then little by little I became aware of the true reason for this general acclamation. It was because I had triumphantly concluded my entire pledge.'

A fitting ending for a most perfectly Goldonian story.

X

'Swift of wit as she was, all the players feared her, sure that she would utterly defeat them upon the stage.'

The chronicler, Francesco Bartoli, writing of the actress,
Maddalena Marliani

The venture took its toll. Beneath the jovial and apparently imperturbable surface of Goldoni's nature there lurked a demon which he describes as hypochondria, and the alarums of the past year awakened it. 'At the age of forty-three I had great facility of invention and in the carrying-out of my projects, but I was a man like any other. The remorseless strain had shaken my health; I fell ill and paid the price of my folly.' What exactly the illness was, he does not reveal – his clinical diagnoses were always cheerfully vague, describing everything as 'hypochondria' – but it was probably what we should call a nervous breakdown, attenuated by Goldoni's equable disposition. Its effects were far-reaching rather than violent; hitherto he had taken his health for granted, but every so often from now on preoccupations concerning it would scud across the sun of optimism that normally shone on his existence.

To his patron, Arconati Visconti, he wrote of the sixteen plays, 'A similar labour I shall never undertake again, and I do not believe that one such has ever been undertaken by another.' And although the feat was not quite so Herculean as it has been painted, it was nevertheless considerable, particularly if one bears in mind that he was also writing opera libretti and occasional pieces, and handling commissions for theatres in other cities. 'I am tied to my desk day and night,' he wrote to a friend about this time, 'and I haven't even been to the theatre for twelve nights. I have two theatres on my shoulders in Venice as well as an order for two comedies a year from Dresden and two from Florence.'

The sixteen-comedy trick was also indirectly responsible for widening a pre-existing crack between Goldoni and Medebac into an open rift. This is how Goldoni puts it: 'I had provided sixteen comedies in the course of a year, and although the manager of the company had not asked for them, he had nevertheless profited well from them. But what profit was there for me? Not a farthing more than the price agreed for a year, not even the smallest bonus; many praises, many compliments, but not even the minimum retribution. It grieved me, but I did not say a word.'

So far history has accepted Goldoni's portrait of himself in the Medebac row as an aggrieved lamb assaulted by a ravenous wolf, forgetting that the only witness present before posterity is Goldoni himself, and that therefore, in default of Medebac's testimony, the hypothesis of two shrewd operators falling out over the loot must be considered as at least equally plausible. Goldoni certainly believed himself to be baulked of his due, and consequently he decided to see what could be raised from the publication of his plays. But once again Medebac blocked the way, asserting that he had bought the rights with the contract. This difference of opinion was to escalate before long into something not far short of real warfare in which it is hard to decide whether Goldoni's conduct was plucky or reprehensible. The verdict must depend to some extent on what one thinks of Medebac. He was a business-man and a Genoese and, as such, was not prodigal with money, preferring to see it flow into his pockets rather than anybody else's. But was he overbearing and dishonest? Before accepting the general verdict that he was, it is worth remembering that Chiari described him as 'worthy, but above all honourable', while a chronicler wrote that he was 'urbane with all, prudent and wise, a compassionate bearer of succour to those in distress, deserving the name of an honourable man and worthy of general esteem'. True, Chiari was then dependent on Medebac and the chronicler – Francesco Bartoli who will later make a walking-on appearance in this story – was a born eulogizer, although he, too, had his fangs. So perhaps a verdict of six of one and half a dozen of the other would be logical. Certainly as far as the publication issue is concerned, the argument might go on indefinitely for the simple reason that the contract contained no clause concerning book rights. *Patti chiari, amicizie lunghe* says an Italian proverb, and in this case the lack of a clear agreement was certainly responsible for the shortening of a friendship.

For the moment, however, a compromise was reached. Medebac offered to let his author print one volume of plays a year, thinking thereby to hold him bound indefinitely, and Goldoni accepted, thinking to break free as soon as the terms of the present contract ended and publish as many plays as he liked. So Goldoni gave the manuscripts of four comedies to a Venetian printer called Antonio Bettinelli and there, for the moment, the matter rested.

In the meantime he followed the company on tour to Turin. 'The uniformity of the buildings in the principal streets creates a most wonderful spectacle for the eye,' he writes in one of those schoolboy-essay type descriptions which he gives in the *Mémoires* of the cities he visits for the first time. 'Its squares and churches are very beautiful, there is a superb walk through the fortified part of the town, and magnificence and good taste reign everywhere in the royal residences, both in the town and in the country.' And he marvels at the fact that the Torinese, 'seeing a Milanese, a Venetian or a Genoese arriving in their city are accustomed to exclaim "Here is an Italian!" ' As Turin was to be one of the hotbeds of the *risorgimento* a century later, this is an interesting example of future events casting their shadows.

King Charles's head, in the shape of the more than usually odorous comparison with Molière, cropped up once again. 'It's good,' said certain Torinese theatre-goers of one of his new pieces, 'but it isn't Molière.' And this, by a process of reasoning which is not as clear as it might seem at first sight, led Goldoni to write a play *about* Molière, of which the best that can be said is that it amply confirms the second clause in the judgement of his Torinese critics, though hardly the first. This did not prevent it from being a great success with the public in Turin and, later, in Venice. As Goldoni himself summed it up with unconscious but deadly exactitude, 'Molière took his place alongside Pamela.'

Having put this piece into rehearsal, he went off to spend the summer in Genoa with Nicoletta, who must have been overjoyed to see her family again at last. This summer is notable for being the only period of any length in Goldoni's maturity during which he did not write any plays. 'Ah, how *dolce* it is,' he says, 'especially after having worked very hard, to spend a few days *senza far niente!*' But with autumn he returned to the sweat-shop in Venice where he was delighted to find, not only that his plays had been published, but that the recipients of the four dedications had presented him with a gold watch and snuff box, four pairs of Venetian lace-cuffs and – what must have delighted him most of all – a silver tray full of chocolate.

He opened the 1751–2 season with another flop, *Il Padre di Famiglia* (*The Father of the Family*) and then, managing as always to jump clear of trouble in the nick of time, followed it up with a success, *L'Avvocato Veneziano* (*The Venetian Lawyer*). There is a Venetian story of a man who, seeing a tombstone which had been set up in memory of 'a lawyer and an honest man', asked how it was that two men could have been buried in the same grave. This neatly demonstrates the Venetian, if not the universal attitude to the law. Quixotically Goldoni ran counter to public opinion by presenting a lawyer of integrity and thus, he hoped, whitewashing the profession. But his one-time colleagues were so accustomed to cavils that they saw them where they did not exist, and now argued that this play could only be a criticism of the profession, presenting an incorruptible lawyer only to make the feebleness and greed of the others stand out more clearly. And, as Goldoni might well have replied, who should know better than they?

In the ten days' Christmas break of 1751 there occurred an event in the Medebac company which set off violent, though conflicting reactions in the breasts of several of its members, and was indirectly responsible for producing one of the greatest comedies in the Italian language. Maddalena Marliani, whose stage name was Corallina, returned to her husband, Giuseppe, the Brighella of the company, whom she had abandoned three years previously 'for some youthful escapades' as Goldoni daintily puts it. The Marlianis were an interesting couple. Giuseppe, like so many of the company, had been a tumbler, and had married the manager's daughter, Maddalena, before Medebac came along to lead the company into higher paths. He not only tumbled and acted, but wrote plays and worked an eccentric musical instrument which was operated by currents of air and which he called the Bells of Manfredonia. Moreover, he studied the Cabala in the hope that it would help him to win the lottery, 'but although he won several times,' says the chronicler, 'he always spent more than he got.' He was also an alchemist, working most diligently to bring about the transmutation of base metals into gold, but only succeeding in producing something 'that looked like silver and was of little value'.

Maddalena, who got tired of waiting for gold and took off for her own 'youthful escapades', might have been made for Goldoni in more than one sense of the word. She was a beautiful young Venetian, as swift and provocative as a wink and, to top up the cup of Goldoni's happiness, she specialized in the parts of serving-maids. 'And so,' he says demurely, 'I did not fail to interest myself on her behalf.'

The effect of Maddalena's arrival on him needs no enlarging upon, while Nicoletta, one imagines, sighed resignedly. As a voracious, but indiscriminate womanizer, Medebac was probably not unduly excited by the arrival of Maddalena the woman, but as a Genoese businessman he must have been overjoyed to see Maddalena the actress who represented a powerful new attraction for his company. It was in Teodora's already dangerously unbalanced mind, however, that the arrival of Maddalena wreaked the most devastating havoc. Here was a deadly rival for the favours of Goldoni, both as man and playwright; and the shadow of total madness, in which she was to die exactly ten years later, began to spread perceptibly.

For Maddalena, Goldoni wrote *La Serva Amorosa* (*The Good-natured Maidservant*). The play is not one of his best and, as he points out himself in the preface to it, Maddalena was to a large extent responsible for its success. But success is always success, wherever it comes from, and this one must have been particularly galling for Teodora Medebac – though nothing in comparison with what was to come. One can imagine the scenes that now racked the company, the venemous looks, the awful rumours. Even Medebac, who had broad shoulders and might be considered a past-master in just this sort of situation, must have quailed at times.

But for the moment Teodora demanded and got her way; or rather – as her unrestrained way would undoubtedly have involved the annihilation of Maddalena – she succeeded in arranging that the next play should be a vehicle for herself. It was *La Moglie Saggia* (*The Wise Wife*), an artificially constructed piece in which the old poisoning device rears its head once again. 'It was generally said in Venice,' writes Goldoni ingenuously, 'that the first scene of this comedy was a masterpiece.' To a tougher and more embittered twentieth-century dramatist, however, it might appear about as artificial as the butler laying character and situations in a telephone conversation at curtain rise. 'In the Marchioness's anteroom,' says Goldoni, 'various servants can be seen, drinking the best wine in the house, describing their masters who had just supped there; so, by tearing them to pieces with their grumbling, they inform the audience about the subject matter of the play and the personalities of the characters.'

Wary of re-awakening Teodora's wrath, Goldoni played safe with the next piece, making it a vehicle for the company's Pantaloon, Collalto, allowing him to display his virtuosity by playing a father with mask and a son without. But all caution was thrown to the winds for the last play of the season which had the unfortunate title of *Le Donne Gelose* (*The Jealous Women*) and an equally unfortunate plot which, for anyone in the know, was plainly based on the situation within the company. Lucrezia, played by Maddalena, is a charming young widow who sends the bourgeois Venetian wives into paroxysms of jealousy, and triumphs over them all in the end. Predictably this piece caused trouble, and the trouble was in no way lessened by the fact that Maddalena scored a triumph. 'So much the worse for Madame Medebac,' says Goldoni somewhat heartlessly; 'The poor woman at once fell back into her convulsions.'

Luckily at this point the bell rang for the end of carnival and the bout was brought to a merciful though temporary halt. Goldoni was struck down at the same time, and no wonder, by a recurrence of his nervous breakdown. To recover he followed the players to Bologna where he stayed with his friend and patron, the twenty-four-year-old Marquis and Senator Francesco Albergati who played an important minor role in Goldoni's life and kept up a correspondence with him lasting for twenty years. This charming young patrician was a passionate amateur of the theatre, writing plays and acting them in a private playhouse which he had built on one of his estates outside Bologna. The authoritative Treccani encyclopaedia is somewhat patronizing about his literary attainments, saying that he 'oscillates uncertainly between classical tragedy and sentimental drama, between the *Commedia dell'Arte* and Goldonian comedy'. It does not cite the judgement of one admirer who, doubtless inflamed by the marquis's generous hospitality, described him as 'the Italian Garrick'.

This same Albergati translated Voltaire into Italian, and exchanged plays and correspondence with the great man. 'I don't know Albergati personally,' Voltaire said to Casanova, 'but he sent me the plays of Goldoni, the *mortadella* of Bologna and a translation of my *Tancrède.*' Whether or not the gastronomical delight of Bolognese sausage had anything to do with it, it is impossible to say, but Voltaire became an enthusiastic admirer of Goldoni and, in 1760, when enemies and critics were baying most savagely at Goldoni's heels, wrote some verses of appreciation *Sur le talent comique de Monsieur Goldoni* which appeared in the *Gazzetta Veneta* to the impotent fury of the anti-Goldonians.

But now, in 1752, the friendship with Albergati was only beginning. Goldoni was able to recover from his nervous breakdown and dabble in amateur theatricals in a trifling, ladylike manner which compromised nobody.

To English readers, accustomed to the yawning chasm which always existed historically between the nobility and Grub Street, the way Goldoni was treated as an equal by the aristocracy may seem surprising.* Nor are the instances of this intimacy limited to Albergati and Arconati Visconti. Goldoni dined regularly in the houses of the great patrician families of Venice, and only a couple of months before the visit to Bologna, he had been invited to the wedding of Giovanni Mocenigo – whose family had already provided the Serenissima with six doges – and Caterina Loredan, the daughter of the then reigning doge. In his invitation to Goldoni, Mocenigo said 'The most serene Doge allows me to invite some of my friends to the wedding. You are of that number. Please come. There will be a place laid for you at table.' 'In the banqueting hall,' says Goldoni of this event, 'there was one table for a hundred people and another for four and twenty at which the Doge's nephew did the honours of the house. I was at the latter, but at the second course we all left our places and went to the great hall where we mixed, stopping to talk now with one, now with another. I in particular was the object of a thousand of those kindnesses which are heaped upon an author who has been fortunate enough to please.'

Some of his experiences of high society were piped into the collected works, and indeed the piece which opened the next season, *I Puntigli Domestici* (*Domestic Quarrels*) contained, in his own words, 'people of quality'. He describes the play which followed it, *Il Poeta Fanatico* (*The Fanatical Poet*) as 'one of my weakest', but the passage recording its inspiration is far from being one of the weakest in the *Mémoires*. 'I had been introduced to a very rich man who had an only daughter, young, beautiful and greatly talented as a poetess. In order that he might enjoy the exclusive rights of her muse, he refused to let her marry. He held literary *salons* in his house which everybody attended gladly, though only in order to look upon the daughter, whose father was so insupportably ridiculous. When the girl read or recited her verses, this infatuated man remained on his feet, looking from right to left, enjoining absolute silence. He flew into a rage if anybody sneezed, and he found the taking of snuff indecent. He made so many grimaces and contortions of his face that it was the hardest thing in the universe to prevent oneself from bursting into gusts of laughter. As soon as the daughter's verses were done, the father was the first

*The patrician Vendramins, as will be seen, were more English than Italian in this respect, but then they employed Goldoni.

to applaud. He would then break away from the circle and, without the smallest consideration for the other poets who were reciting their compositions, he went up behind all the chairs saying in a loud voice and most outrageously, "Did you hear my daughter? What did you think of her? She's a very different proposition from these others!" I myself was present more than once at similar scenes, and the last I saw finished badly because the other authors took umbrage and brusquely stamped out of the *salon*. This fanatical father wished to go to Rome so that his daughter might be crowned in the Campidoglio, but her relatives prevented the project and the government itself had a hand in the affair. The girl was married in spite of him and he, after fifteen days fell ill, and melancholy and anger killed him.'

Just before Christmas 1752 Goldoni told Medebac that he intended leaving the company when his contract expired at the end of the current season, and at almost exactly the same time as that conversation handed over to him *La Locandiera*, translated into English at one time or another as *The Mistress of the Hotel, The Fair Hostess, Mine Hostess*, and even, in 1805, as *The She-Inn-keeper, or the Landlady*. So it was that by only a few months Goldoni's masterpiece fell to Medebac rather than the proprietors of the San Luca theatre.*

Maddalena was its inspiration. Or, as Goldoni unkindly puts it, 'Seeing that the leading lady was in no state to appear on stage for the opening of Carnival, I produced a comedy for the maidservant.' Indeed, poor Teodora's condition was alarming, nearer now to madness than mere 'temperament'. 'Her hypochondrias had become more and more of a trial,' says Goldoni. 'She laughed and cried at the same time, hideous shrieks issued from her mouth, she made a thousand grimaces and contortions of her face. The good folk in her family, believing her to be possessed, fetched exorcists to her and she, hung about with relics, played with these pious objects like a little girl of three or four.' It is typical of Goldoni that he can describe this scene so vividly, without caring a jot for the horror of it or even realizing that he was at least indirectly responsible for it.

So *La Locandiera* was staged for the first time on Boxing Day 1753. It was immediately a triumph, and there was no telling for how long it would have run had Teodora not intervened. 'What with the jealousy already fermenting in her soul for the success of Maddalena, this last play should have been enough to put her underground for good, but since her vapours were of an unusual type, she left her bed for two days after the first night of *La Locandiera* and demanded that its run be cut short and *Pamela* be put in its place.' Of course she had her way.

Goldoni's comment on the affair is almost unctuous. 'These little scenes

La Locandiera is unquestionably his masterpiece among plays written in Italian, or as he puts it, Tuscan. Its supremacy is more arguable if one includes the Venetian-dialect plays.

occur in almost all those places where despotism leads reason by the nose. But as far as I was concerned I had no complaints; two of my daughters were involved, and I was a tender father as much to one as to the other.' There is no telling whether he is referring to the plays, the actresses, or both.

In all Goldoni's vast gallery, which contains some very dismal old masters indeed, no portrait is sharper than that of Mirandolina, *La Locandiera*. She is scheming, quick, malicious, witty and fickle, yet possessed of all female sense and sensibility, with her feet, in the last resort, planted with almost peasant firmness on the floorboards of her *locanda*. If it is true that the test of a great play is whether it can survive transplanting from age to age, then *La Locandiera* has triumphantly passed it. For too long it was staged in the celebrated lace-cuffs style of Eleonora Duse; then in 1971 it was presented in an Italian production with randy and impoverished noblemen guzzling and tumbling fly-blown actresses against the background of a sleazy inn. Far from suffering from this violent treatment, at which Goldoni, a great moralist on paper, would have been the first to be horrified, the play emerged with greater strength and vigour than before.

Goldoni, understandably vexed with La Medebac, somehow persuaded her husband to take off *Pamela*. Indeed, although he does not say so, it is probable that *Pamela* was doing poor business which would be hardly surprising after *La Locandiera*. In its place went *L'Amante Militare* (*The Military Lover*) for which Goldoni drew upon his experiences of war. In the preface to this play he attempts to make up for his own lack of martial background by waving the career of his brother at the reader; this, one might say, was the only occasion in his life when the wretched Gian Paolo was of some assistance to Carlo. The whole play holds up well, but its happiest moments occur in the sub-plot concerning Harlequin, a young recruit who attempts to desert disguised in a dress of Corallina. He is caught and condemned to death, and the scene of his execution when a reprieve arrives as the rifles are pointed at his breast is *Commedia dell'Arte* at its joyous best.

The next play, and the last he wrote for Medebac, focuses the attention of posterity onto the interesting fact – though of marginal importance – that Goldoni was almost certainly a Freemason. Two Englishmen of his acquaintance had recently founded a lodge in Venice into which, for lack of any inconfutable evidence, we can only assume he was received. Goldoni's sense of humour would not have allowed him to put up for long with the bizarre hocus-pocus of Cagliostro's Egyptian rite, but the goings-on in the Venetian lodge, to judge by the evidence of the play, were altogether more homely and down-to-earth – a sort of comfortable, all-male, clubby atmosphere which Goldoni sometimes enjoyed as an escape from the brawlings of actresses and even, perhaps, the tender solicitude of Nicoletta. The play – *Le Donne Curiose* (*The Curious Women*) – is a veiled defence of Freemasonry, or at any rate a theatrical demonstration, prudently set in Bologna, that Freemasonry, far from being the personification of the Great Beast as the Jesuits were proclaiming it, was a harmless enough affair. The plot could hardly be thinner: the women, curious about the men's secret activities, bribe Brighella to hide them behind the arras where they discover that there is nothing to be discovered. But the play is first-class Goldoni, and it allowed him to end his years at the Sant' Angelo on the crest of the wave.

The Medebacs do not appear to have been unduly put out by his departure. Medebac had almost certainly signed up Chiari as Goldoni's successor, though whether the retiring author was aware of this – or how he would have reacted if he had been – there is no telling. As for Teodora, she must have realized by now that all her hopes of holding Goldoni – man or author – were vain and, that being so, the sooner he was out of her sight altogether the better. Only Maddalena reacted, but her fury was enough for three. When she had rejoined the company after her escapades, Goldoni must have seemed to her a Prince Charming – tubby, married and forty-three it was true, but those were mere details – who would make a queen of her; and, indeed, in *La Locandiera* he had given her the dramatist's equivalent of a royal crown. And now, little more than a year later, he was abandoning her. She pleaded with him, she used every argument that a woman and an actress and a mistress can have recourse to, and when she saw that it was all in vain, she swore undying hatred for him. This was the sort of situation that left Goldoni as unmoved as a Christmas pudding in brandy flames. He took an old script – now lost – that he was leaving behind him, made about as many alterations in it as Hamlet made in the script of the players to suit his particular domestic purposes, titled it *The Vindictive Woman* and, more than satisfied with his little joke, walked off to the San Luca theatre.

XI

'Whether they be comedies, tragi-comedies or dramas, they pleased one and all ... And so if they have not sufficient merit to be esteemed, at least one cannot deny them the homage that is generally accorded to success.'

Goldoni's judgement of his *Persian Bride* trilogy

Things were very different at the San Luca theatre, and although Goldoni puts a good face on it in the *Mémoires,* he must have found the atmosphere unpleasantly chilly after the bawdy, brawling, animal warmth at Sant' Angelo. Medebac had his faults, but he was an old-fashioned actor-manager, the sort of man – as the definition has it – you could go out for a drink with. But you would never have dreamed of going out for a drink with Francesco Vendramin, nor he with you. (In fact, the San Luca theatre was jointly owned by Francesco Vendramin and his brother, but the brother seems to have been a sleeping partner.) Far from being an actor-manager, he was a patrician who stood most firmly on his rank, expecting to be addressed as Your Excellency by such common rabble as actors and writers; his family after all was of the nobility of Venice and had included one of its doges. Goldoni he addressed as 'Master Carlo' and on one of the occasions when Goldoni importuned him for money, the sum was sent, but with an accompanying note that must have made even Goldoni wince. 'Master Carlo,' wrote Francesco Vendramin, 'I am a gentleman and a Christian, two words of great significance. I who write them understand their meaning; I hope that, on reflection after having read them, you will understand them.' If Medebac had been mean, at least he was a man of the theatre; the Vendramins were business-men who ran a theatre as today they might run a night-club or a garage, counting and stacking away the takings and giving as little as possible to the employees who, understandably, did their best to cheat them in return. So on the whole Goldoni's transfer might be considered as a jump, not so much from the frying-pan into the fire as from the frying-pan into the deep-freeze.

Two of the most immediately apparent drawbacks concerned the theatre itself and its leading lady. San Luca was one of the oldest theatres in Venice, built in 1622, burnt down and rebuilt in 1653. But it was far too big. Goldoni was accustomed to comparatively small and intimate playhouses, and his doll's-house reality was swamped in San Luca. This was responsible for the disastrous beginnings he made in his new life and for the most improbable turn his writing took before he became adjusted to his new surroundings.

As for the leading lady, Teresa Gandini, she was exactly half as old as the rebuilt playhouse, and her husband, Pietro, the Brighella of the company, was a pompous prickly little man who stood on his wife's dignity even more than on his own - although he was said to be an actor of exceptional ability who, in the course of a single play, changed costume, appearance and accent eighteen times.

The actor who co-ordinated the company, serving as a sort of foreman for the Vendramins, was a one-time barber from Bologna called Giuseppe Lapy who, to judge by contemporary accounts, was not a very attractive or savoury character. The chronicler says of him that he was 'successful at a time when very little was needed to get laughs', that he walked like a duck, and that it would have been impossible to find a more insufferable actor than he. Moreover he earned a lot, which seems improbable under the Vendramins, spent nothing, and had no respect for anybody, even Goldoni, 'to whom he owed everything he had on earth'. The chronicler, however may have been a little prejudiced as far as Lapy's professional attainments were concerned for the actor apparently played some of Goldoni's loud-mouthed old women with uproarious success.*

But for better or worse, Goldoni's move was now made, and he was to stay at San Luca for the next ten years, his last decade in Venice. And, after a disastrous start, it was for this company that the richest plays of his maturity were written. Finally, in this theatre he was to be the protagonist of one of the most vicious and ear-splitting literary squabbles of all time.

Goldoni opened the batting at San Luca with *La Donna di Testa Debole* (*The Weak-headed Woman*) which is a sort of poor man's *Précieuses Ridicules* and flopped most resoundingly. He tried to remedy things with *Il Geloso Avaro* (*The Jealous Miser*) and floundered even more alarmingly, by which time he, the Vendramin brothers and the company must have all been wishing most fervently he had never come over from Sant' Angelo. He himself puts the blame on the size of the theatre and the fact that the company was not yet versed in his

---

* This pantomime dame tradition in Goldoni lapsed entirely, which is a pity as some of the plays emphatically lend themselves to it. Fortunately it was revived by Gino Cavalieri who was most wickedly funny as the mother in *La Buona Madre* who is prepared to sell her daughter for a cup of coffee.

'new style'. There is more or less truth in both these defences, although, in the case of the second, at least five of the actors had worked with him before. But the multi-headed monster in Venice needed more than good excuses to appease it, and Goldoni – always at his best in that sort of situation – came up with an expedient which had the monster rolling at his feet overnight and begging to have its tummy tickled. But before dealing with the bizzarre trilogy of plays which allowed Goldoni once more to breathe the heady air of success, there comes a dramatic episode in the long serial dealing with the publication of his plays.

Now free of all obligations towards Medebac, he went to Antonio Bettinelli, the publisher, with manuscripts for the third volume of the collected works. 'But what was my surprise when this phlegmatic man told me plainly and in cold – indeed icy – blood that he could no longer take my scripts from me because he was now receiving them from Medebac on whose behalf he was continuing the publication.'

Goldoni claims that in the eyes of the law he was in the right and Bettinelli and Medebac in the wrong. But, he says, to obtain a decision to that effect would have involved taking the matter to court, 'and litigation is the same all over the world'. It is more probable, however, that he was in doubt about the outcome of legal proceedings, for if the contract with Medebac gave the rights of the plays to the director of the Sant' Angelo theatre, then the law would almost certainly have decided that those rights, for want of specification, included publishing rights.

But whatever he may have thought about it, Goldoni most improperly took the law into his own hands by having a rival edition published in Florence. Then, when Bettinelli managed to obtain an order banning the importation of this edition into Venice, Goldoni – probably much savouring the cape-and-dagger smack of it all – organized a network for the smuggling of the Florentine edition into the territory of the Serenissima, a deserted fisherman's hut on the banks of the Po being used to store the volumes before they were picked up by a group of 'high-born Venetians' who then carried them over the border. These high jinks, however, might have seriously altered the whole shape of his life, for while he was organizing the job in Florence, the authorities in Venice threatened to refuse him re-entry if the contraband were to continue. But nothing came of it, the Republic by now being soft and fundamentally indifferent to what went on, although such insubordination a century before might have brought him a nasty spell in the leads or worse.

All the excitement probably took his mind off the work for San Luca, but after the failure of *Il Geloso Avaro* he was forced to concentrate or lose for ever the attention of his fickle monster. He concentrated and came up with a five-act abomination in verse called *La Sposa Persiana* (*The Persian Bride*). Even Goldoni's most enthusiastic hagiographers tend to look a little askance at this play and the two which followed it and made up his Oriental trilogy, but they ignore the fact that these plays, which admittedly do nothing to augment his stature as a dramatist, represented a manoeuvre which was both astute and successful. Goldoni, switching theatres, had staked heavily and it now looked as though he were losing everything; if he could hit on something which would turn this loss into triumphant gain, he certainly was not going to let a trifle like the good opinion of posterity – even assuming he could foresee posterity's reprobation, which he could not – stand in his way. What he needed was a play which would fill up the daunting space of San Luca and give him time to think. Obviously nothing of the type of *La Putta Onorata* or *La Locandiera* would do it. So he hit upon the idea of an Oriental hotch-potch – full of lurid, clashing colours, Circassian slave-girls, seraglios, disguise, violence and intrigue – and it worked like the flamboyant artificial magic it was.

And if the plays were not enough by themselves to fan the public interest, there was also a lively scandal behind the scenes. What was ostensibly the leading female role in *La Sposa Persiana* – Fatima, the daughter of a high-ranking officer – went to the fifty-year-old Signora Gandini, but the far more attractive part of the little slave-girl, Ircana, went to a girl in the company on whom Goldoni had his eye, Caterina Bresciani, a pretty young Florentine who still retained her native accent. She was apparently wild and unaccustomed to acting from memory, 'with a body', as Goldoni said in a letter, 'full of furious fits and starts'. Moreover she was fiercely jealous of popularity and would not tolerate applause going to another actress. For all this, she was obviously worth the taming, and Goldoni went about it with a will.

La Sposa Persiana was a wild success, running for thirty-four nights and signalling the downfall of la Gandini and the triumphant ascent of la Bresciani who from then on, says Goldoni, came to be known by the name of her part, Ircana.

The Gandinis, of course, were gibbering with rage, and the husband went about accusing Goldoni of 'treachery worthy of the gallows'. He then went to Francesco Vendramin, an ill-calculated move as His Excellency was the last person on earth to receive the anger of a social inferior sympathetically. And so, finding no satisfaction there, poor Gandini, on his way out, hurled his watch through the glass panes of a door. Finally, having obtained a contract at the court of Dresden, which seemed to have an inordinate appetite for Venetian actors, he simply walked out with his wife, leaving the field open for Caterina Bresciani who went on to star in the sequels *Ircana in Julia* and *Ircana in Isaphan.*

Apart from the charms of Bresciani and the whiff of scandal, it was probably above all the Venetians' insatiable lust for novelty which was responsible for the apparently incredible success of these plays. But this same lust was a dangerous animal to ride as Goldoni was to be balefully aware before too long. For the moment the aptest footnote to the trilogy is provided by the *Mémoires* which dedicate three entire chapters to it whereas *La Locandiera* for example gets a bare two pages. No better example could be given of Goldoni's incapacity to judge his own work.

The Persian trilogy was spaced out over two years during which, of course, other plays were written including another English one *Il Filosofo Inglese* (*The English Philosopher*), inspired by Venetian lady fans of Addison's *Spectator* and producing another spate of what Goldoni presumably thought were English names like Milord Wambert and Jacobbe Monduil. Also over these two years the Goldoni–Chiari hostilities were continued, though Chiari, unable to grasp the initiative, limped petulantly behind Goldoni, producing *The Chinese Slave* for Medebac in an attempt to counter *La Sposa Persiana,* and a Venetian philosopher who he hoped would pull the carpet from under the English one's feet.

Shortly after this, in 1755, Goldoni wrote *Le Massere* (*The Maidservants,* though not the sort that he found so irresistible, but rather the boisterous battleships of Venetian domesticity) and with this play at last he began to regain the equilibrium he had so disastrously lost with the move to San Luca. It is one of those studies of aspects of Venetian life – in this case the servant problem – in which he excelled. There is a difference which is hard to define between this play and the best of those he wrote for Medebac; observed closely it proves to be an increase in size, an amplification in volume to fit the new theatre. *Le Massere* – together with *Donne de Casa Soa* written in the same year – are the first really Goldonian plays to be written for San Luca. The Oriental trilogy had served its purpose.

All Goldoni's Venetian plays are in dialect which explains why their author has never been fully appreciated outside Italy, or even, it could be argued, outside Venice. Anybody who has only glimpsed Goldoni through the non-dialect *Locandiera,* masterpiece though it is, could not perceive where his real power lies; to do so one must see – or at least read – plays like *I Rusteghi, Sior Todero Brontolon* and *Le Baruffe Chiozzotte* which are all but untranslatable and certainly never have been even approximately adequately translated.* Goldoni himself was well aware of this problem and refers to it as early as the preface to *La Putta Onorata* where he says that, with 'the flavour of the sentiments' being lost in a little understood tongue, he feared that the play itself would become 'insipid or perhaps downright unpleasant'. And now in the preface to *Le Massere* there appears a project which he was to propose to himself

---

* As for seeing as opposed to reading, Goldoni – like all playwrights, but possibly to a greater degree than most – needs staging and reveals only a small part of his magic to the reader. This explains why so many academics and men of letters have been patronizing, if not downright hostile, towards Goldoni; they were all viewing from their study chairs, and it took a critic like Goethe, who could actually be bothered to go to the theatre, to appreciate Goldoni. I had a most vivid personal experience of this when I first went to the tiny open-air

every so often throughout the rest of his life. 'I am now preparing a dictionary,' he says, 'with explanations of the terms, phrases and proverbs of our language for use with my plays . . .' Alas, he never finished it, for it would have been as spirited and diverting a piece of lexicography as Dr Johnson's dictionary.

At about this time brother Gian Paolo erupted again, having given no signs of life for more than a decade. He announced his presence in a letter from Rome, to the overwhelming joy of their mother who was close on eighty and within a few months of her death. In the intervening years, he said, he had married a lawyer's widow who had presented him with a boy named Antonio, now four years old, and a little girl now five called Petronilla. His wife had now died and so – with a naturalness that showed he had lost nothing of his inborn cool – he proposed handing the children over to his brother and sister-in-law. Goldoni had his share of human frailty, but his behaviour on this occasion was little short of saint-like. He immediately invited his brother to come and stay with them in Venice, and arranged for money to be paid to him in Rome for the fare; though perhaps he is overloading it a trifle in the *Mémoires* when he describes how he finally embraced 'that brother I had always loved'. But whatever he may have felt about Gian Paolo, he and Nicoletta adopted little Antonio and Petronilla and brought them up as though they were their own children.

Shortly after this – though whether as a result of it there is no telling – Goldoni had another nervous crisis and, in order to distract himself, he set off with Nicoletta, Gian Paolo and the children to follow the players who were now on tour. When they were in Milan, there occurred an event which was scarcely calculated to tranquillize him. The company had acquired a new and apparently excellent Brighella, in place of Gandini. This actor was named Giuseppe Angeleri and came from a Milanese legal family and had himself practised law before going on the stage. Angeleri was a fellow hypochondriac, and he and Goldoni had had long chats together in Venice about their health. On the present occasion, Angeleri had been abstaining from acting for some while for unspecified medical reasons, but at the same time had been chafing for the limelight. Finally, giving rein to his passion, he decided to perform. '. . . He acted,' says Goldoni, 'was applauded, went off into the wings and dropped dead on the spot.' The news spread through the theatre like a hushed but rustling wind and finally reached the box where Goldoni was sitting. 'Oh Heaven! Angeleri dead! My companion in melancholy! I rushed out of my box like one

---

Goldoni festival at Roverè near Verona. For some reason this glorious little festival is not – or was not then – widely known, and the audience consisted largely of children and people from the mountain villages around, many of whom may probably have only had a sketchy idea of who Goldoni was. And yet I have rarely, if ever, seen theatre so much enjoyed. The two plays that year were *I Rusteghi* and *La Buona Madre*.

possessed, went I know not whither and found myself in my own house without having perceived anything of the way I had taken.' He fell genuinely ill as a result of this and was only fully cured when the doctor gave him a disquieting little sermon which would probably only alarm most patients the more. ' "Consider your complaint", said he, "as a child who attacks you with a naked sword in his hand. If you stay on guard, he will not wound you, but if you offer your breast to him, then even this child will be enough to kill you." ' Apparently this somewhat alarming consideration served to keep Goldoni in more or less robust health for close on another forty years.

After this disconcerting episode he returned to the treadmill and produced one of his more resounding failures, *Il Vecchio Bizzarro* (*The Eccentric Old Gentleman*). The play, he said, crashed in the cruellest and most humiliating manner and the final curtain, which they scarcely reached at all, fell amid whistles and cat-calls. The author, to avoid physical violence he assures us, donned his mask and mixed with the milling crowd in the *ridotto* where, he says, everybody was talking about him. 'Goldoni is finished,' was the burden, 'Goldoni has emptied the sack'; and they even suggested – not entirely without truth – that everything he had written hitherto had been copied from other sources, and he had now run out of material to plagiarize. Such a situation in a Goldoni script – and his life story was his script *par excellence* – could only be a prelude to triumph, and so it was. He rushed off home and wrote a play called *Il Festino* (*The Party*) which was memorized and rehearsed by the company act by act as he threw them off, and staged – all five acts in verse – in a fortnight flat. The somewhat Shavian device employed, on which he had fallen back in other emergencies, was to make the characters discuss *Il Vecchio Bizzarro,* repeat the unkind comments he had overheard in the *ridotto* and triumphantly confute them. This gambit of mocking the mockers succeeded, not so much because of any inherent merit in the play, but because it represented the sort of harmless, much-ado-about-nothing controversy which was meat and drink to the Venetians of the eighteenth century.

When this season ended he set off for Bologna and was arrested for smuggling – of all things – chocolate, but of course the customs man turned out to be a fan and the whole thing ended amicably. A little later he stayed at the estate near Padua of another aristocratic admirer and dabbled in some more amateur theatricals, getting a little huffy when the ladies, having persuaded him to play the part of a lover, giggled at the results.

Then back to Venice and another machine-gun burst of plays before setting off – in the spring of 1756 – for Parma (at that time considered the Athens of Italy) at the invitation of the Spanish Infante, Don Philip, who wanted him to write libretti for a comic opera company he maintained at court. There was also a French theatrical company there, and this gave Goldoni his first opportunity to watch French actors at work. He says he was enchanted by their acting and full of admiration at the silence which reigned during the performance, as well he might be after the clamorous uproar of Italian theatres. It was also the first time he had seen a mouth-to-mouth kiss on the stage – such licentiousness being forbidden to Italian actors – and he was so enthusiastic that he cheered out loud which momentarily upset the aristocratic audience.

The three libretti didn't cost him much fatigue as they were patched together from existing material, and they brought him a handsome down payment plus an annual pension and the title of poet laureate to the court.

The stay in Parma awoke memories of the battle he had watched there more than twenty years before and so, for the San Luca company back in Venice, he wrote *La Guerra* (*The War*) which, with its scenes of camp life, is the nearest Goldoni ever comes to Brecht. Also in Parma he had made friends with yet another fellow-hypochondriac, and the chats they had about their health inspired him to write a play on the subject called *Il Medico Olandese* (*The Dutch Doctor*), which goes to show once more that Goldoni could and did make plays out of anything.

Just before his return from Parma yet another Goldoni scandal was sweeping Venetian society and preparing the scene for the great controversy that was soon to break over his head. He had become the lover of the then celebrated dialect poetess, Cornelia Barbaro Gritti whose Arcadian name was Aurisbe Tarsense and whose boudoir was hung with other literary scalps including that of Metastasio. At the time when Goldoni was calling there, however, there was another visitor, Carlo Innocenzo Frugoni, poet and erstwhile monk who had been released from his vows by the pope. Goldoni never took kindly to these *ménages a trois,* and on this occasion his exasperation came to a head while he was in Parma. He wrote Cornelia a letter denouncing the whole situation and thoughtfully sending copies to various friends. This was just the sort of thing the Venetians liked best, and it was enthusiastically taken up on all sides, with Frugoni himself jousting in Cornelia's defence and calling Goldoni a 'clown and doggerel-merchant'. All sorts of rumours must have been blowing through the salons, for Goldoni alleges that on his return many people confidently believed him to be dead and a monk even went so far as to say he had attended the funeral.

Finding, for better or worse, that he was alive, his critics sent up the cry – which far from abating with time was to swell in volume – that he couldn't write decent Italian. Even when he was writing the *Mémoires* thirty years later, poor Goldoni was still a little baffled by these accusations. 'I was taught, and I cultivated by reading, the language of good Italian authors, but first impressions [he is referring to Venetian dialect] make themselves felt in spite of all one's efforts to thwart them. I made a journey to Tuscany where I stayed for four years to make myself familiar with the language, and I had the first edition of my works printed in Florence under the very eyes and censorship of the learned men of that city, so that they might be purged of linguistic defects. But all my precautions were insufficient, and still they would reprove me for the original sin of Venetian-ism.'*

During his life and after it, Goldoni's critics have always been particularly acrimonious about his use of Italian. Even Indro Montanelli, (significantly a Florentine) cannot resist the temptation to take a punch at it. The *Mémoires*, he says, were written in French 'because he didn't trust his Italian (and how right he was).' But the critics – and Goldoni himself – miss the point which is that his Italian didn't matter a rap, and that his supreme asset – some might say his only one – was the original sin of Venetian-ism. *I Rusteghi* is not (or are not if one is to respect Italian niceties) *I Promessi Sposi.*

Goldoni tried to face these criticisms in the only way he knew how – with a play; vaguely remembering that Torquato Tasso had also been reproved for incorrect Italian, he thought to silence his critics by waving that poet under their noses in a play called *Tasso.* His opponents were not noticeably put out by this evidence that the immortals, too, could fall short of the purest Tuscan, but he tells us that the play was a success which, on his own admission, is more than it deserved.

At this point of his life one sometimes has the impression of plays flashing past like telegraph poles outside the window of a railway carriage, and some of them scarcely more memorable. Goldoni himself must have felt this, for he says in the *Mémoires,* 'Are you perhaps beginning, my dear reader, to grow weary of this immense collection of play synopses? To tell the truth I feel tired and bored myself . . . ' But however tired or bored he may have been, the relentless bombardment of synopses does not flag for an instant. Elsewhere he says that by now playwriting had become such second nature to him that, having conceived the idea and the characters, 'the rest was no more than an easy game.' The results of this 'easy game' were unpredictable; often they were flat, but sometimes they were vintage Goldoni, and in fact 1756 saw the first performance of *Il Campiello* (a *campiello* is a small square in Venice) in which Goldoni is at his glowing best. 'This *campiello,*' he says, 'which is the only set in the play, is surrounded by little houses lived in by the lower orders. Here they play, here they dance, here they quarrel.' That is just about all it is, but it is perfect.

A few months after this Goldoni received an invitation to go to Rome. It came from a young count who owned the Tordinona theatre there. Business was feeble and the count, having heard of Goldoni's magical powers of pulling in the public, must have thought that if anyone was capable of attracting audiences to the Tordinona it must be he.

* The four years he is referring to are those he spent practising law in Pisa. Tuscany and its capital, Florence, are traditionally held to be the source of pure Italian. Alessandro Manzoni went to Florence *'a lavare i panni in Arno',* 'to wash his clothes in the Arno', before setting about the massive task of shaping modern Italian in *I Promessi Sposi.*

Vendramin's consent was obtained, and Carlo and Nicoletta set off, stopping on the way at Loreto of which Goldoni gives an unforgettable account. It seemed, he says, 'a non-stop market of rosaries, medals and holy pictures, and it appears that everybody who passes through is obliged to buy some of this pious merchandise for their acquaintances.' Making his purchase along with everybody else, Goldoni asked the stall-holder how business was. ' "Alas, sir," said he, "there was a happy time when, thanks to the grace of the Blessed Virgin, those of my calling made rapid fortunes. But for many years now the mother of God, irritated by our sins, has turned her back on us. Sales are going down day by day, we can barely live, and if it wasn't for the Venetians, we should have to shut up shop altogether." ' After this touching speech, the man wrapped up Goldoni's purchase and handed it to him, naming a price which Goldoni paid without discussion. 'The good man then crossed himself with the money I had given him, and I went away much edified.' But shortly afterwards he learnt from a native of Loreto that the stallholder, seeing that his customer was a Venetian, had charged him exactly a third more than the standard rate. 'As it was late and I was eager to leave, I did not have time to go back to my pious friend and show him that he was a rogue.'

As soon as he arrived in Rome, Goldoni realized that he was in trouble. He was invited to dinner with the count to meet the Tordinona players who turned out to be Neapolitan knockabouts, neither suited for nor well-disposed towards the fancy new ways of the Goldonian reform; and, to complete Goldoni's desolation, the women's parts – including those of the maidservants – were played by men, such being the law in the papal states.

This unhappy situation did not, however, put Goldoni off his sightseeing, a pursuit he followed avidly throughout his life. He sought for and obtained an audience of the reigning pope, Clement XIII, who was a member of the Venetian family of Rezzonico and received him in private for three-quarters of an hour, chatting about things Venetian. Finally he tinkled a little bell on the table beside him which was the sign that the audience was at an end. 'Rising to go, I made my reverences and expressed my thanks, but the Holy Father didn't seem to be satisfied. He shifted his arms and legs about, coughed, shot glances at me, but said nothing. Oh, what a booby I was! All taken up by the honour I was receiving and ecstatic with joy, I had forgotten to kiss the foot of the successor of Saint Peter. Finally I came to myself and, having prostrated myself at the holy foot, Clement XIII overwhelmed me with blessings, and I left mortified at my stupidity and edified at his indulgence.'

One of the most lasting benefits of the Roman visit – although Goldoni didn't realize it at the time – derived from the character of his host, a certain Pietro Poloni, four rooms of whose house in Via Condotti the Goldonis occupied. Poloni seems to have been rendered gently insane by the presence of such a celebrity in his house. He insisted on cooking all Goldoni's food himself, and every day would prepare him a new exotic dish, warning anyone else who happened to be at table – including his own wife and very beautiful daughter – that 'that was the dish for master lawyer Goldoni prepared for him by his servant Poloni, and no-one was to touch it without the express permission of master lawyer.' Indeed everything in the house was orientated towards master lawyer, and Poloni was extremely upset if his guest were to dine out. 'One day when he came back home and heard that I would not be eating with him that morning he flew into a fury and shouted at my wife. Nobody, he said, shall eat of the dish that I have prepared for master lawyer. Then going into the kitchen he looked compassionately upon the delicacies he had prepared with so much joy and care, but rage swept over him once more and he threw the stew-pot into the courtyard.' Another scene occurred at carnival. A procession was due to pass along Via Condotti, and Poloni had reserved the principal balcony of the house for Goldoni, placing on it a card which said, 'Balcony reserved for master lawyer Goldoni.' Unfortunately, his native extravagance had further prompted him to invite sixty people for the occasion, and a group of these, to the fury of Poloni, successfully invaded and occupied the balcony. A year later Goldoni casually immortalized his host in the character of Fabrizio in *Gl'Innamorati* (*The Lovers*). Fabrizio is one of the funniest and most vivid characters in the whole range of Goldoni's plays. His vice is that he will insist on transmuting base metals into the most shining gold, whether the base metals like it or not. Thus his pictures – poor copies paid for as if they were originals, as his niece points out – are '. . . treasures, stupendous masterpieces such as the king of France himself does not possess'. Of his daughter he says, to her embarrassment and irritation, that 'she dances in such a way that prima ballerinas have been struck dumb with amazement. She sings so perfectly that the hearers die of ecstasy. And as for conversation, there has never been her equal since the world began.' And when he speaks of food, one seems to hear – indeed one probably is hearing – the very words of Poloni. 'Show me that capon. Look. Since the very beginning of the world has there ever been a capon like it? Show me that veal. What do you say to that? Isn't it a picture? Isn't it something rich and rare? Ah, nobody else in Milan is allowed to have the veal that I get. This veal, Master Ridolfo, is butter – it's balm!'

But in spite of assiduous sight-seeing and the goings-on in Via Condotti, Goldoni did some work for the Tordinona theatre. He had knocked up for the actors a piece called *La Vedova Spiritosa* (*The Witty Widow*), and this now went into rehearsal with a carpenter's apprentice and a barber's boy in the leading female roles. 'Oh heavens, what hamming! What clumsy gestures! And not a spark of intelligence. I made some general observations about their poor declamation, and the Pulcinella of the company who was always their spokesman replied, "Everybody has their way of doing things, sir, and this is ours."' Goldoni took about the only course of action open to him: he cut the play by a third 'to reduce the torment of listening to them'.

Predictably the first night was a disaster. As the Tordinona audience was traditionally made up of coal-heavers and sailors, the only thing that prevented actual bloodshed was that, word having got about that the new play was a bit highfalutin with no Pulcinella in the cast, most of the regulars stayed away and there were only about a hundred people in the house. 'The curtain rose, the characters appeared and acted as they had done at rehearsals. The audience began to lose patience and call for Pulcinella, and the play went from bad to worse.' Unable to bear it any longer, Goldoni fled to the opera where Nicoletta – who had presumably been warned off the Tordinona by Carlo – had gone with their host's daughter. It may have been some small comfort to Goldoni that the opera was also a resounding flop. 'The theatres of Rome are terrible indeed!' comments Goldoni, '. . . No guards, no police. Whistles, howls, laughter and insults can be heard on all sides . . . What would have become of me if I had stayed at the Tordinona until the end of my play? The very thought makes me tremble.' *The Witty Widow* was immediately whisked off the boards, no doubt a little trembly at the knees, and her place was taken by the old *Commedia dell'Arte* farces and musical intermezzi which doubtless pacified the coal-heavers and sailors.

Not all the Roman audiences, however, had such low tastes; at the Capranica theatre they had been enjoying the awful *Pamela* for some years, and so Goldoni, once again leaping agilely on to his own band-waggon, knocked together for them a *Pamela Maritata* (*Pamela Married*) who deservedly fell flat upon her virtuous face.

Goldoni left Rome in the summer of 1758. As he and Nicoletta drove out of the eternal city he may have felt, in spite of his normal breezy optimism, a slight premonitory twinge of unease. Certainly the future looked none too cheerful. Relations with Vendramin – never cordial at the best of times – had become more than strained, partly because the plays which Goldoni had left behind him in a sort of literary deep-freeze to keep the Venetians going while he was in Rome had all done badly, and partly because Vendramin was understandably vexed at Goldoni's repeated demands for money. But whether or not he had a sense of foreboding, Goldoni dawdled on the journey back to Venice, stopping at several cities on the way. 'I was beginning to take leave of my Italy,' he said, 'without yet knowing that I was to abandon it for ever.'

Four years, in fact, were left to him in Italy and during the course of them he was to meet his most powerful and dangerous enemy, Carlo Gozzi.

XII

'There he is, boys, squat and fat! Chase him, trip him, nip him in the bum!'

Carlo Gozzi's exhortation to his fellow testicular academicians

During the four years between his return from Rome and his final departure for Paris, Goldoni produced an almost uninterrupted series of masterpieces, an achievement nobody appeared to notice – least of all himself. Indeed, so careless was he of these plays that, in the *Mémoires,* he mistakes the dates of many of them, ante-dating *I Rusteghi,* arguably the greatest of them all, by three years. Not that one expects or even particularly cares about accuracy in the *Mémoires* (one would be sadly disappointed if one did), but one is surprised that he can have been so careless about such an intense concentration of genius in such a short period of time, a literary triumph which is infinitely greater than the superficially dazzling feat of·producing sixteen new plays in a year.

Goldoni may be considered to have lived on two completely different levels during these last four years of his life in Italy. On the one – in that secret part of the subconscious where the artist creates – everything was at last in complete harmony. But on the other, that level immediately visibie to historians and even gossip-writers, everything was at odds. They were years of ceaseless and soul-destroying conflict.

He was back in Venice by October 1758 as one of his letters demonstrates, and the reunion between him and the Vendramins must have been embarrassing for relations were now so bad that one is surprised they were kept up at all for another four years. Goldoni's demands for money were the principal, though by no means the only bone of contention. He had taken under his protection the young man who copied his plays for him, Giovanni Simoni (that same young man who was later to be known as Goldoncino because of the author's patronage) and he wanted a place for him in the company. The Vendramins, or rather the one who spoke on their behalf, refused. Goldoni offered to resign over the issue, but the offer was icily rejected.

Then there was the sad affair of Goldoni's project for a series of nine mythological plays, collectively titled *Mount Parnassus,* with each play dedicated to one of the nine muses. He had been cherishing this idea for some while and, during his absence from Venice, it had been the subject of a protracted correspondence with the Vendramins who at first wouldn't hear of it because it was too expensive. In the face of Goldoni's insistence they gave way, though reluctantly, and as it turned out they were all too right, for *Mount Parnassus* toppled and fell.

A happier prospect was yet another publication of the plays, this time in the definitive Pasquali edition. Goldoni first announced this publication to eighteen fellow guests at a penitential dinner party on Ash Wednesday with the tables groaning under 'everything that the Adriatic sea and Lake Garda could provide in the way of fish'. Goldoni made his announcement when the company was flushed with wines and liqueurs and, mellowed by the abundance of food and drink, they agreed to take ten complete editions each which, given the number of volumes ultimately involved, was handsome. Thus, says Carlo, 'with a single casting of my net I caught 180 subscriptions'.

Another fortunate event was the success of the first play he wrote on his return, *Le Morbinose (The Merry Ladies),* a Venetian frolic which, in a sense, sets the key for the great dialect comedies that follow it.

But the happy moments were scarce, and Goldoni's days were increasingly filled with bitterness. The great battle which was to come now, reaching unprecedented heights of violence and scurrility, was preceded by the interminable quarrel which had started nearly ten years before in 1749 when Chiari had written *The School for Widows* as a parody of Goldoni's triumphant *The Artful Widow.* This quarrel had been going on ever since, reaching its own particular climax when Goldoni moved from Sant' Angelo to San Luca and Medebac hired Chiari. Venice was divided into Goldonians and Chiarites, this being the sort of dispute the Venetians loved most dearly, and the elegant battle – every bit as deadly as a battle of flowers – was waged enthusiastically in streets and *caffès* and drawing-rooms. Giuseppe Baretti, who was later to flail into the conflict with almost lunatic savagery, wrote that 'None of Goldoni's and Chiari's productions can really stand the test of criticism. They were both born without wit, and educated without learning. Yet an epidemical frenzy in their favour seized the Venetians, both high and low, and quickly spread itself from Venice to almost all parts of Italy.'

But however juicy the Goldoni — Chiari quarrel may have been, it could not be squeezed for ever; already it had lasted for close on a decade which was very good going, but the Venetian public would soon have been clamouring for more novelty if a newcomer had not appeared on the scene in the nick of time and re-awakened the flagging interest to a pitch it had never reached before, by belabouring indiscriminately both Chiari and Goldoni and forcing them into a rather unconvincing alliance which, even at a distance of over two centuries, is scarcely edifying. Chiari called Goldoni 'Most worthy playwright, bard, poet, friend' and Goldoni replied with a little verse which went:

> Yea, thou art the eagle,
> I the ant,
> Thou with all ease soarest to the heights,
> While my poor Muse
> Cannot reach the door-hinges.

The man who brought about these most improbable changes of heart was Count Carlo Gozzi, whose characteristic comment on the reconciliation was 'Chiari lowered himself to embrace Goldoni, and Goldoni lowered himself to accept the embrace.' So before embarking on an account of this new and infinitely bloodier battle which was eventually to drive Goldoni from Venice, it would be as well to examine the lives and characters of Carlo Gozzi, of his henchman, Giuseppe Baretti, and of Carlo's brother, Gasparo, who also played a part in the drama.

By no particularly odd coincidence both Gozzi and Goldoni bore the same Christian name, but that is about all the two men had in common except for the fact that they both wrote their memoirs in old age, and these two works together make up a unique portrait of the Italian theatre in the eighteenth century. But in every other sense the two autobiographies could hardly be more different. Goldoni's is simple in style and immediately establishes a friendly relationship with the reader; Gozzi's is an intricate and contorted soliloquy. Goldoni – either for his own peace of mind or out of innate good-will – avoids mentioning his quarrels whenever possible; Gozzi uses his memoirs for the almost exclusive purpose of venting his spleen on the world at large. Goldoni, while certainly enjoying the composition of his *Mémoires,* also and frankly expected them to make money, like everything else he wrote. But Gozzi titled his autobiography *Useless Memoirs* partly because, as a patrician, he would not take money for it any more than he would for his other literary works.

The difference in character of the two men is evident from their very opening words. 'I was born in Venice,' says Goldoni, 'in the year 1707, in a fine, large house between the Nomboli bridge and the bridge of the Honest Woman, at the corner of the street of the Hundred Years' Old House, in the parish of St Thomas.' In the admirable journalistic tradition he gets his who, what, where and when into his opening sentence, and, surprisingly enough, they are even accurate. He goes on to say how his mother bore him without pain and loved him the more for it, and his naturally equable and cheerful nature was immediately shown by the fact that he did not cry on his first entrance into the world. Gozzi's beginning is very different. 'My name', he says, 'is Carlo, and I was my mother's sixth confinement, born into what I don't know whether I should describe as the light or the shadow of this world.' And while Carlo Goldoni says he was born under the influence of a star of comedy, Carlo Gozzi writes, 'An evil star has always persecuted our family.' Gozzi, whose mother was a Tiepolo, was of the Venetian nobility while the Goldoni family was recognizably bourgeois. As boys, both Carlos displayed precocious talents, though in somewhat different ways. Carlo Goldoni wrote a play which apparently caused various people to foretell a great future for him. Carlo Gozzi wrote a sonnet to console a lady who was mourning for the death of her dog. 'Do you remember,' he asks in the poem, 'how he sometimes pissed in the bedroom or the kitchen and how you would gladly have killed him?'

Goldoni may not have been a model son, but he was always devoted to his family, sometimes – as in the case of Gian Paolo – above and beyond the call of duty. Gozzi, who admittedly had little reason to love his nearest and dearest, describes his family tree as 'Legitimate, covered with spiders' webs and dust, and not without woodworm', while he remembers his paralyzed father as an 'arrogant spendthrift' and his mother as 'irresponsible'. He found refuge from his family first in playing the guitar, and then in literature which he 'shaped into a weapon to defend his principles'. But neither activity could isolate him sufficiently from the wailing and bickering of his home life and so, at the age of twenty, he ran away to be a soldier.

At the outset of his travels he saw some prisoners condemned to row in the galleys, and his description of the scene is striking. 'There were perhaps 300 wretched creatures, loaded with chains and condemned to live in misery and torment sufficient in themselves to cause death. A merciful epidemic of malignant fever rescued several every day from the water, the biscuits, the starvation, the irons, the whiplashes: and accompanied as they were by the thundering voice of a Franciscan friar, sun-scorched and always jolly, their souls, I believe, flew straight to Paradise.' The friar is unforgettable.

After three years of wandering he returned home to find his family ruined and, having extricated himself from them with some difficulty, he went on to devote the rest of his lonely life – he was known as the Bear and the Solitary One – to literature and quarrelling. One of the first things he did was to join, as a founder member, in 1747, a literary club known as the *Accademia dei Granelleschi*, or Testicular Academy, with the ostensible aim of defending the purity of the Italian language. Its meetings were held in the bookshop of a certain Paolo Colombani in the Merceria, and its coat of arms showed an owl clutching a pair of balls in its right claw. The chairman was a semi-imbecile priest named Giuseppe Secchellari who had the formal title of *Arcigranellone*, or Arch-big-ball. 'An idiot', says Gozzi, 'who filled pages with atrocious rubbish which you couldn't hear without braying with laughter.' This poor fool, Gozzi suggests with a sneer in his pen, was elected chairman 'to denote literary humility' which if one has ever come across a congregation of writers grouped together, is not such a silly idea as it may seem on the face of it. Then, says Gozzi, 'there followed the solemn coronation of that rare imbecile with a garland of plums . . . and the best of the comic scene was to see him so proud of the honour, thanking academicians for about twenty compositions which were ironic burlesques on him and which he took for elogies and paeons of praise.' He was provided with an enormous throne which 'this prince with the stature of a dwarf had to jump three times to get on to.' In the heat of summer when the academicians sipped iced drinks, Secchellari was served boiling hot tea, and in winter he had iced water while everybody else had coffee. This somewhat nasty club was the headquarters for the attacks which were to be launched on Goldoni, so it is hardly surprising that the attacks themselves were almost unparallelled for viciousness.

Gozzi was an aristocrat, a cynic and a hypochondriac who loved to hurt but seemed invulnerable to those hurts which life might inflict on him. Or almost invulnerable. Life took its revenge on Gozzi when he was already over fifty and totally unprepared for it. The cause was a woman, and it is not hard to tell from his memoirs how successfully she succeeded in piercing his defences. The battle with Goldoni was over by then and the playwright was in Paris, never to return, but Gozzi was still working with the Antonio Sacchi company which had been the theatrical regiment he had used to hurl against Goldoni. One day Sacchi asked him to audition an actress named Teodora Ricci who had come to the theatre accompanied by her husband.

'I saw this young woman with a very fine figure,' said Gozzi, 'although somewhat altered by pregnancy. Her face, though pitted with smallpox, was always somewhat theatrical in its expression. But her lovely hair made up for this defect. Although her clothes told of poverty, she wore them with such cunning art that one did not think whether they were of wool or silk, new or threadbare. She seemed somewhat ill at ease in the new company, but I could not bring myself to judge whether her manner was the result of timidity or cunning. I thought I could also detect a feeling of impatience. She feared that her husband would do her little honour in that company. As for him, he continued to sleep soundly in spite of the glances she threw at him.'

It is a most curious stroke of fate that all the players of that period, except the most outstandingly famous, owe such immortality as they have to that same husband who so embarrassingly slept through the audition in his broken shoes and muddy socks, and woke to spit blood. His name was Francesco Bartoli. He dreamed vainly of being a philosopher; he had failed, first as a bookseller then as an actor, and as a husband his only virtue was complaisance. But by piecing together experience, knowledge and gossip he produced his *Comici Italiani* which is the only contemporary record in existence of the lives of the Italian players of the age – including that of his wife which is a masterpiece of marital dissimulation and diplomacy. Poor Francesco Bartoli – who pathetically told Gozzi 'My silence and my scolding are one and the same thing for my wife' – died of consumption in 1806.

Gozzi probably fell in love with Teodora at that first audition, and she continued to torment him in one way or another for the rest of his life. She was, he said, 'impetuous and fervid and as ambitious as Lucifer.' Faced with opposition or failure, she 'trembled, wept, took to her bed with the fever of a lion and cursed the moment she had ever agreed to enter Sacchi's company or come to Venice.' Furthermore, she felt nothing but 'disgust and boredom' for all studies, and despite Gozzi's efforts to improve her, sitting at her dressing table for whole days at a time, 'six years of trying were not worth a piece of straw compared with the principles in which she was soaked.'

Gozzi was an aristocrat and proud of it, and he was now in the clutches of a slut who had been thrown on to the streets in her early teens and combined prostitution with acting ever since. It was an old, old story, but then so are all the most pitiful human dilemmas, and Gozzi can have received little consolation from the fact that he was not the first to be in such a ridiculous and painful position. Money was the only way he could reach what served Teodora for a heart, and so he poured it upon her, at the same time persuading Sacchi to pay her a vastly inflated salary – and Sacchi, of course, took his own recompense for this in Teodora's bed. But the actor-manager and the author were merely sources of gain for her and, as for her husband, he was as inept in bed as he was everywhere else. So for her pleasure, Teodora went to a handsome young junior diplomat named Pietro Gratarol, and this – perhaps because the rival was of his own class – Gozzi would not tolerate. The affair quickly blew up into one of those endless, rowdy and, in the end, quite pointless rows that the Venetians so much enjoyed. Gozzi left Teodora and Teodora used every wile at her command to get him back. (One is strongly reminded of the Passalacqua—Goldoni scandal.) She even sent her wretched husband as an ambassador, but he failed in that as in everything else. The next twist of the story would only have been possible in eighteenth-century Venice. Sacchi staged a script of Gozzi's called *Le droghe d'amore* (*The love drugs*) which, in villainous and cynical consort, he and Teodora made appear like a literary revenge. In other words, by tricking up one particular performance, they convinced the public – never slow to believe these things – that Gozzi had been abandoned by Teodora (instead of the contrary) and was now taking his revenge with a vicious theatrical parody of Gratarol. In fact, of course, the parody lay entirely in production and performance, not in the script which had been written before the affair had blown up, though nobody bothered about details like that. So everybody, including the young diplomat himself, believed that Gozzi was publicly insulting Gratarol. The noisy bickering went on interminably, and interminably it is recounted by Gozzi in his memoirs. In fact he must have had some inkling himself towards the end that the abuse had become merely monotonous, for his closing words are simply 'Good-bye my long-suffering, benevolent readers!' But the very fact that he could go on about it at such length, so long after the quarrel had ended, showed that he was still obsessed with Teodora. She died, mad, in 1824 at the hospital of San Servilio in Venice. Carlo Gozzi, embittered and querulous, had preceded her to the tomb eighteen years before on 4th April 1806. It is doubtful whether his passing would have been particularly cheered if he had had known that Schiller was to judge him 'a very great man, and worthy to be imitated'.

Strangely enough Carlo's brother, Gasparo Gozzi, was one of Goldoni's warmest defenders, and it was to Gasparo that Carlo entrusted the revision of the Pasquali edition of his plays when he went to Paris. Gasparo was no less odd a person than his brother, though he lacked Carlo's incisiveness. Like him, he was a hypochondriac and, although he had a morbid terror of doctors, he was never comfortable without one about. He was incorrigibly lazy, and rarely rose from his bed before mid-afternoon. His great moment came in 1760 when, already close on fifty, he was offered the editorship of a newspaper called the *Gazzetta Veneta*. The task gave free rein to his one real talent which was for gossip-writing. His editorship only lasted for a year, but it was a year at the height of his brother's attack on Goldoni and, although Gasparo was a member of the Testicular Academy, he nevertheless defended Goldoni in the *Gazetta*. Such was the curious ebb and flow of the age that he was succeeded in the editorship by none other than the Abbé Chiari.

His ending is characteristic of his strange, largely ineffectual life. At the age of sixty-three he tried to commit suicide in rather a half-hearted way by throwing himself out of a window in a villa at Padua where he was staying. But his fall was broken by the branches of a nearby tree. He was nursed over his injuries by the French governess of his hostess and later, on the death of his own wife – whom he had already abandoned – he married the governess, who reared chickens and lovingly tended poor Gasparo until his death nine years later.

Giuseppe Baretti, who seconded Gozzi's attack on Goldoni as well as most ably mounting his own, was an even more clamorous and eccentric character than Carlo Gozzi himself. 'Sir,' said Dr Johnson, who was a close friend of his together with Mrs Thrale, Garrick and Sir Joshua Reynolds, 'I know no man who carries his head higher in conversation than Baretti. There are strong powers in his mind. He has not, indeed, many hooks; but with what hooks he has, he grapples very forcibly.'

This huge, roaring quarrelsome man with his shaggy mass of red hair was far too much larger than life-size, too outrageously direct, above all too real for the dainty powdered and prattling world of Venice where corruption and decay were so lovingly disguised with silks and perfumes. He came, indeed, from Turin where the air has always been colder and more penetrating than in Venice, a brawling literary barbarian who could lay about him with words and not only words, but – God help us all! – with his fists.

Detail from 'The kitchen' (style of Pietro Longhi). Maidservants like this played an active part in Goldoni's life and works.

'Rustic scene' (Pietro Longhi). They might be playing *piquet* or *faro* – both very popular at the time – or *tresette,* a game Goldoni learned from his mother.

'The quack dentist' (Pietro Longhi). A Goldonian scene in the streets of Venice.

'The seller of essences' (Pietro Longhi). With dominos like these there is no distinguishing a marchioness from a maidservant – unless, perhaps, you look at the feet.

Like Gozzi, he had an unhappy childhood. His mother died when he was six, and his father immediately set up house with a girl introduced into the family by the cicisbeo. Giuseppe, as soon as he was old enough to realize what was going on, challenged the cicisbeo to a duel and was chased out of the house as a result. After a brief stay with an uncle he moved to Venice and struck up a friendship with the Gozzi brothers, eventually joining them in the Testicular Academy where the air of violent malice must have suited him and where he was able to vent for the first time his great, life-long hatred of Goldoni.

In 1751 he went to London for the first time, and found what was in many ways his spiritual home. There was a viciousness in the streets which must have been exhilarating after the sweetness of Venice. A girl to whom he taught Italian introduced him into Dr Johnson's literary set, and once ensconced there he set about compiling an Italian—English, English—Italian dictionary, the second ever to be published, but the first of any quality, even though it is marked by Baretti's characteristic defect of carelessness.

He also wrote one of the first English grammars for Italian students. The work is too rigidly scholastic for our tastes, but it is exhaustive and could profitably be followed by an Italian student today, though the English he would acquire might sometimes be a little quaint. Like all good teachers he knew where the obstacles lay. 'Many of our women', he writes, 'would take me for a wizard if I told them that to take, to shake, to forsake, to wake, to awake, to stand, to break, to bear, to shear become in the preterite took, shook, forsook, woke, awoke, stood, broke, bore, shore.' But he also knew how the obstacles could be overcome. 'Master reader, I say and repeat if you want to learn English, study and then study and then go on studying and then you will learn, as many have before you, all these extravagant variations of preterites.'

His useful phrases are sometimes revealing. Starting modestly enough with 'The fleet is come in. I go to court. I come from court. Did you see the king? Have you seen the queen?' he moves on to examples of more general use like, 'I cannot bear cheese. My head akes. He is a sad dog. She is a fine girl. I have drank too much. I am but sixteen years.' And then, particularly revealing and useful, 'Let us drink this bottle out.' Finally, having dealt with the merely practical, he concludes with a fine spate of phrases in the true Baretti vein: 'He is as great a rogue as any in London. I never saw such hypocrisy as there is in that old dog. He ought to be kicked out of every company. Get you gone, you booby.'

He also regales his students with dialogues of such charm that one can only reflect that development in the field of linguistic text-books has not been all forward. One of these dialogues is between two young ladies.

1st Lady: Your most humble servant, Miss.
2nd Lady: I'm yours; I hope, Miss, you're well.

1st Lady:	I'm very well thank God; but what's the matter with you? You seem you wasn't well.
2nd Lady:	I'm very well; but I'm very much afflicted.
1st Lady:	Why so?
2nd Lady:	Because my mamma isn't well.
1st Lady:	What ails 'er? Or what is the matter with 'er?
2nd Lady:	She has a violent pain in her head.

Two gentlemen at table in another dialogue give the impression that they may shortly become co-sufferers with the second young lady's mother. 'Butler,' calls one, 'bring us a bottle of Madera, and ask the housekeeper if she has nothing cold for starving huntsmen.' Then, waiting presumably for the housekeeper to stir herself, he continues, 'Let's drink King George's health', and his guest replies, 'I'll pledge you with pleasure.' The housekeeper apparently comes up trumps, and the host is able to say, 'Choose, that cheese, those fruits, and sweetmeats you like best.' But for all his magnanimity he appears to have the weaker stomach and head of the two, for his next remark is, 'I've eat too much. I can drink no more.' But he gives way to the insistence of his foreign friend and concludes, 'I'll do it to have the honour of drinking to the Grand Duke's health, as you so kindly drank to my lawful sovereign King George!'

But Baretti was not content with teaching English to the Italians. In search of bigger game he went to the prime minister, Pitt the elder, and offered him an alliance against the Austrians in the name of the house of Savoy. Pitt made enquiries of the British ambassador in Turin, and the information he received about Baretti was so damaging that it took all the graces of his literary friends to save him from prison.

After further travels in Spain and Portugal, he returned to Venice and founded his famous review *La Frusta Letteraria* (*The Literary Scourge*), the aims of which were abundantly clear from the title. It is somewhat reminiscent of a scene from a western in which one solitary cowboy dashes about the barricades from propped-up corpse to propped-up corpse, firing at the Indians from each and thus giving the impression that the barricades are manned by a small army; for although Baretti declared that he had a variety of collaborators, he in fact wrote the whole thing himself under a variety of pseudonyms. But he certainly struck at the enemy, and indeed at anybody else who happened to be within range, and those whom he struck at rose against him, hissing and indignant. *La Frusta* ran in all for twenty-five fortnightly numbers from 1st October 1763 to 15th January 1765 and was finally closed down by the Venetian state on the instances of a huffy monk. Baretti retreated to Ancona and brought out eight more numbers almost exclusively dedicated to venemous attacks on that same monk.

In 1766 Baretti was back again in London, and once again in bad trouble. One night in Conduit Street he was solicited by a whore, he struck her, she called three lurking pimps to her aid and as a result of the struggle that followed, one of them – a Welshman named Evan Morgan – died of knife-wounds inflicted by Baretti. The following morning he appeared before Sir John Fielding and was committed for trial at the Old Bailey for murder. Once again the whole of literary London rallied to his defence. 'Never', said Boswell, 'did such a constellation of genius enlighten the awful senate house.' And the evidence tended to show that Baretti had acted in self-defence, including the fact that the knife with which he inflicted the wounds was a fruit knife, 'an instrument which foreigners generally carry about with them.' He was acquitted, and Sir Joshua Reynolds got him a job dealing with foreign correspondence at the Royal Academy. At the same time Dr Johnson persuaded Mrs Thrale to employ him as tutor to her children. This post brought him the last huge scandal of his life. Mrs Thrale had a daughter to whom Baretti was devoted. This child got appendicitis and her mother, instead of relying upon conventional medical aid, insisted on giving her own treatment. The girl died as a result and Baretti – characteristically un-hair-splitting – branded Mrs Thrale a murderess which understandably strained the bonds of affection that bound them. The next series of events, however, snapped these bonds altogether. Mr Thrale died and Mrs Thrale immediately ran off with an Italian tenor named Piozzi. This aroused all Dr Johnson's xenophobia and he promptly broke off relations with all Italians, including his friend Baretti who, for once, was in no way to blame. Mrs Thrale then wrote a volume of memoirs fiercely attacking Baretti. Baretti, of course, replied with even greater violence, and the quarrel mounted in volume until half Europe had its ears cocked to it. Somebody even wrote a play about it.

In 1789 Baretti died alone and in misery. The Royal Academy had decided to give him a small pension, but too late, for the first £50 only arrived in time to pay his funeral expenses. His executor destroyed all his papers for fear that some new scandal might be smouldering amongst them.

Thus died the man who made the famous observation *'Inglese italianato, diavolo incarnato'* – 'an Italianized Englishman is the devil incarnate'. The Welsh pimp in Conduit street would probably have put it the other way round.

Why, apart from the fact that they were both natural haters, did Baretti and Carlo Gozzi feel such violent antipathy towards Goldoni? It is rather as though two eminent Edwardian art critics were to have carried on an uninterrupted and virulent campaign against Beatrix Potter. Baretti's case is the simpler of the two; like so many eminent critics since he was quite simply blind to the good in Goldoni while the bad was anathema to him. '. . . His language is the most nauseous medley of words and phrases, taken from several of the Italian dialects, and Tuscanized in the most ridiculous manner, besides being seasoned with abundance of Gallicisms. His sentences are constantly so trite and so vulgar, whether he makes a duchess or a footman speak, that those of one may full as well fit the other. Goldoni knows no art, no science. His blunders in law and ethics, in physic and anatomy, in geography and natural history (for the fellow talks of everything) are numerous beyond conception.' Allowing for Baretti's habitually wild exaggeration, there are two grains of truth in this: Goldoni's Italian was not classical (it wouldn't have been Goldoni if it had been) and Goldoni – like Baretti himself – was never over-scrupulous about accuracy. To criticise him for these things, however, is like criticizing a bird in flight because it is illiterate. But in the last resort, perhaps the overriding cause of Baretti's dislike, and the very motive power which gave the man his demonic force, was that he was totally lacking in humour.

So, of course, was Gozzi, but his motives were altogether more complex, and in some cases he was probably not even consciously aware of them. Certainly, in so far as he was capable of it, he loved the *Commedia dell'Arte* and was most violently indignant that a vulgar little plebian like Goldoni should, as he believed, be wantonly destroying it. All his affection and indignation come through when he writes, 'Improvised comedy known as the *Commedia dell'Arte,* has always most faithfully served the Italian players. It has been going for three hundred years. It has been attacked in every age, but it has never perished. It seems unbelievable that one or two men who pass for authors in our times do not realize that they are making themselves ridiculous by lowering their dignity to a facetious rage against a Brighella, a Pantaloon, a Doctor, a Tartaglia, a Truffaldino. This rage, which seems to be the effect of too much wine, demonstrates beyond all doubt that *Commedia dell'Arte* still survives in Italy, and in full possession of all all its powers, in spite of the persecutions which are infinitely more ridiculous than anything in the *Commedia dell'Arte* itself. This truth, redoubling the blind fury of these writers, makes them fall into a wild delirium which renders them the more ridiculous.'

But elsewhere he wrote, 'He [Goldoni] has often made true Noblemen the mirror of all that is iniquitous and absurd, and he has made the common people a model of all the virtues.' Here lies the true motive for Gozzi's fury: Goldoni's world was a democracy in which gondoliers might be good while marquises were bad, and this, for Gozzi, the aristrocrat, was the ultimate and unforgivable heresy. For him the only true form of theatrical expression was the *Commedia dell'Arte* where, between the nobility and the people, a great gulf was fixed, and the lower orders could never be anything except villains or buffoons or both.

Gozzi's formal declaration of war on Goldoni may be considered his publication of a mock almanac entitled *The Tartana of Influences for the Leap Year of 1756.* This almanac, Gozzi does not fail to point out, is written 'in strictly literary Tuscan, in a style inextricably bound to that of the ancient Tuscan masters', and it purports to catalogue the various disasters threatening Venice that year, all of which directly or indirectly concern Goldoni and Chiari who are represented as two charlatans battling with wooden swords to attract the groundlings. Goldoni is given the name of Original and Chiari that of

Pillager. The satire of this almanac is very leaden-footed, but in snatches it gives a vivid idea of the fervour aroused by the Goldoni—Chiari quarrel.

> In number every day supporters grew,
> 'Original!' they cried here, 'Pillager!' there;
> The whole country fell into an uproar
> Which was very far from a joke.
> Brother fought against brother,
> Between husbands and wives it was worse.
> Everywhere the combat was bitter,
> Chaos reigned, dissension everywhere . . .
> Thus, keeping the people in an uproar,
> Those two charlatans made a handsome profit.

Goldoni unwisely replied with an equally mediocre piece of verse in which he describes the Tartana as 'rancid and insipid' and ended by saying that he who couldn't support his allegations was as ineffective as a dog barking at the moon. This predictably enraged Gozzi the more, and the battle was on. The very air of Venice became dense with the pamphlets and lampoons, in verse and prose, which now started to fly. Gozzi seemed almost insane with fury and frequently descended – as Goldoni never did – to personal insults and obscenities. 'There he is, boys, squat and fat!' he hysterically incited his fellow testicular academicians, 'Chase him, trip him, nip him in the bum!'

Gozzi's next major offensive which, of course, immediately went the rounds of Venice, was entitled *The Comic Theatre at the Pilgrim's Inn, in the Hands of the Testicular Academicians.* The action takes place during carnival at a then-existing inn of that name in St Mark's square, where the academicians are making merry. Their merriment is interrupted by the entrance of a hideous, lumbering monster with four faces and four mouths, but only one tiny brain. Needless to say, this monster symbolizes the Goldonian theatre. The first mouth opens to imitate the masks of the *Commedia dell'Arte*, but 'with little grace and a great deal of dishonesty'. Then as soon as the public begins to get bored with this, the second mouth opens to give vent to the comedy of character, and grotesquely unnatural characters are represented speaking flaccid prose. There is more applause and more yawning, and the third mouth opens for romantic comedy in verse which in turn gives way to the fourth mouth uttering plebian comedy. At this point the camera of Gozzi's satire zooms in for a close-up of a fifth mouth in the monster's belly, and this mouth addresses the academicians saying, 'Champions and defenders of the truth, of your charity forgive the strange and manifold things said and done by the four mouths in my head . . . You should know that they were all said and done exclusively for love of me, the belly.'

In spite of all this, however, Gozzi, unlike Baretti, did have some faint inkling of Goldoni's true quality, though at the time of the battle he was very careful to harp exclusively on what he called 'Goldonian bestiality'. Only in the *Useless Memoirs,* when Goldoni had already been dead for four years and the quarrel had been finished for over thirty, did he hint that Goldoni (though never Chiari) might have been less than objectionably mediocre. Having said that 'Only our Testicular Academy stood against this Goldonian and Chiarist epidemic' and gone on in his best polemical style to refer to 'Those two wearers-out of pens . . . those showers of ink . . . the lowest, most awkward and clumsy writers in our idiom' – only after these by now habitual insults does he cautiously admit that Goldoni 'was born with the capacity to write excellent plays' and that he (Gozzi) had been 'indeed a martyrdom for that good man'.

But the stream of Baretti's hatred ran undiluted. In the *Frusta Letteraria* he accused Goldoni of 'aping the philosopher and the moralist without having studied either morals or philosophy' and went on to say, 'He deserves the French title of *empoisonneur public* rather than that of reformer of corrupt drama and customs awarded him by the ignorant mob which rarely knows what it is talking about.' Elsewhere in the *Frusta* you can still feel the hot blast of exasperation as Baretti cries out that he cannot understand how the wretched plays could please 'all the nobility and all the people, the entire male sex and the entire female'.

To what extent Goldoni was wounded by the hail of poisoned arrows that were shot against him in these years it is impossible to say, for he gave no sign of pain or even discomposure, and his comment on Baretti is, under the circumstances, almost sublime. 'Whether I am good, bad or indifferent,' he wrote in a letter, 'Baretti can neither give nor take anything away from me.' And indeed from a box-office point of view this was entirely true, for the public continued to crowd out the San Luca theatre.

Then at the very height of the battle help and comfort came from a source that was as eminent as it was unexpected. The great patriarch of European literature, Voltaire, expressed himself openly and warmly in Goldoni's favour.

> En tout pays on se pique, [he wrote,]
> De molester les talens;
> De Goldoni les critiques
> Combattent ses partisans.
> On ne savait à quel titre
> On doit juger ses écrits;
> Dans ce procès on a pris
> La Nature pour arbitre.
> Aux critiques, aux rivaux
> La Nature a dit, sans feinte:
> Tout auteur a ses défauts,
> Mais ce Goldoni m'a peinte.

And Gasparo, Carlo Gozzi's brother, went so far as to print this seal of semi-divine approval in his *Gazzetta Veneta*, leaving one speculating as to what may have passed between the two brothers as a result.

Furthermore Voltaire wrote a letter to Goldoni in very bad Italian, but quite unmistakable terms. 'My dear sir, painter and child of nature,' he wrote, 'I have loved you ever since I first read you. In your works I saw your soul. I said to myself: here is a good and honest man who has purified the Italian stage, who creates with fantasy and writes with sense. Oh, what fecundity!, my dear sir, what purity! You have rescued your country from the hands of Harlequin. I should like to entitle your collected plays 'Italy Freed from the Goths'. Your friendship honours, delights me . . . I wish you, my dear sir, the longest possible life since you cannot be immortal as is your name . . .'

Goldoni would have been less than human if he had not allowed this to go the rounds, and one can only imagine the fury it must have aroused in the enemy camp. But Baretti was not to be put off. 'This heterogeneous Italian wit, who, as I said, has rendered himself the idol of the Venetian *canaille;* this same Goldoni is one of the greatest men of the age with Monsieur de Voltaire.' Elsewhere he went so far as to suggest that the letter was a forgery and then, just in case it wasn't, added that 'Voltaire had no right to judge things written in Italian.'

The next and most famous phase of the battle came about, like so many other momentous events, by sheer chance. One day Gozzi and Goldoni met accidentally in a bookshop. It has been suggested that the bookshop was the one in the Merceria run by Paolo Colombani, but as this was the headquarters of the Testicular Academy, it seems unlikely that Goldoni should have deliberately stuck his nose into a hornets' nest. Baretti is hardly an impartial observer, but his account of the momentous meeting is by far the most vivid that exists, and it has the smack of truth about it. Gozzi's account is comparatively dull, and Goldoni makes no mention of it. 'It happened one day,' wrote Baretti, 'that Carlo Gozzi met with Goldoni in a bookseller's shop. They exchanged sharp words; and in the heat of the altercation Goldoni told his merciless critic, that it was an easy task to find fault with a play; but desired him to observe, that to write a play was a very difficult one. Gozzi replied, that to find fault with a play was really easy: but that it was still easier to write such plays as would please so thoughtless a nation as the Venetians; adding with a tone of contempt, that he had a good mind to make all Venice run to see *The Tale of Three Oranges* formed into a comedy. Goldoni, with some of his partisans, then in the shop, challenged Gozzi to do it if he could; and the critic, thus piqued, engaged to produce such a comedy within a few days.'

'Who could ever have thought,' Baretti continues somewhat extravagantly, 'that to this trifling and casual dispute Italy should owe the greatest dramatic writer that it ever had!' He refers, of course, to Gozzi.

In fact, although the meeting in the bookshop certainly took place, the creation of *The Tale of Three Oranges* cannot have been quite as spontaneous as all that. It is obvious from his *Useless Memoirs* that Gozzi planned a deliberate campaign against Goldoni, and chose the Sacchi players for the purpose, rather as a warring king might select an army of mercenaries; his very terminology is military, and he refers to Sacchi as 'the Colonel'. 'To *attack* the above mentioned poets [Chiari and Goldoni] and to divert the public, I chose for my team the Sacchi company . . . I had chosen that family of actors for recreation in my hours of idleness . . . and before long I had studied the ways and the characters of *my soldiers* so well that their parts seemed entirely natural to them and consequently they pleased doubly.'

Although Sacchi himself was notorious for his lechery and Gozzi probably had more than one mistress from the company, including Sacchi's niece, Chiaretta, his description of the prevailing moral climate would put any convent to shame. Life, if we are to believe him, was made up of union, harmony, domestic duties, study, subordination and discipline. The women were all forbidden to receive visits and, abhorring presents from seducers, divided their time between work, prayer and works of mercy. 'If any actor or actress deviated from the path of strict morality, they were instantly dismissed.' And while actresses in other companies spent their time wheedling money out of their lovers, in this company they were 'foreign to venality'. As for Gozzi, he reigned over these paragons like a benign monarch, standing godfather to their children, creating characters that would suit them, writing their letters for them, teaching them French and 'educating them generally'. And they, in their turn, wrote him 'loving' letters while on tour. Most of this is so wildly improbable that one wonders whether even Gozzi could have expected his readers to believe a word of it.

But he also says, 'The comics I protected considered me their guiding genius. They exclaimed with delight when they saw me. They told all the world that I was the lucky star of their revival. They protested they owed me an unpayable debt and eternal gratitude.' And, leaving aside what they probably said about him behind his back, there is some truth in this, for the Sacchi players undoubtedly did owe Gozzi an enormous debt.

They had returned from Portugal as a result of the great earthquake of 1755 to find the theatrical scene in Venice entirely dominated by the Goldoni—Chiari quarrel. The public tumbled over itself to see the plays at the San Luca and the Sant' Angelo theatres, but it was indifferent to the Sacchi *Commedia dell'Arte* productions at the San Samuele. Then Gozzi put into their hands a script which enabled them to wrench away the victory in one evening. On 25th January 1761 there broke out at the San Samuele theatre what Gozzi described as 'an uproarious and mirthful revolution with such delight among the public that the two poets [Goldoni and Chiari] saw their own decadence as in a mirror'.

The Love of Three Oranges was, and indeed still is, a fairy story told to Italian children, and it comes originally from Abruzzo, though Gozzi's version is considerably embroidered. The protagonist, Prince Tartaglia, who is suffering from a mysterious illness which prevents him from laughing, represents the Venetian public, reduced to a stupor of boredom by the plays of Goldoni and Chiari who are themselves satirized in the 'evil' characters, the Fata Morgana (Chiari) and the magician Celio (Goldoni). And the masked figure of Truffaldino, who finally succeeds in making the prince laugh, was specifically Sacchi who played the part, and also a general symbol of the *Commedia dell'Arte* as a whole.

Tartaglia and Truffaldino set off together for the castle of the giantess, Creonta, in search of three magic oranges, and during their countless adventures they are always bumping into the Goldoni and Chiari figures. Finally, having obtained the three oranges, Truffaldino cuts open the first and a beautiful young girl steps out of it, only to die immediately of thirst. Truffaldino cuts open the second orange to bring her succour, only to find himself with a second lovely girl on his hands. He is about to open the third orange to save her from the fate of the first when the prince seizes it from him and carries it to the shore of a lake from which the third girl is able to restore herself as soon as she emerges from her orange. Then, having rescued her from the jaws of death and overcome all his enemies, the prince marries the girl of the third orange.

It was a nonsensical piece of work and Gozzi's fellow Testicular Academicians begged him not to let it be staged for the sake of his reputation. But they were wrong, and *The Love of Three Oranges* was by no means the first or the last example in the history of entertainment of a load of trash sweeping the public off its feet.

There were various reasons for this enormous success. First, and probably foremost, there was the overriding Venetian love of novelty, the same love which had made the public flock to the bizarre *Persian Bride* trilogy. Indeed, Goldoni had successfully ridden that beast, novelty, on many occasions; now it turned and rent him. *The Love of Three Oranges* seemed excitingly new (although it was only something very old rehashed); it was brash and gaudy and colourful, having a great deal in common with the English pantomime, and whereas Goldoni's work attempted to mirror the real world, Gozzi's created an unreal, flashing, almost psychedelic world into which the public could escape, and where *'tout arrive et où se pose l'Oiseau bleu.'*

Then of course there was the scandal. The fable contained an almost uninterrupted flow of verbal darts winged from Gozzi's poisoned blowpipe at Goldoni and Chiari, and the Venetians always enjoyed a strong flavour of personal unpleasantness in their entertainments. Or, as Baretti puts it, 'It may easily be imagined, that Goldoni and Chiari were not spared in the *Tre Aranci*. Gozzi found means to introduce in it a good many of their theatrical absurdities, and exposed them to public derision. The Venetians, like all other Italians, do not greatly care for the labour of searching after truth, and their imaginations run too often away with them, while their judgement lies dormant. But point out sense to them, and they will instantly seize it. This was remarkably the case on the first night that the comedy of *The Three Oranges* was acted. The fickle Venetians forgot instantly the loud acclamations with which they had received the greatest part of Goldoni and Chiari's plays, laughed obstreperously at them both, and applauded the *The Three Oranges* in a most frantic manner.'

The piece, too, was brilliantly played with masterly performances by Sacchi (one of the greatest actors of the age) as Truffaldino, and Cesare D'Arbes as Pantaloon. It is ironical that these were the two men whose careers were so notably forwarded sixteen years earlier when Goldoni, at their most urgent requests, wrote a play for each of them during the period when he was practising law in Pisa.

Encouraged by this success, and no doubt most ardently solicited by Sacchi and his players, Gozzi went on to write nine more fables – including *Turandot* – which were received by the Venetians with slightly diminishing rapture as they went along, in spite of the almost deafening drum-beating that Baretti did for his fellow Testicular Academician whom he not only considered the greatest dramatist Italy had ever seen, but even paragoned with Shakespeare, claiming to see some resemblance between the fables and the romantic comedies like *The Tempest*.

Such was the success of the fables, says Baretti, 'that in about two seasons Goldoni was utterly stripped of his theatrical honours . . . ' This was untrue, but at the time it must have seemed to be so, to Goldoni himself, to his friends and enemies, to the actors and the Vendramins. What is so extraordinary, however, is that this was the richest creative period of his life. In 1759 he wrote *Gl'Innamorati* (*The Lovers*) and in 1760 *I Rusteghi* (*The Cantankerous Men*) – to name only the plays which are peaks in the Goldonian range. In 1761, the year of *The Love of Three Oranges,* there were five major Goldoni premières – those of *La Buona Madre* (*The Good Mother*), *La Casa Nova* (*The New House*) and the holiday trilogy consisting of *Le Smanie per la Villeggiatura* (*The Craze for the Holidays*), *Le Avventure della Villeggiatura* (*The Adventures of the Holidays*) and *Il Ritorno dalla Villeggiatura* (*The Return from the Holidays*). And in the year after what appeared to be his total downfall he wrote three more masterpieces, *Sior Todero Brontolon* (*Master Todero the Grumbler*), *Le Baruffe Chiozzotte* (*The Chioggia Squabbles*) and his farewell to Venice, *Una delle Ultime Sere di Carnevale* (*One of the Last Evenings of Carnival*). In the same year of 1762 Gozzi countered these plays with two fables, *Il Re Cervo* (*The Deer King*) and *Turandot,* and the Venetians preferred them.

I Rusteghi (*The Cantankerous Men*) is quintessentially Goldonian, a marvel of dramatic harmony and the most vivid portrait that even he, the master portraitist, ever painted of the respectable merchant class of Venice. It is also a social document (just the sort of faintly pompous description that Goldoni would have relished, in his old age at any rate) for it illustrates the clash between the old conservative, puritanical tradition of the Venetian middle classes and the new frivolity which was the downfall of the Republic.

The play is dominated by four merchants of Venice who have more than a little in common with Shylock, and indeed their domestic behaviour can be most aptly summed up in the Jew's instructions to his daughter.

> What, are there masques? Hear you me, Jessica:
> Lock up my doors, and when you hear the drum
> And the vile squeaking of the wry-neck'd fife,
> Clamber not you up to the casements then,
> Nor thrust your head into the public street
> To gaze on Christian fools with varnish'd faces;
> But stop my house's ears, I mean my casements,
> Let not the sound of shallow foppery enter
> My sober house . . .
> Do as I bid you, shut doors after you:
> Fast bind, fast find,
> A proverb never stale in thrifty mind.

If one cut the adjective 'Christian' and substituted Lucietta for Jessica, the passage could be transposed bodily into *I Rusteghi.*

As always in the best Goldoni, the plot has scarcely more substance than a soap-bubble. Lunardo – one of the *rusteghi* of the title, and the most cantankerous of them all – wants to marry his daughter to the son of a fellow merchant, and not only will he not hear of the couple meeting before the wedding, he also refuses to tell the girl or her step-mother who the young man is. But the wife of another merchant smuggles him into Lunardo's house dressed as a woman. The couple fall in love at, literally, a glance (for that is all they are allowed), but the device is almost instantly discovered and the resulting uproar could not be more frightful if they had been caught in bed together. When the first pandemonium has died down, Lunardo sits in company with the boy's father and another merchant, morosely contemplating the tragedy as if all the corruption and decay of eighteenth-century Venice were stretching out before their eyes. But they have to give way in the end, indirectly to the course of history, and directly to the wiles of that same woman who smuggled the boy, Felippetto, into Lunardo's house. 'You see?' she tells them, 'This cantankerousness, this bearishness of yours, it's been the fault of all the trouble that's blown up today; and it makes you – all three of you, huh? I'm talking to all three of you – it makes you furious and odious and miserable and public laughing-stocks! Can't you be just a little civilized, friendly, human? Look at your wives – and then if you find them honest and faithful, then for heaven's sake give them a little freedom, bear with them a bit . . . And as for clothes, if a woman doesn't run after every fashion that's going, if she doesn't ruin the whole household, then there's no harm in her being neat and tidy – a woman ought to be well dressed. What it boils down to is this – if you want to live in peace, if you want to be on good terms with your wives, then behave like men, not wild beasts. Command, but don't tyrannize. And love if you want to be loved.' The *rusteghi* agree, though reluctantly one imagines.

The least important character in the play, who could be dispensed with altogether from the point of view of pure plot, is a certain Count Riccardo, a 'foreigner' from Milan, who aids and abets the smuggling of Felipetto into the house. Socially he is a cut above the others; he carries with him the whiff of another and less healthy world – for the world of the *rusteghi* was robust for all its harshness. And Lunardo's last words in the play refer to this Count Riccardo. 'Tell that foreigner', he says to his wife, 'that he can stay to supper with us.' The resistance of the old order fails at last and the gates are opened to the enemy.

Of *La Buona Madre* (*The Good Mother*) Goldoni writes that it was 'neither despised nor applauded. It was coldly received and only had four performances. A well-made play that failed honourably.' It deserved better, for this story of a tough but doting mother and an apparently goody-goody son who is courting behind her back is supremely funny and could only be the work of a master of comedy.

La Casa Nova (*The New House*) is generally ranked alongside *I Rusteghi* and *Le Baruffe Chiozzotte* as one of the pinnacles of Goldoni's work, and for once Goldoni himself accurately anticipated the judgement of posterity. 'If I had written no other comedy but this,' he says, 'I believe that it would have been sufficient to win me the fame that I have acquired with so many others. Reading and re-reading it, I cannot find a fault in it, and I would be so bold as to propose it to others as a model if I could flatter myself that my works were worthy of imitation.' As a past master at the art of utilizing any material, however banal, that lay to hand, Goldoni once more took an episode from his own life at that period and wove a play out of it which also happened to turn out a masterpiece. 'I had just moved house,' he said, 'and as I always kept my eyes open everywhere for subjects for plays, so I found one here in the upheavals of a move.' At the same time, he must have delved into the past for, in the intrigues and diplomatic clashes between two families living on different floors of the same house, there is more than an echo of his own youthful adventure when he managed to conduct affairs simultaneously with the attractive Venetian spinster of the aquiline nose and her 'ugly' niece with the Harlequin mask and the mischievous black eyes who lived on the floor above. Once again the plot is thin: there is an all-but broken marriage with the husband drowning in debt and the wife indulging every caprice that the heart of a foolish woman can devise, there is a pleasant, tripping love affair carried on from one floor to the other, there is the chaos of the move itself with furniture being shifted from room to room as opinions change concerning the lay-out of the house, and finally there is a convenient rich uncle who settles all problems in time for the third-act curtain.

But Goldoni handles this material in such a way that, unless you set out to analyze it cold-bloodedly, it never occurs to you that it is less than exceptional. There are five female characters, and they are drawn with such skill that one realizes, almost to one's surprise, that Goldoni possessed – and the phrase would surely have made him chuckle – an astonishing insight into the female mind. One of these women – the wife, Cecilia – is probably the most all-round venemous bitch that Goldoni ever created, and the only flaw in *La Casa Nova* – which one must nevertheless accept for it represents a vital facet of the author's character – is that she becomes good in harmony with the general happy ending.

Switching, with the holiday trilogy, from Venetian dialect to Tuscan, Goldoni's touch becomes instantly less sure, and the habitual thinness of plot – which goes unnoticed in the Venetian plays because they transcend mere events – becomes all too evident, Goldoni having taken what is scarcely sufficient material for one play and divided it among three. In the first play the characters prepare to leave for their country villas, in the second we see them in the country, and in the third they come back. The whole thing is intended as a satire on the reigning passion for ruinously expensive country holidays during which, as one of the characters points out, the holiday-makers bleed themselves white in order to do exactly the same things as they do in the town. It is undoubtedly material for satire, but it calls for a crueller wit than Goldoni's; he never could bring himself to wound.

There were still three plays to go before he left Venice for ever, and appropriately they were all Venetian, or, strictly speaking, two were set in Venice and the third across the lagoon in Chioggia. Writing of this third play, *Le Baruffe Chiozzotte* (*The Chioggia Squabbles*), Goethe most neatly summed up both the play itself, and – in so far as it is possible – Goldoni's genius. 'Never in my whole life', he wrote in his diary, 'have I witnessed such an explosion of joy as that which was vented by the public on seeing itself portrayed so naturally. It was one long laugh of wild delight from beginning to end ... The author deserves great praise for having got such exquisite entertainment out of a trifle – something which can only be done by an artist who lives in the midst of his people, and of such a mirthful people as this. Anyway, the play was written by a master.' In fact, the characters are scarcely mirthful during the course of the play, for they do nothing but quarrel until, of course, the final curtain when the heroine, Lucietta, calls the attention of the audience to their true nature. 'I should be sorry if there was some stranger here,' she says, 'and he went away talking badly of us, and the word got about that the women of Chioggia do nothing but quarrel. Because what he's heard and seen this evening was all a mistake. We're respectable women, looked up to by one and all. But we're cheerful, and we like a good laugh, and we like to dance and jump about. And we want everybody to be able to say – long live the women of Chioggia, long live the women of Chioggia!'

To get his material, Goldoni delved back over thirty years to when he was a magistrate's clerk in the town, and in fact the *deus ex machina* of the play is a magistrate's clerk, and the scenes in which he interrogates Chioggians are obviously based on personal experience. In the first act the quarrels are aroused by the tattling of the women and the resulting jealousy of the men who are all fishermen and have just returned from the sea; but although stones are hurled and knives and pistols brandished, nobody is hurt, and one would be very surprised if they were. In the second act the quarrels are taken to law, and in the third, thanks to the good offices of the magistrate's clerk, they are settled out of court. The couples are blissfully reunited, faiths are pledged, the lights of Chioggia twinkle across the lagoon, and the sounds of music and dancing and the clinking of wine-glasses spread on the evening air.

Of *Sior Todero Brontolon* (*Master Todero the Grumbler*), Goldoni writes in the *Mémoires*, 'There was an old man in Venice, I don't know exactly when, whose name was Todero. He was the harshest, rudest, most irksome old man in the world, and he left behind such a good reputation that even today when somebody meets a grumbler in Venice, they call him "Todero the grumbler". I knew one of these old men of such a black disposition that he wouldn't give his family a minute's peace. He particularly persecuted his daughter-in-law, a delightful and most beautiful woman, who was made even more unhappy by her own husband who trembled with terror at the mere sight of his father. I wished to revenge this excellent woman, whom I often saw, by painting in the same picture the portraits of her father-in-law and husband. She, being in the secret, was more than delighted at the success of the play, because the originals recognized themselves, and she saw them returning home, one humbled and the other in a great rage.' Both the situation and the play are eminently Goldonian.

Was it pessimism about life in Venice or optimism about that in Paris which finally induced Goldoni to abandon the one for the other? There is evidence to support both theories. Certainly there was little to offer him comfort or cheer in Venice; he had been soundly trounced by Gozzi, or at least so it must have seemed; his plays were now considered out of date, and his relationship with the Vendramins, never warm, was now icy. On the other hand, the prospects in Paris, if they were not examined too closely (and Goldoni rarely gave more than the most perfunctory examination to any situation before plunging into it) might well have appeared rosy. He had no illusions about a possible return to Italy, for he writes in the *Mémoires,* 'It is true I was invited to France for only two years, but my intuition told me that once I had left my country, I should be most unlikely to return to it.' And the motive for the final decision, according to him, is matter-of-fact, if a trifle melancholy. 'My condition was precarious, I was obliged to maintain it with continual and toilsome labours, and I feared the cruel days of old age when one's powers diminish and one's needs increase.'

Certainly, for this or for a variety of reasons, the decision was finally made, and Goldoni, at the age of fifty-five, bade farewell to Venice in characteristic style – he wrote an allegorical play about his own departure called *Una delle ultime sere di carnevale* (*One of the last evenings of carnival*). It is odd that Goldoni, whose titles are so often no more than labels, should this time have chosen something so haunting and – in Italian at any rate – poetic.

In the *Mémoires* he meticulously accompanies the announcement of most of his plays with summaries and these summaries, like the little schoolboy-type essays in which he describes new towns, are often rather less than faithful portraits of the originals. But the summary of *Una delle ultime sere* conveys the spirit of the play and contains a touching little mistake which must have escaped both Goldoni and Nicoletta. 'Zamaria, a cloth-maker, gives a feast for his colleagues, and also invites Anzoletto who provided them with their designs and patterns. The gathering of cloth-makers represented the actors, and I was the designer.

'A French embroideress named Madame Gâteau [maturity had not made Goldoni any defter in his choice of foreign names] happening to be in Venice on business, meets Anzoletto, and is attracted to him and his designs. So she persuades him to go with her to Paris. This was a problem that was not difficult to solve. The cloth-makers learn with regret of Anzoletto's new engagement. They do all they can to prevent him from going; but he promises them that he will not stay away longer than for two years. With a soul full of gratitude he receives their intimations of regret, but he answers their reproofs resolutely. Anzoletto pays his respects and offers his thanks to the guests, and it is Goldoni who is bidding farewell to his public.' And indeed, so much was Goldoni taken up with the allegory that he overlooked the fact that it was to Moscow, not Paris, that Anzoletto was going.

All rancour was left aside for this last encounter, for *Una delle ultime sere* was apparently well received, and the theatre 'echoed with cheers, among which one could clearly make out shouts of *"Bon voyage!* Come back soon! Don't forget." '

With these ringing in his ears, Carlo Goldoni set off for his long, self-imposed exile.

The Last Night
of Carnival
or
The Contented
Exile

XIII

'I was at court, but I was not a courtier.'
Carlo Goldoni

Although, as events were soon to prove, Goldoni had not made the enquiries about conditions in Paris that would have been prudent, the decision to go there had been maturing for some while. He and Nicoletta finally left Venice in April 1762, but the idea had first been mooted a year before when Francesco Antonio Zanuzzi, actor-manager of the *Comédie Italienne* in Paris, had written offering him a two year contract with the company. But what Zanuzzi – a thirty-four-year old Paduan – did not make clear in his letter and what Carlo did not discover until it was too late was that the *Comédie Italienne* was on its last legs.

A company of Italian players had first been called to Paris about the middle of the sixteenth century, and the masks of the *Commedia dell'Arte* had had a warm following for well over a century. But public interest had eventually begun to wane and finally in February 1762, only two months before Goldoni set out, the company had been merged with the *Opéra Comique*, although the merger seems to have been more like a take-over. '... The new type of entertainment had the best of the old,' says Goldoni, 'and the Italians, on whom the theatre had once entirely depended, were now no more than an appendage ... The theatre was packed out on the days when the *opéra bouffe* was playing and deserted for the Italians.'

Obviously Zanuzzi hoped that Goldoni would pull his company out of the slough; and indeed the author's name was already known in Paris. *I pettegolezzi delle donne* had been played there the year before, and the *Commedia dell'Arte* scenario *Il figlio di Arlecchino perduto e ritrovato* (*Son of Harlequin, lost and refound*) in 1758 – both with success.

When he received Zanuzzi's letter, however, Goldoni was unaware that he was being called upon to undertake an almost hopeless task. Indeed, he found the idea of going to Paris extremely attractive, but first he thought that he might use the invitation as a gentle means of blackmailing the Venetian authorities into giving him a pension. But the trick didn't work. 'Where pensions are concerned,' he said, 'the useful arts always have the better over the pleasant ones'; and with this wistful reflection he set about his preparations for departure.

The Vendramins might have held him in Venice, for his contract had not yet expired, but such resistance as they put up was overcome without great difficulty and, indeed, they were probably only too glad to see the back of him. As for his other affairs in Venice, they presented no great problems. His mother had died eight years before in 1754. His niece-cum-adopted daughter, Petronilla, was put to board in a convent school while her brother, Antonio, now twelve years old, went with the Goldonis to Paris. As soon as she left the convent, Petronilla went to live with a married couple named Chiaruzzi and, on the death of the wife, she married the widower. Such money as Goldoni left behind him in Venice he had passed, with amazing generosity, to his brother Gian Paolo who, incredibly, didn't manage to spend it all before his death because Goldoni mentions in the *Mémoires* that it went on to Petronilla. The proofs of the Pasquali edition of his plays were entrusted to Gasparo Gozzi, the brother of Carlo.

Goldoni still enjoyed his travels as much as ever, and he took a leisurely four months to go from Venice to Paris. He stopped first in Bologna for two months where he fell ill with rheumatic fever and stayed at the home of his old friend, the Marquis Albergati. They bled him by candle-light for the fever, and he had the satisfaction of seeing his own blood 'as black as blackberries . . . strong and robust, gushing up like a fountain'. He also wrote a comic opera, 'but the opera felt the fever as did its author'. However, he comments, 'fortunately the only thing to be buried in Bologna was my work'.

From Bologna they went to Parma, where they stayed for a month, and then on to Genoa for a last farewell to Nicoletta's family. 'We spent eight days of great happiness in my wife's native town, but when the time came to leave the tears and lamentations never seemed to finish. Our separation was the more painful because our relatives despaired of ever seeing us again. True, I promised to return at the end of two years, but they didn't believe it. Finally in an orgy of farewells, embraces, tears and lamentations we embarked on the *felucca* for France and sailed for Antibes, hugging the coast by Genoa.'

Such regret as they surely felt was quickly dispelled by more pressing concerns for they were swept off their route by a hurricane and – if Goldoni is to be believed – nearly lost their lives. But however desperate the situation, comedy was never completely out of earshot in a Goldonian story, and it was provided on this occasion by a French Carmelite monk 'who murdered Italian as I murdered French'. 'This monk was frightened when he saw one of those mountains of water coming towards us from the distance, threatening to overwhelm us altogether, and he yelled at the top of his voice, *"La voilà! La voilà!"* I thought that the Carmelite was shouting *"La voile"*, in order that the sailors should double the sail, and so I tried to point out his mistake to him; but he maintained that what I was saying was not common sense.' This difference of opinion kept them busy – and one hopes that it kept Nicoletta occupied, too – until the danger was passed and they reached land where they disembarked and waited forty-eight hours for the storm to pass. Then they sailed, without further mishap, to Nice. A day later they set off again by carriage and forded the River Varo which divided France and Italy. 'I bade my country farewell once more,' says Goldoni, 'and invoked the shade of Molière that it might guide me in his.'

At Antibes, the customs official, in true Goldonian style, turned out to be an admirer, and waved aside the passport saying that Paris was impatiently awaiting its bearer. But Goldoni enjoyed lingering over his journeys, and the impatience of the capital was not going to put him out of his ways. They first stopped at Vidauban and the little incident which he records as taking place there is indicative of a leisurely frame of mind which the actors awaiting him in Paris might have found a trifle irritating if they had been aware of it.

'Supper was served. But there was no soup on the table; my wife needed soup, my nephew wanted it. They asked for it in vain. In France they do not serve soup in the evening. My nephew maintained that *souper* (to sup) derived from *soupe* (soup). The inn-keeper didn't understand a word and withdrew with a bow.

'Basically, however, the young man wasn't mistaken, and I enjoyed myself giving a little lecture on the etymology of *souper* and on the elimination of the *soupe.*' And more than twenty years later he enjoyed himself once more repeating the little lecture for the benefit of his readers and adding that his nephew, who had started keeping a diary of the journey, did not fail to include the 'eloquent dissertation' in it.

In Marseilles they were persecuted by bed-bugs, but took refuge with the Venetian consul and stayed for a week. In Avignon he admired the pontifical palace and noted that it was so well kept-up that 'if the pope wanted to come there, he could move in with all comfort.' In Lyons a letter was awaiting him from Zanuzzi, the manager of the *Comédie Italienne,* reproving him for his delay. Lack of seats on the diligence prevented the Goldonis from leaving Lyons immediately, but such a banal obstacle was no use to Carlo who, as usual, had to make a story of it. 'The letter . . . should have made me leave without delay. But how could I leave one of the most beautiful cities in France without having a look at it? Could I fail to visit those workshops which furnish the whole of

Europe with fabrics and designs? I took rooms at the *Parc Royal* and stayed there for ten days. Were ten days necessary, you may ask, to see the most interesting things in Lyons? No, but they were not too many to accept all those invitations to dinners and suppers that the rich cloth merchants outbid each other to shower on me.'

It was also in Lyons that he first had news of the merging of the *Comédie Italienne* with the *Opéra Comique*, but he did not immediately realize, he says, how much trouble he would run into as a result.

Finally on 26th August 1762, he reached his destination. At Villejuif he, Nicoletta and Antonio were met by Zanuzzi and the leading lady of the *Comédie Italienne*, Elena Savi, who, five years previously, had played the parts of maids with the Medebac company and therefore almost certainly knew Goldoni although she had not worked with him. Elena's husband, Bartolomeo, had also worked with Medebac, playing Harlequin, and now in Paris, having aged somewhat, he had graduated to the Doctor. Elena died in Paris only three years after Goldoni's arrival there, but her husband, after a spell at manufacturing fireworks, returned to Italy and made a modest fortune running a puppet show.

Zanuzzi and la Savi escorted the Goldonis to Faubourg Saint-Denis where they both had apartments and where, later in the day, their arrival was celebrated by the full company with one of those uproarious and bibulous meals that the Italian players so greatly delighted in. There were at least two other familiar faces from the past to cheer Carlo, if he had need of it. One of the most talented actresses in the company was Camilla Veronese, daughter of that same Carlo Veronese of the glass eye, who had run the company of players which had so delighted Carlo more than thirty years before when he was clerk in the criminal court at Feltre. And there was also Antonio Matteuzzi, nicknamed long-neck, the one-time soldier from Vicenza who had taken over the Pantaloon parts from D'Arbes in the Medebac company. He was still playing Pantaloon when Goldoni arrived in Paris, and it was said to be only his talent which kept the tottering company going at all.

Before attempting to remake the company's crumbling fortunes, however, Goldoni was determined to see Paris, and there is no doubt that, whatever regrets he may have felt later, his immediate reaction on arrival in the French capital was an upsurge of enthusiasm and excitement. One can feel this mood both in retrospect (in the *Mémoires*) and in all its immediacy (in a letter written by Goldoni shortly after his arrival).

'Here I am in Paris at last!' says the letter, which has all the breathless exhilaration of a schoolboy recounting an adventure. 'I arrived on the 26th of last month, and I haven't written a line to anybody so far, although I had every intention of writing immediately, because in the reigning confusion the hours and the days passed without my realizing it. Now I am just beginning to get a hold of myself. The chaos is beginning to diminish, I am beginning to make out where I am, and I am in the finest situation in the world. I will not tell you of the city of Paris because you know it, I will only tell you that it surprises me more every day and that it surpasses any conception I might have formed of it.'

In the *Mémoires* the situation is, as usual, invigoratingly dramatized. 'Tired by the journey and restored by that exquisite nectar which might give to Bourgogne the title of promised land, I spent a peaceful and happy night. And the awakening was as delightful as had been the dreams of the night. I was in Paris, I was overjoyed, but as yet I had seen nothing, and I was dying of the desire to see everything. I spoke to my friend and host. "First," said he, "We must begin by paying calls. Let us wait for the carriage." "Not for all the world," said I, "In a carriage I shouldn't see anything. Let's go on foot." "But the distances are great." "It doesn't matter." "It's hot." "We shall have to put up with it." In fact that year it was as hot as it is in Italy, but I didn't mind in the least. I was fifty-three years old. [In fact, he was fifty-five.] I was strong, healthy, vigorous. Curiosity and impatience gave me wings.' There follows an outpouring of delight that would leave the most gushing American matron gasping. 'I went into the Palais Royal. What a crowd! What a gathering of people of every sort! What an enchanting assembly! What a delighful promenade! But what a stupendous spectacle struck my senses and my soul when I drew near to the Tuileries! . . . And on leaving this enchanted spot, behold there was another spectacle which held me enchained. A majestic river with wide-spreading bridges which seemed to multiply one upon another, most ample river-side walks, a great concourse of carriages, an uninterrupted crowd. I was stunned by the uproar, worn-out by the walking, exhausted by the excessive heat; I was pouring with sweat and yet I did not even realize it.'

Nor did all this make him the least reluctant to plunge into the delights of society. He and Zanuzzi went (by coach at last, it is true) to the apartment of Camilla Veronese where they were expected for dinner. 'It would be impossible to be more amiable and vivacious than was this actress. Playing the parts of maidservants in Italian comedies, she was the delight of Paris on the stage and the idol of conversations wherever one had the fortune to meet her. Dinner was served. The guests were numerous, the dinner exquisite, the company most entertaining. We took coffee at table and only rose from it to go to the play.' The *opéra bouffe* was playing that day and Goldoni found it, too, quite delightful.

Indeed, the enchantment of Paris seemed to touch everything in those early days, even the failing *Comédie Italienne*. 'The sight of this *Comédie Italienne* is most beautiful,' he wrote in a letter, 'Last night they did *L'Enfant d'Arlequin*, which is my *Birth of Harlequin's son*. The applause was great and, to tell the truth, Harlequin was excellent, and the maidservant is a skilful actress, witty, vivacious and an excellent mime.' But disenchantment was to follow very quickly.

Perhaps due to the excitement of Paris, he did not appear unduly anxious to start writing. First of all he announced that he had to study the characters of his actors, and to this end he took an apartment near the theatre in Rue Comtesse d'Artoise where one of his neighbours was a retired actress turned novelist, Marie-Jeanne Laborras de Mézières, who had married the Italian actor, Antonio Riccoboni. Goldoni describes her as 'a charming neighbour whose company was both useful and pleasant'. She knew the actors through and through, he said, and was able to give him detailed descriptions of them all. And indeed, many of them were talented; the trouble, he decided, lay in their material. 'My dear compatriots', he said, 'only played trite comedies, the sort of bad scenarios that I had reformed in Italy. "I", I said to myself, "will give them characters, sentiment, movement, behaviour and style." ' But either the actors didn't particularly want characters, sentiment, movement, behaviour and style (which would have meant changing their ways and learning their parts by heart) or Goldoni was not anxious to start work. Whatever the reasons, the great reform showed no signs of taking over the *Comédie Italienne* and its author, splendidly ignoring the fact that he had only just arrived, asked for four months' leave 'to sound the public taste'.

He started this sounding by following the court to Fontainebleau, not perhaps the most probable choice for an investigation into the tastes of the Parisian groundlings, but nonetheless enjoyable. 'I saw the royal family every day, the princes of the blood, the great ones of the kingdom, the French and foreign ministers. Everyone gathered at the castle. It was the custom to attend the king's *lever* and the royal meals. One followed the court to mass, to the hunt, to the theatre without restraint or embarrassment, without confusion.'

But if he felt no embarrassment in following the court, he may have felt at least a trace when the *Comédie Italienne* presented his own *Son of Harlequin* scenario at Fontainebleau where it received the sort of icy reception that only an aristocratic audience can give. He claims that it was the fault of the actors who mixed in gags from Molière's *Cocu imaginaire*.

Back in Paris he moved into a much bigger apartment overlooking the Palais Royal gardens and spent 4,000 francs furnishing it which, given the way things were going, was less than prudent. 'Just in front of me was the famous chestnut tree known as the Cracow tree, around which the gossips would gather, swapping news, tracing trenches, encampments, military positions in the sand and carving up Europe at their will.'

Eventually he persuaded the reluctant members of the *Comédie Italienne* to stage one of his new-fangled comedies of character and so now, when he could tear his eyes away from the lovers in the Palais gardens and the goings-on around the Cracow tree, he started to write it.

The play was *L'amore paterno* (*A father's love*), and the reluctance of the *Comédie Italienne* appeared to be all too well founded for it was a resounding flop and had to be taken off after four performances. 'I wanted to leave without delay; but how could I leave that Paris which so enchanted me?' he wrote, and it is the only hint in the *Mémoires* that he ever had any second thoughts about his decision. But notes of regret can be detected elsewhere in his writings. '*De solo*

'The happy couple' (Pietro Longhi). Many of Longhi's paintings reflected scenes from Goldoni's plays: this could be one of the girls in *The Chioggia Squabbles* – 'We're cheerful, and we want to go on being cheerful, and we want to dance, and we want to jump about.'

'The faint' (Pietro Longhi). But it might be a faint from *The Woman Sick for Subterfuge*.

'The *ridotto*' (Francesco Guardi). The open doorway on the left leads to a bar dispensing hot chocolate, tea and coffee; at another bar on the right, cheese, salame and fruit are served.

'The cicisbeo' (Giandomenico Tiepolo). The woman was accompanied by her husband and her cicisbeo who was sometimes, but by no means always, her lover. A common theme with Goldoni.

pane non vivit homo,' he wrote to his friend Albergati, 'Reputation is food and drink for a gentleman, and the want of it will make me return to Italy as soon as possible.' And a little later he wrote that if the players of the *Comédie Italienne* were tired of their author, then he was no less fed up with them. But these remarks might be no more than expressions of injured pride. Goldoni's true melancholy and the deep sense of nostalgia he felt for Venice, which he normally kept most carefully veiled, stand truly revealed in a little piece of dialect verse that he wrote during his last years in Paris.

> Da Venezia lontan do mille mia
> No passa dì che no me vegna in mente
> El dolce nome de la patria mia
> El lenguazo e i costume de la zente.

> (Two thousand miles away from Venice
> Not a day passes when I don't remember
> The sweet name of my country
> The language and the customs of the people.)

Not a thousand years of being *bien amusé* in Paris – as surely he was – could ever have expunged this sentiment in the most Venetian of hearts ever to beat.

So a little underground stream of sorrow there was, but it could never have overflowed its banks and borne him back to his homeland. The attractions of Paris, *amour propre,* the thought of the dreadful Vendramin brothers and Carlo Gozzi, above all perhaps Goldoni's own triumphant optimism – all these made him stay on and compose for the players one of the old *Commedia dell'Arte* scenarios, which was a betrayal, in theory at any rate, of his most cherished principle.

But any reluctance he may have felt over the betrayal was speedily overcome when he saw what a successful betrayal it was. At last he seemed to have struck gold again. *Les amours d'Arlequin et de Camille* was such a triumph that he was able to tell Albergati that his reputation in Paris was made. 'Tous nos acteurs sont contraint d'avouer que depuis Molière il n'y a pas eu de génie semblable,' wrote Charles Simon Favart, the librettist for the *Opéra Comique,* with perhaps just a pinch of partiality given the fact that he was the great friend of Goldoni's old age and was already an enthusiastic supporter even before Carlo arrived in Paris. True, *Les amours* was not well received at court, but then it was cut down from two hours to three-quarters of an hour to suit the royal time-table, and the court was so effectively isolated from the ordinary public that this disfavour was not even noticed, let alone taken into account. Audiences continued to flock to the *Comédie Italienne* and Goldoni, always ready to strike while the iron was hot, followed up *Les amours* with *La jalousie d'Arlequin* and *Les inquiétudes de Camille,* then going on to lump all three together as a trilogy called *Les aventures de Camille et d'Arlequin*. He cheerfully accepted the fruits of these pieces, but, as a small tribute to rectitude and theatrical reform, did not go and see them.

Instead he went to the *Comédie Française* and was rapt in admiration. ' "Ah!" I said to myself, "If only I could see one of my plays presented by such actors!" ' That satisfaction he was to have.

In the meantime he was able to enjoy his first literary squabble on French soil, though it was a mild affair compared with those that had raged in Venice. The word was going about Paris that Diderot had filched material for two of his plays from Goldoni, and the great man flew huffily into print, branding Carlo as a hack composer of farces. It was the sort of situation that could have festered indefinitely, had not Goldoni had the good sense to beard Diderot at a *soirée*, and the whole thing ended with reciprocal professions of mutual esteem.

Women could still twist Goldoni round their fingers as was clearly shown by two episodes that occurred about this period. He and a group of other men, all in late middle age and mostly writers, had formed a club which met at the homes of the various members in turn every Sunday for good food, drink and conversation. Women were barred from these parties, but when, one Sunday, the pretty singer, Madeleine-Sophie Arnould, invaded their ranks Goldoni allowed himself to be whisked off by her to the *Opéra Francais* where he opined – unfortunately in the hearing of the composer – that the entertainment was 'Paradise for the eyes and Hell for the ears.'

There is none of that minuet-like charm about the second episode which is understandably not mentioned in the *Mémoires*. A certain Catherine Lefébvre, 'known as Méry', brought a charge of sexual assault against him, but then withdrew it saying that she had been 'amply recompensed', as indeed she probably had. Nothing more is known of the affair, but there is a sinister ring about it, as though somebody had accidentally switched on the wrong lights in the theatre and one suddenly saw that the Arcadian shepherd was a fifty-seven-year-old lecher.

The scandal, such as it was, did not prevent Goldoni from moving in the best society, dining out with the Venetian ambassador, Giandomenico Tiepolo and, later, his successors, with the Dutch ambassador and the plenipotentiary from the court at Parma, Count d'Argental. And while he was thus engaged, poor Nicoletta stayed at home. 'She enjoys herself little in Paris,' he wrote to Albergati, 'because she can't understand the language and she can't make herself understood. I, on the other hand, either well or ill, speak, understand and enjoy myself.' One can recognize them both very clearly in this description.

In 1764 Goldoni's contract with the *Comédie Italienne* expired, and both he and the theatre were only too glad to see the back of each other. Apart from the brief moment of glory resulting from the Harlequin trilogy, Goldoni had not succeeded in pulling the company out of the doldrums, and all the contempt he felt for their *Commedia dell'Arte* knockabout, they felt for his comedies of character.

The *Comédie Italienne* wobbled on for another sixteen years until in 1780 Louis XVI put it out of its misery. Only the name of *Comédie Italienne* lived on in the French company which continued to present farce and comic opera at the *Hôtel de Bourgogne,* the *Comédie's* old home. Then three years later this company moved to a new theatre which, oddly enough, was named after Carlo's greatest friend in Paris, the librettist Charles Favart. The only person who can be said to have made anything like a fortune out of the *Comédie Italienne* was its director, Francesco Zanuzzi, who went back to Italy with enough money to buy a large villa in Treviso surrounded by land which he farmed in retirement.

In 1764, however, Goldoni was in a dilemma. He was glad enough to leave the *Comédie Italienne,* but what were he and Nicoletta to live on? He had opened negotiations with theatres in Lisbon and Vienna, but these had fallen through. The Venetian ambassador, Tiepolo, urged him to return home, but the thought of the Testicular Academy and the Vendramins immediately soured any sweetness this idea might have had. He was in an awkward position that might rapidly have degenerated to catastrophic if it had not been for a most improbable stroke of fortune.

Mademoiselle Sylvestre was a lady-in-waiting to the Dauphine, Marie Josephine of Saxony, mother of the future Louis XVI, and she was also a great admirer of Goldoni's and had communicated her enthusiasm to her royal mistress. So now that Mlle Sylvestre heard of Goldoni's plight she interceded with the Dauphine on his behalf. Marie Josephine would probably have taken him on as Italian master for her own children, but as they were considered too young for the study of foreign languages, Goldoni was passed on to Princess Adelaide, the eldest living daughter of Louis XV. 'Providence', wrote Goldoni in a letter, 'has shown me signs of her favour, and God has freed me from the players.' Money was not mentioned, but Goldoni must have gambled that it would have been forthcoming sooner or later; or, as he himself more discreetly put it, he reckoned that 'so honourable a post resounded of itself to my glory'. And indeed, as wily a diplomat as Andrea Gradenigo, who had succeeded Tiepolo as Venetian ambassador, must have believed that Goldoni was in a strong political position, for he introduced him to the Duke of Choiseul, one of the most powerful ministers at the court of Louis XV. But Goldoni was not shaped for politics and he never became more than a humble Italian teacher at the French court. He summed it up perfectly himself in the *Mémoires* when he wrote: 'With so honourable a post and such influential protectors, I should have made a magnificent fortune in France. It is my own fault if I only made a modest one; I was at court, but I was not a courtier.'

As was his custom, he started this new phase of his life badly, this time with a monumental *gaffe*. Arriving for his first lesson he was received at the door by the Dauphine, whose good offices had obtained him the post in the first place, and he mistook her for a chamber-maid of Princess Adelaide's. He must have behaved with more decorum than was his wont with chamber-maids, however, for the awkward moment was passed over without too much embarrassment, and lessons began. He gave five a week, lasting two or three hours each and divided into four parts – reading, grammar, translation from his own plays into French, and conversation.

Perhaps because some Italian was spoken at court, Nicoletta seems to have been a little happier there. In a letter Carlo describes finding Princess Adelaide and her lady-in-waiting, the Duchess of Narbonne, talking in Italian to Nicoletta. 'You can imagine', he says, 'how the poor woman felt and how her heart must have beaten with joy and awe!' 'Thank God,' he adds, 'there never has been and never will be a trace of pride in either of us.'

After he had been teaching for six months, Goldoni was assigned his own apartment in Versailles, but in the meantime a carriage would pick him up every morning in Paris. It was during one of these rides from the capital that he nearly went blind. He was reading Rousseau's *Lettres de la montagne* when his sight suddenly failed him, leaving only the capacity to distinguish between light and darkness. With remarkable *sang-froid* he descended at Versailles and groped his way up to the royal apartment. When he was unable to read the book, however, he was obliged to admit the truth to Princess Adelaide who showered him with devoted attention which, he says, brought back some vestige of sight. After a few days the use of the right eye was back to normal, but the left had lost all sight. The cause is thought to have been either a fallen retina or a cataract.

His reaction to this catastrophe was perhaps more characteristically Goldonian than anything else in his life. 'I am one-eyed,' he wrote. 'It is a slight inconvenience which puts me in no great embarrassment and which is scarcely noticeable. But there are circumstances in which this handicap emphasizes my defects and ridiculous qualities. For example, I am a great pest for my companions at the card-table. The light has to be put on my good side, and if there is a lady in the game who is in the same position as myself, she does not dare confess it, but she considers my pretensions absurd. At the game of *brelan* the candles are placed in the middle of the table and I cannot see. At whist and *tresette* partners are changed and I have to carry my own light with me.'

For him no melancholy or metaphysical speculation about how his light was spent; just a consideration on the disadvantages at the card table. That was eighteenth-century Europe for you. That was Goldoni.

XIV

'. . . if you will permit me, you are far too old to start writing and composing in a foreign language.'

J. – J. Rousseau to Goldoni

Goldoni had been assigned his apartment in Versailles in 1765. It had four rooms with its own kitchen and was 'very properly furnished and with excellent beds', as he said in a letter. Thus Italy's greatest playwright came to form part of a vast army of royal servants. The *Almanach de Versailles* of the period sets out to list this army, and it runs to 165 pages in small type. There were sixty musicians (including a grandson of the great Couperin who was one of the two organists) and one functionary whose duties were limited to carrying the musicians' instruments; there was a spit-mender, two wine-carriers and one clock-winder whose only job was to wind the king's watch every morning; there were even commode-carriers who were made redundant when English water-closets were installed.

In May he went to Marly with the court and was deeply impressed with everything, particularly the gambling-hall. He watched the great ones of the land playing there one evening and his description ends with a delightfully cocky personal intervention on the scene. 'It was said that Louis XV was lucky; I waited until he was the banker, put down six louis to play on my behalf in favour of the bank, and won.' Gaming was the dominant passion at court, and Goldoni noticed one lady who stayed at the same table for thirty-six hours uninterruptedly, keeping herself going on chocolate and biscuits.

Lessons, however, were not interrupted, and Goldoni said that what little French he had was acquired during his three years with the royal princesses. (Although Adelaide remained his principal pupil it seems that her three sisters also took Italian lessons from Goldoni) They read the writers of poetry and prose in Italian; I stuttered out a bad translation in French; they repeated it with grace and elegance; and the teacher learned more than he could teach.' He was not the first or last emigrant to teach his own tongue in a foreign land and realize at the same time that he was acquiring far more than he was giving.

While it lasted Goldoni revelled in the high life at court, travelling to Compiègne and Fontainebleau, observing the great occasions and mingling with the courtiers, *ce cher petit italien,* just important enough to be accepted socially, but not so important as to run the risk of being toppled by intrigue. Then on 20th December 1765, the thirty-six-year-old Dauphin, husband of Goldoni's protectress, died of tuberculosis at Fontainebleau, and the event marked the beginning of the end of the carefree period of Carlo's court life. Two days later, on his return to Versailles, he had to hand over the keys of his apartment which, on the death of her husband, ceased to be in the gift of the Dauphine. He moved into the town of Versailles.

Now things became really difficult. Lessons were suspended on the Dauphin's death, but Goldoni did not dare leave Versailles for fear they should be resumed again. He had no money and didn't know how to go about asking for some; and, as often happens at courts, it never occurred to anybody that he might be in need. This miserable situation dragged on for more than a year and was not improved when the Dauphine died, of grief it was said, in March 1767 and plunged the court into further mourning. The Goldonis lived on credit.

And then, after three years unpaid service, when he had given up all hope, the princesses remembered him. They gave him a carved gold snuff-box with a hundred louis inside and they created a paid position for him as *Instituteur d'Italien des Enfants de France.* They asked for 6,000 francs a year for him, but ministry officials objected that it was too much (the royal family was by no means omnipotent even before the revolution); finally after a great deal of red tape the officials compromised on 4,000 less tax.

It was 1,400 less than he had earned with the *Comédie Italienne.* In the *Mémoires* he professed himself contented with this, but, it should be remembered, the volumes were dedicated to Louis XVI on whose protection he was relying. 'I could not live in great state,' he said, 'but to be fair, what had I done to deserve it? I had left Italy to come to France. And if the *Comédie Italienne* didn't suit me, then I could perfectly well go back where I came from. But I had grown fond of France; three years of most seemly and delightful service now enabled me to stay there. Should I not count myself happy? Should I not be content?' And although he had had three years of work without earnings, he was now able to earn without working, for, apart from a vague promise from the princesses that they would send their nephews and nieces to him, there were for the moment no more Italian lessons at court, and he was able to enjoy a pleasant, if somewhat restricted *dolce vita* at Versailles where, he said, he was enjoying himself too much to return to Paris.

He did go back there, however, in 1769, keeping on, in spite of restricted circumstances, a *pied à terre* in Versailles because 'It was in my interests to pay court to my august patronesses and try to win supporters for the Italian language and literature among the young princes and princesses.'

In the meantime, he was sending plays back to Venice and dismally, one after the other, they all failed. Only a somewhat insipid little fable *à-la*-Gozzi, titled *The good fairy and the wicked fairy* met with anything like success, running for twenty-six nights during carnival 1767.

Goldoni's nephew-cum-adopted-son, Antonio, was the cause of some anxiety at this time for, although the boy was amiable enough, he was not very bright, and there seemed to be no chance of ever employing him. But Goldoni was far too Italian to be unaware of the magical powers of *raccomandazioni*, and a word with Princess Adelaide quickly resulted in an Italian teaching post being made vacant at the *École Royale Militaire*. Unfortunately, no sooner was Antonio installed there (and Mademoiselle Adelaide occupied with other things) than the post was made redundant and the Goldonis were back where they started. Various other posts were found for him at and around the court, each one, less stable than the last. His final recorded action was the official notification of his adopted father's death, after which he was borne away upon the swirling tide of events out of our sight, taking with him, it is believed, what was left of Goldoni's papers.

Returning, however, to the heyday of Goldoni's Parisian life, it was during this period that his name began to appear on the theatrical scene in London; not, however, as the author of *I Rusteghi*, but as a hack writer of comic opera. 'They wanted me in London,' his account of this episode begins somewhat grandiosely, but 'They' made no mention of money. Their intentions, however, must have been honest for a collaboration continued for some years and only ended when the direction of the opera house in London passed into other hands. The people for whom Goldoni worked were women, he says, 'and women are amiable all the world over'. *Vittorina,* staged in London in 1763, was set to music by Niccolò Piccinni, one of the greatest comic opera composers of the eighteenth century who, some years before, in 1760, had written the music to another Goldoni comic opera, *La Cecchina, ovvero la buona figliuola (Cecchina, or the good daughter)* which triumphed in theatres all over Europe for thirty years.

At about the same time Goldoni also wrote *Il ventaglio (The fan)*, which, in the early part of this century, was done more in Britain and the United States than any other of his plays. In 1756 – the year when Gozzi launched his attack upon Goldoni – a play of Goldoni's appeared for the first time in England. It was *Pamela*, which may have suited the taste of the age but was hardly the best way of introducing Goldoni. And since then not one of the great dialect comedies has ever been performed, and all too often British and American audiences have been fobbed off with second-rate Goldoni. Only *Il servitore di due padroni* and *La locandiera* have been performed more than once with any success in Britain. The former first appeared at the Theatre Royal, Drury Lane in 1776 under the title *The hotel, or the double valet.* Seven years later, a certain Robert Jephson re-adapted it as a farce of his own called *The hotel, or servant with two masters* and it was performed in Dublin, and then, in 1791, at Covent Garden 'with great applause' under the new title of *Two strings to your bow.* *La locandiera* had a great vogue in the 1890s and was produced several times. It was also specially translated for Ellen Terry, but unfortunately she never did it.

The preference for *Il ventaglio* in the United States and Britain may partly account for the indifference with which Goldoni is often viewed in English-speaking countries, for it is a strange play which seems in places to be almost a caricature of Goldoni. It is a *moto perpetuo* of loves and jealousies and squabbles in which, as in *The rape of the lock,* there is a quite disproportionate fuss over a trifle – in this case the possession and whereabouts of a fan. It is dexterously constructed and contains at least one character who can stand among Goldoni's most vivid – Giannina, a pretty, quarrelsome peasant girl who defies everybody for the sake of her love, including the love himself; this Giannina is in that class of aggressive yet irresistible maidservants that was always so dear to Goldoni. At first it is hard to understand why the play does not communicate that warm glow of delight which comes from so many of its predecessors. But if one can close one's ears for a minute to the endless bubble and squeak of it all, one perceives the truth: *Il ventaglio,* like its author, is rootless, and if Goldoni never explicitly bewails his exile, he does so implicitly in this play. There is even the suggestion of another and darker shadow over it, as though Goldoni were subconsciously aware of the storm that was building up about him in Paris and that was to break nearly a quarter of a century later in the French Revolution. For if the aristocracy is seen as more or less futile throughout Goldoni's work, it reaches a climax of futility in *Il ventaglio,* and the lower orders, for the first time, do not even show a nominal respect for it. There is a count who is a good character in himself although he is also a feeble caricature of Carlo Gozzi (Goldoni was never a caricaturist), always taken up with 'exquisite fables'. And there is a surly peasant called Moracchio (Giannina's brother) who, in his attitude to the nobility, is much closer to the mob that stormed the Bastille than to the Harlequin he would have been some years before. Goldoni's aristocrats are always offering their 'protection' to less well-born characters, and there was a time when that protection was a very valuable asset. But by the time of *Il ventaglio* it had been devalued to a point of total collapse. At the very end of the play, the count offers his protection to Moracchio who walks straight off muttering 'Bread, bread – not protection!' It could be one of the first, almost imperceptible rumbles of the French Revolution.

But time had not yet quite run out, and indeed in 1770 when Goldoni had been in France for eight years he was able to witness the fairy-tale magnificence of the marriage of the fourteen-year-old Marie-Antoinette to the new Dauphin. He was particularly struck by the firework display in which, he said, the art of pyrotechnics reached its greatest height. It is typical of Goldoni that he forgot to mention that it ended in tragedy when the vast crowd was suddenly seized with panic and 130 people were trampled to death in the stampede.

It was in the balmy atmosphere of Marie-Antoinette's brief spring that Goldoni's last theatrical triumph flowered. He had never been daunted by obstacles and he now set out to overcome two, either of which would have been enough to put off anybody else. First of all he decided to write the play in French and then to have it staged by the *Comédie Française* 'The word temerity is no exaggeration,' he says, 'It was truly an act of temerity for a foreigner who had arrived in France at the age of fifty-three [fifty-five], with a confused and superficial knowledge of the language, to dare at the end of nine years to write a play for the first theatre of the land.'

It is an example of the sheer force of Goldoni's self-confidence that he succeeded abundantly, and the piece stayed in the repertoire of the *Comédie Française* until 1848 – nearly eighty years. *Le bourru bienfaisant* (*The soft-hearted despot*) contains nothing new; there is the usual crusty old man dealing with problems, amorous and financial, of the younger generation. Perhaps the secret of its success is simply that it conveyed the true Goldoni flavour, albeit somewhat diluted, in French for the first time, and enabled audiences to see, not how similar, but how different their Italian guest was from Molière. For the first time they saw him as he was and, like the Venetians before them, they liked what they saw.

Later on Goldoni was to get a little touchy when people suggested that he had written *Le bourru* in Italian and then translated it into French. He both thought and wrote the play in French, he insists, although he did 'take advice' from experts. One of those to whom he went for advice was Jean-Jacques Rousseau. Having prudently written first of all for an appointment, Goldoni went to the Hôtel Plâtrière, climbed up to the fourth floor and knocked, whereupon the door was opened for him by a woman 'neither young nor old, neither pretty nor pleasant' who was, in fact, the washerwomen, Thérèse Lavasseur, whom Rousseau had recently married after having lived with her for many years. On being asked if Rousseau were at home, she replied that 'he was and he wasn't', but opted for the positive when Goldoni gave her his name. 'A moment later I went in; I saw the author of *Émile* copying music; I had been warned, and yet I shuddered in silence. He received me in an open and friendly way; he got up, holding an exercise book in his hand: "You'll see if anybody else can copy music as well as I do. A score would only come from the press as neat and elegant as it comes out of my house. Let's go and warm ourselves." ' But Goldoni could not get over the poverty of the spectacle. 'To see Rousseau working as a music-copyist and his wife as a servant was a most distressing spectacle for my eyes, and I could not hide my sorrow and dismay. I said nothing. But he, being no fool, realized that something was afoot in my spirit; he put questions to me and I was obliged to confess the reason for my silence and dismay. "What?" he exclaimed, "You pity me because I work as a copyist? You think I would do better to write books for people who cannot read, and provide articles for malicious journalists? You are wrong. I love music with a real passion, and I copy most excellent models. This gives me enough to live on, and I enjoy myself; that is enough for me." ' Goldoni makes no comment on this, but he surely never glimpsed the profound truth of Rousseau's words.

He went on to broach the subject of the play he had just written. ' "You have written a play in French?" he [Rousseau] went on with an astonished air, "What do you want to do with it?" "Put it on." "At what theatre?" "At the *Comédie Française.*" "You have just blamed me for wasting my time; it is you who wastes it without any profit." "But my comedy has been accepted." "Really? But then I am not surprised. Actors have no common sense. They accept things or turn them down as the fancy takes them. So perhaps it has been accepted. But it won't be performed. And it would be the worse for you if it were." "How can you judge a play that you do not know?" "I know the taste of the Italians and that of the French; they are altogether too dissimilar. And, if you will permit me, you are far too old to start writing and composing in a foreign language." "Your reasoning is correct, sir, but difficulties may be overcome. I have entrusted my work to people of understanding, to connoisseurs, and it seems that they are satisfied with it." "They are flattering you. They are cheating you. And you will be the victim. Show me your play – I'm French and I'm sincere, and I'll tell you the truth." '

Few other men would have borne such a trouncing without any reaction, but Goldoni was unmoved. It had been his intention and desire to show Rousseau the play, but – perhaps because of the great man's contemptuous attitude and perhaps because Goldoni feared that Rousseau might find a portrait of himself in *Le bourru* – he changed his mind, and the two men never met again.

The atmosphere can have been scarcely warmer when he read the play, before its performance, at the *salon* of Madame du Deffand, who wrote to her friend, Horace Walpole, that it was 'La pièce la plus froide, la plus plate qui ait paru de nos jours.'

Fortunately it was a different story with the actors. According to Goldoni – and nobody has contradicted him for once – the traditional secret ballot among the actors of the *Comédie Française* resulted in unanimous and enthusiastic support for the play, and it was put on for the first time on 4th November 1771 with Pierre-Louis Préville – whom Goldoni ranks with Garrick and Sacchi as one of the three great actors of the age – in the part of the old despot, Géronte.

The author watched the first night from the wings and, at the final curtain-fall, was horrified (or so he says) when they tried to drag him on-stage for an author's call, such not being the custom in Italy. 'I could not understand,' he says reasonably enough, 'how a man could tacitly say to the audience, "Here I am, ladies and gentlemen, applaud me!" '

The next day the play was repeated for the court at Fontainebleau and was also a success, Goldoni receiving 150 louis from the king. Finally – though for all too brief a period – his name in France was established. Royalties started to pour in. 'I saw myself overwhelmed with honour, with delights, with joy: I am telling the truth without hiding anything – false modesty seems as odious to me as vanity.' It must have seemed as though a second summer were upon him, with all the rich fruitfulness of the first, but without Chiari or Gozzi or the Vendramins.

He waited for five years – until 1776 when he was already in his seventieth year – to write another play. To friends he said that he was resting on the laurels which he had won with *Le bourru,* but the real reason, he admits in the *Mémoires,* is that he was afraid of failure – a fear that was only too well founded. Age had done nothing to cure him of the habit of trying to jump on to successful band-waggons, and as a 'paradoxical' title had brought him luck with *Le bourru bienfaisant,* he decided to try another one, *L'avare fastueux (The spendthrift miser).* It ran into trouble as soon as it left his desk when the *Comédie Française* somewhat coolly agreed to accept it 'subject to rewriting' – a decision which stung the author who had never rewritten a word in all his long life. But he swallowed his pride and reworked the piece which was finally billed for production at Fontainebleau where it was received in chilly silence and taken off after a single performance. In the *Mémoires* Goldoni uncharacteristically tries to edge the blame off on the actors, but the play itself was tired, with too easily recognisable echoes of Molière, and the brilliant star of Beaumarchais rising on the horizon dimmed such novelty as was left in the prospect of an Italian dramatist writing in French. 'Je compte ma pièce tombée,' wrote Goldoni in a letter, 'Je ne suis ni avare ni fastueux et je la retire tout à fait.' It was the last play of his life.

But this failure never for an instant lessened Goldoni's bubbling enthusiasm for life about him. Paris he still loved, and he spent hours walking about it, going to the theatre or – supreme delight of the sage tourist – just watching life go by. 'Endless crowds of people, an amazing amount of carriages, hawkers, throwing themselves under the wheels and the horses, with every conceivable type of merchandise; chairs on the pavements for the people who like to watch and those who like to be watched; attractive looking *cafés* with orchestras and French and Italian singers, pastry-shops, inns, restaurants, puppet-shows, acrobats, hucksters bawling out the attractions of giants, dwarves, wild beasts, sea monsters, waxworks, automatons, ventriloquists . . .' Apparently there were some people who put about the extraordinary rumour (current in some circles even today) that life was too expensive in Paris. 'False,' says Goldoni, 'nobody has less money than I have, yet I enjoy the city, I amuse myself and I am happy.'

Throughout the first fifty-five years of Goldoni's life, time was of the essence, and one often wonders how there was enough of it for him; in that first half century it flashed past, and the events followed each other as rapidly as the telegraph poles outside a train window. But during the last thirty years when he was in France, time seemed to slow down more and more, pottering aimlessly about him and bringing little of greater moment than cups of chocolate and games of cards to mark its passage.

But destiny reserved for him another bout of teaching in the royal family. Shortly after the death of Louis XV in 1774 it was announced that Marie-Clotilde – sister of the new king, Louis XVI – was to marry the Prince of Piedmont, the future Carlo Emanuele IV. The girl had no Italian and Goldoni was asked to give her what would nowadays be called a crash course in the language. He agreed, but was doubtful about the results. '. . . What could she learn in seven months?' he asked. 'I would certainly be careful to avoid traditional methods. She knew French grammar well, and I only made her learn the auxiliary verbs in Italian grammar. But I made her read a lot. The reflections and brief diversions which I interpolated into the reading were much more useful, in my opinion, than a long, boring rigmarole of rules and scholastic difficulties.' A point of view that could be taken with profit in some language teaching circles even today. The princess was a good student, 'but our conversations were often interrupted by goldsmiths, jewellers, painters, merchants. Sometimes I came into her room to witness the choice of materials, the pricing of jewels and the judging of similarities in portraits. I tried to take advantage of these very drawbacks. I made her repeat in Italian the names of the things she had seen, that had been bargained for on her behalf, that had been bought or refused.' And the result of all this, linguistically at least, was satisfactory for both master and pupil.

Less satisfactory was Marie-Clotilde's younger sister, Elisabette, to whom Goldoni was called shortly afterwards. As he himself delicately put it, she was 'more at an age for enjoying than applying herself'. He tried to sugar the pill with play-readings from his own works in which he and a lady-in-waiting would take part with the princess, and then, when these palled, he turned to Metastasio. But for somebody as vivacious as the princess, it was not so much the text-books that needed changing as the teacher. And anyway it was time for Goldoni to go. 'I was getting old; the air at Versailles was bad for me. The wind, which always prevailed and blew everywhere, made my nerves jangle, awoke all my old ailments and gave me palpitations'. He withdrew from the court, leaving the Italian lessons of the lively Elisabette – who was to die on the guillotine fourteen years later – to his nephew, Antonio. This final move from Versailles to Paris was in the spring of 1780.

Unfortunately, the royal exchequer had been no more open-handed than in the days when he had taught Princess Adelaide, and he left court without a franc more than the original and by no means munificent pension that had been awarded to him. He was forced to sell his library – including a precious volume of Corneille given him by Voltaire – to the secretary of the Venetian ambassador. This, of course, is not mentioned by Goldoni himself. Just as the early parts of the *Mémoires* are edited to transform the common-place and to reassure Nicoletta, so the latter parts are presented in order that the misery may never show through.

XV

'I almost always accept invitations to lunch, I avoid whenever possible those to dinner, and I never refuse a game of cards.'
Carlo Goldoni

When Goldoni made his final move from Versailles to Paris he was well into his seventies. Hitherto there had been little routine or regularity in his life; he had lived first at the behest of managers, public, actors and – not least of all – actresses; then he had moved on the whim of princes. But now nature, to whose voice he had always had one ear cocked, demanded a little peace, and he conceded it to her.

'I rise at nine o'clock, breakfast on a cup of chocolate, work until midday, go for a walk until two: I like society and seek it, dining often with friends, or at home with my wife . . . I do not like to work or walk after dinner. Sometimes I go to the theatre, and more often I play cards until nine in the evening, always returning home before ten where I take two or three *diablotins* [chocolate-covered sugar almonds, dotted with hundreds-and-thousands] with a glass of wine and water; that is my supper. I talk with my wife until midnight. In winter we sleep in a double bed, and in the summer in twin beds in the same room. I go to sleep very quickly and pass the night tranquilly.'

This regime was a success for, in his eightieth year when he was nearing the end of the *Mémoires,* he was able to say, 'I am well, thank God, though I must be careful to keep up my strength and health; every day I read and study with attention the *Traité de la vieillesse* by Master Robert, head of the medical faculty in Paris.' Apropos of this volume, Goldoni goes on to make a very shrewd remark. 'Our normal doctors treat us when we are ill and try to cure us, but they do not bother about our way of living when we are well. This book teaches, guides and corrects me; it tells me the degrees of vigour that still may be left to me and shows how best I may husband them.'

Like many people before and since, Goldoni had a marked dislike for the drivers of public conveyances whom he considered to be chosen from 'the most ill-mannered and vulgar of fellows'. But thanks to his regime and Master Robert's *Traité*, he usually managed to avoid them by walking which he still greatly enjoyed, not only in Paris, but also at Belleville, Passy and Clignacour.

But he did suffer from what he describes as 'palpitations'. 'They surprise me several times during the year, at all hours and weathers, before, during and after meals, but rarely during the night.' When an attack was about to come on he felt a movement in his bowels, his pulse quickened with alarming violence, his muscles were in convulsion and his heart was 'oppressed.' Such symptoms, one would think, would be enough to carry off most men of his age or even younger, but not Goldoni who never lost his calmness in front of even the most violent manifestations. When the attack ended he just felt a jolt in the head and his pulse suddenly became normal. He even had one attack in his late seventies which, he says, lasted uninterruptedly for thirty-six hours; this 'seemed to be serious', and so he went to a doctor who put him right for the occasion. Normally, however, he did nothing about it. 'Accustomed to this inconvenience, more disconcerting than painful, I had learned to bear it without fear. Thus I sought means to distract myself. If it assailed me at table, I continued the dinner; if it surprised me in company, I went on playing cards. Nobody was aware of my state, and since at my age one must learn to live with one's enemies, I sought no means to cure it for fear of falling upon Scylla to avoid Charybdis.'*

Nor was all well with Nicoletta. On leaving the court, which had never suited her anyway, she had had an attack of pleurisy, and its effects had stayed with her. 'Many of my friends', wrote Goldoni, 'go to the country in the summer while I stay in Paris. I should be very happy to pass a few days with some or other of my friends, but the uncertain state of my wife's health forbids me to go far from her.' And he adds a little tribute which those who gloat over his infidelities prefer to overlook. 'My poor wife has shown me so great consideration that I must also show consideration for her.'

Goldoni, as he said, did not suffer from insomnia, but 'It happens to me as it happens to everybody that occasionally my mind is obsessed with a thought which delays sleep. In this case I have a sure remedy, and here it is.' In fact it was a remedy that he must have had to hand for all of thirty years, for it was in the 1758 preface to *Le massere* (*The maidservants*) that he had first promised his public a dictionary of Venetian dialect. Alas, he never wrote it, but he did extract from it a number of verbal sheep to jump over his nocturnal fences.

*Medical opinion is somewhat baffled by this and doctors, faced with the symptoms, say they would have to see the patient to give an accurate diagnosis. One doctor, however, suggested that the cause could have been a tumour.

'Whenever I feel my spirit disturbed for some reason, I select at random a word from my native dialect, I translate it into Tuscan and French; then in the same way I pass in review the words that follow it in alphabetical order. I am sure to be asleep by the third or fourth word. My sleeping draught has never failed.'

Goldoni had always been generous to a fault – one has only to remember the prompt and loving consent he gave to the adoption of the two children of his hapless brother, Gian Paolo; and this generosity did not wain when the cold winds of age, poverty and ill-health began to blow about him. In his eighties he translated various works, dedicating the entire proceeds to indigent compatriots or friends. When that same retired actress turned novelist, Marie-Jeanne Laborras de Mézières, was widowed and living in very straitened circumstances, Goldoni – at the age of eighty-four, with the French Revolution raging about his head and his own pension in imminent danger of being withdrawn – calmly settled down to translate into Italian a novel of hers called *La storia di Miss Jenny.* It was his last literary work, and while he was engaged upon it there occurred the death of another great artist of the eighteenth century whose genius was not entirely alien to that of Goldoni at his best – Wolfgang Amadeus Mozart.

Another characteristic which never deserted him was his passionate interest in life about him, and the latter chapters of the *Mémoires* are crammed with details about the births, marriages and deaths of the nobility and the royal family and about the life and institutions of Paris.

He writes of the Louvre in which commissioned works could then be seen and adds, in a typically Goldonian aside, 'There are those who commission painters and sculptors so that in the catalogue may be written "This picture was painted for Monsieur So-and-so", "This bust was sculpted for Madame So-and-so". And there are some who have their portraits painted so that their faces may be seen in the *Salon.'*

He chronicles the furore that blew up when the Duc de Chartres ordered that celebrated avenue of trees in the Palais Royale to be cut down. The whole of Paris was in an uproar, he said. 'People lamented that magnificent avenue in which huge crowds had gathered on fine days, where the beauties of Paris had paraded their charms, the young men had run risks and found fortunes, and the prudent had sometimes amused themselves at the expense of the heedless. Every tree that fell was a painful blow in the souls of the spectators.' But Goldoni was no sentimentalist – except when he thought it would pay him to be, as in *Pamela.* In his early days in Paris when he had had an apartment over the Palais Royale his window had looked out directly over the famous chestnut tree known as the Cracow tree. Now, some quarter of a century later, he happened to be there when that same tree was cut down. 'Pushing through the crowd,' he said, 'I was lucky enough to be able to seize a branch which still had some leaves, and, taking it into the house of an acquaintance of mine, I saw all the ladies about to cry and the gentlemen in a fury. Everyone was inveighing against those who had destroyed it, but I was secretly laughing, for I had faith in the new project, and I was not wrong.' Though perhaps we, who know only too well what the wholesale cutting-down of trees can mean, would rather be on the side of the weeping ladies and the furious gentlemen.

Another aspect of Parisian life he touches on casts an indirect light on his own straitened circumstances which he never consciously reveals in the *Mémoires*. The gambling mania, which had played such a large part in the life of Goldoni and his Venice, hit Paris, and the French Government banned it, partly, it seemed, on the persuasion of a book called *De la passion de jeu depuis les temps anciens jusqu'à nos jours*. This somewhat severe tome denounced both heavy public gambling, and private card games for small stakes. Politely, wittily and – if you read between the lines – rather pathetically, Goldoni disagrees. 'It seems that small games have become necessary. One cannot pass the evening without doing anything. After the news of the day, after the scandal at the expense of one's neighbours and friends, one must perforce turn to play. It is an honest pastime, a pleasant occupation, but not everybody enjoys themselves in the same way; this depends on differences of character. There are the mildest of people, courteous and pleasant in the extreme, who altogether change in tone, character and even physiognomy at the card table. A generous man sometimes flies into a rage over a modest loss; not because of the money, he says, but for *amour propre*. This may well be; but I, too, play, and to be sincere I prefer to win six francs rather than lose them. I note exactly my gains and losses, and I am very happy when, at the end of the month, my accounts show a few crowns to the good. And this is not my *amour propre* which is flattered; but a louis more or less in my purse makes a small difference which in turn involves either a small pleasure or a small sacrifice.' And then having unwittingly revealed to his reader that he was by then in such a state that a louis more or less *did* make a difference to him, he concludes in typically Goldonian fashion, 'I am speaking for myself; nobody can apply to himself what I say or think.'

He had been keenly following the fads and fancies of the Parisians for many years – indeed long before he left the court – and was much interested by the visit, in 1778, of Franz Anton Mesmer, the Austrian doctor who had invented the doctrine of animal magnetism and the healing of all disease by touch. 'Nothing more delightful', comments Goldoni, 'than to get one's health back without the disgust of medicine.' He also watched the first balloon ascents with a touch of indulgent cynicism. 'M. Montgolfier was the first to hurl such a globe into the air; this globe rose until it was out of sight, flew where the wind took it, and kept up until the flame and smoke that fuelled it went out.' And of the men who later flew in the little baskets, he wrote, 'I cannot see them without trembling. Besides, what is the point of the risk, the courage? If one is obliged to fly according to the direction of the wind, if one cannot steer oneself, the discovery will remain admirable, but useless. It will always be a game.'

Paris, like so many other cities that had nothing better to occupy their minds, was swept by a passion for the supernatural and – with more gullibility than any capital has a right to show – raised a subscription to bring a man from Lyons who claimed that he could walk bare-foot across the Seine. Predictably, having pocketed the subscription money, the man didn't turn up. But three years later, no doubt impelled by this example, a man arrived who did in fact cross the Seine on foot in the presence of an enormous crowd. But he was careful that nobody should see what he had on his feet. Some form of floating equipment, Goldoni assumes, adding that the whole thing is quite impractical anyway as it is much easier to cross a river by boat.

In February of the same year that Mesmer came to Paris, Voltaire – the undisputed intellectual monarch of Europe – arrived there from his country home at Ferney. And Goldoni, together with practically the whole of intellectual and artistic Paris, went to pay tribute at the house where he was staying – the home of the Marquis de Villette, the husband of an adopted daughter of Voltaire's. The mystery about this visit is why it had never been paid before. Voltaire had been Goldoni's most illustrious and faithful admirer and supporter for over a quarter of a century. His verses of praise, written in honour of Goldoni, represented a decisive shot in the Goldoni—Gozzi—Chiari battle, and it was partly thanks to Voltaire's unstinted praise that Goldoni was famous beyond Italy. Nor had the great man's enthusiasm waned over the years. When *Le bourru bienfaisant* first appeared, Voltaire wrote, 'Un vieux malade de 78 ans, presque aveugle, vient de recevoir le charmant phenonène d'une comédie française très gaie, très purement écrite, très morale, composée par un Italien. Cet Italien est fait pour donner dans tous les pays des modèles de bon goût.'

Goldoni had been invited by Voltaire on more than one occasion and could easily have paid a visit sixteen years before in 1762 on his way to Paris. He claimed that he did not do so because he was so anxiously awaited in Paris by the *Comédie Italienne.* but that had not stopped him from lingering in Lyons for fifteen days, accepting invitations from total strangers. To Voltaire himself he gave the somewhat odd excuse that he was accompanied by his wife and Voltaire, most charmingly and wittingly, took him up on this. 'Il caro Goldoni, il figlio della natura, veut donc me laisser mourir sans me donner la consolation de le voir. Il m'a écrit de Lyons, qu'il n'avait pu passer chez moi parce qu'il a sa femme: mais certainement je ne lui aurais pa pris sa femme et je les aurais reçu tous deux avec autant d'empressement qu'il le sera ailleurs.' The reason for the delay and Goldoni's feeble excuses must remain a mystery; it is conceivable that Goldoni, who was always modest about his own intellectual capacities, was a trifle in awe of Voltaire.

The reception accorded by Parisian society to the great man was overwhelming. Every day several hundred people crowded into the house of his adopted daughter, and the strain was so great that he collapsed at the end of a week, but against his doctor's orders he continued to receive all comers. Goldoni called on 17th February 1778 and, thanks to the *Journal de Paris*, we have a brief account of the meeting. Voltaire renewed his praise of Goldoni as the restorer of grace and good taste to Italy. 'We were dumbfounded,' wrote François de Neufchâteau in his piece in the *Journal*, 'to see M. de Voltaire speaking Italian with as much ease and facility as he spoke French. M. Goldoni increased our amazement by informing us that once M. Voltaire had written him a letter, not only in Italian, but in Venetian dialect.' Less than three months after this encounter Voltaire was dead. In the *Mémoires* Goldoni suggests that it was the transfer from the peace of Ferney to the hurly-burly of Paris that precipitated his end. 'Alas!' he says, 'the *dulcis amor patriae* had seduced him away, and philosophy had surrendered to nature.'

In the same year Rousseau also fell off the perch, and Goldoni, if he had been given to much speculation, might have begun to ruminate on the imminence of his own departure, but he was far too interested in the goings-on about him, the gossips, the journals, the institutions of Paris, the doings of the great. Even the theatre. But it is clear from the *Mémoires* that his interest here is academic rather than passionate; he writes of the theatre rather as he writes of the *Académie Royale de Chirurgie* to which he also dedicates a study. For the sad truth was that as a man of the theatre he was a back number. His work was scarcely seen at all.

Un curioso accidente was put on at the *Théâtre Italien* in 1786 and was a resounding flop. Goldoni assigns part of the blame to the translation which is odd as there is good reason to believe that the translator was none other than Goldoni himself. But there is a revealing and highly Goldonian aftermath to this failure. 'I had given some people balcony and stall tickets for the first night,' he writes, 'but nobody called to tell me how it had gone – a bad sign. However, I went to bed without any news of the result, and it was my barber the next day who, with tears in his eyes, told me the details of this clamorous failure. I withdrew the play without delay; and as I was feeling particularly well, that day I dined with excellent appetite.' The years had worked no radical changes in his character; this was the same Goldoni who, exactly fifty-three years before, after the fiasco of his *Amalasunta* and its ceremonial consignment to the flames, 'began to reflect that whatever disasters had befallen me, I had never before gone without my supper'.

An earlier project for staging *Le bourru bienfaisant* was put off no less than three times to make way for Beaumarchais' *Le mariage de Figaro,* and although *Le bourru* remained in the repertoire of the *Comédie Française* until 1848, it was never again put on during the author's lifetime. It was not in Goldoni's nature to bear grudges, but this might conceivably have accounted for his somewhat cool attitude towards Beaumarchais whom he damns with faint praise. 'Nobody better than M. de Beaumarchais knows the defects of his work. He has given proof of his talent in this *genre,* and if he had wished to make his *Figaro* a comedy according to the rules of art, he would have done it as well as anybody else; but he only wished to entertain the public, and in this he succeeded perfectly.' Coming from Goldoni this is downright hypocritical. And later, of *Le mariage* and *Le barbier de Séville*, he had the face to say, 'Connoisseurs and lovers of the fine *genre* made loud lament over these works which, in their opinion, were only designed to lower the level of the French theatre.'

'In these *Mémoires* of mine I go by leaps and starts,' wrote Goldoni and, in the Parisian part at least, he most certainly did. The reason is that in these last thirty years of his life there is no underlying, harmonic chronology. It is all chit-chat, often highly diverting and an excellent though superficial portrait of the world about him. With one major exception there is no outstanding event between his departure from Venice and his departure from the world, except, of course, for the French Revolution which hardly counts as Goldoni cannot in any real sense be said to have been even aware of it. The exception is the composition of the *Mémoires,* or to give them their full title *Mémoires de M. Goldoni, pour servir à l'histoire de sa vie, et à celle de son théâtre, dédiés au Roi.*

The *Mémoires* were written in French between 1784 and 1787 and published in three volumes in August of the year of their completion *chez la veuve Duchesne libraire, rue S. Jaccques temple du goût.* In his preface to the work Goldoni explains, with what one might consider to be an excess of modesty, his reason for writing it. 'The story of my life offers no particular interest; but maybe, sometime or other, in the corner of an old library, somebody will come across a collection of my works. And then curiosity may be aroused to know who was this singular man who proposed the theatrical reform of his country, who staged and printed 150 comedies, in verse, in prose, of character and of plot, and who saw in his own lifetime eighteen editions of his theatrical works.'

Why were the *Mémoires* written in French? The simple answer is that he was aiming principally, if not exclusively, at a French market. Moreover, after nearly quarter of a century he had gained a dexterity in the language of which he was probably rather proud. His compatriots have never been slow in claiming that the real reason was that he didn't trust his Italian. 'And very rightly, too,' they add with (usually Florentine) malice. But they miss the point; the prose style of the *Mémoires* is no more important than that of the plays, and it was never remotely the vocation of Goldoni – as it was of Dante and Manzoni – to forge a language.

Another, and superficially more solidly founded criticism, is that the *Mémoires* are wildly inaccurate, and here there is ample ammunition to be fired at him. 'This is what I have to say to my readers,' he says at the end of his preface. 'I beg them to read my book and do me the courtesy to believe me.' But his readers must politely beg to be excused. He gets his dates wrong, both of historical events and of the composition and production of his own plays; he even mistakes the date of his departure for Paris, and he frequently mixes up people and events. According to him, his paternal grandfather had an uncle who was, in fact, his brother, was married to two women he never knew, and finally died nine years after the actual date of his decease. These mistakes, of course, could be put down to old age and absent-mindedness. But then there is the apparently more serious charge of the stories which were deliberately falsified, like the tale of the examination which, in his telling of it, he passed so triumphantly in the face of terrible odds, whereas in fact he was failed. And these errors may be pardoned, too, by all but the most pedantically-minded readers, on the grounds that a well-rounded story is more entertaining than an if-and-a-but-and-a-might-have-been story. But basically those who criticize the book because of its errors and distortions (and in Italy there are battalions of them who look upon it as an Italian text-book gone raving mad) are missing the point every bit as much as those who condemn Goldoni for his lack of prose *finesse*.

The real point is that it is one of the most entertaining autobiographies ever written and that, on the only level that really matters, it reveals the truth about its author and the people and places about him far more clearly than thousands of other books which are superficially more accurate. Gibbon, after reading it, said that Goldoni's life was vastly more entertaining than his plays — a back-handed compliment, but true enough as far as some of the plays are concerned. Even Indro Montanelli who (as the Italians put it) has no hairs on his tongue, says, 'The *Mémoires* reproduce all Goldoni's defects: they are unreliable, thrown off slap-dash, full of inaccurate references and mistaken dates. But these defects are amply made up for by the vivacity, the immediacy, the accuracy of observation, and that good-natured humour which constituted his fascination as a man.'

The immediacy. This is perhaps the key-word to the immortal quality of the *Mémoires*. Just as in the best of the plays, he takes you by the hand and leads you into his own time and world. Nobody who has read the account of the escape from Rimini to Chioggia with the actors, or the interview with Vivaldi or that with Rousseau (to mention only three examples) can ever for the rest of their lives entirely escape the impression that they were personally present at those events. At one point in the third volume this sense of immediacy is heightened in a different but no less startling way. It happens like this. In the twenty-seventh chapter of the third volume, he is writing tranquilly away about the advent in Paris of the Italian composer, Piccinni, and the warfare between the supporters of Piccinni and Gluck, when he suddenly cries out (and it seems a cry rather rather than a printed word), 'Alas! At this moment I am being struck by a violent palpitation . . . by now it is an ailment common to me; I cannot go on writing . . .' So the reader is able to have the doubtful pleasure of being present at the very moment when Goldoni is seized by an attack of his mysterious malady. The next day he picks up where he left off. 'Now I take up again the chapter interrupted yesterday. This time my palpitation was more violent and longer than usual; it struck me at four in the evening, and did not cease until two in the morning.'

One striking omission in the *Mémoires* adds much to one's appreciation of Goldoni's character. The long, literary squabble in Venice, which reached such extremes of hysterical virulence, occupied a fair part of his life and thoughts, but never once in his autobiography does he name the three men who libelled him for so long with such prolonged and vicious malice — Chiari, Gozzi and Baretti. In this it may be said of him that he made no claim to Christianity, but merely demonstrated it in his life.

Perhaps nowhere does Goldoni reveal himself more clearly than in the closing paragraph of the *Mémoires*. After conceding that criticism of his plays might lead to their improvement, he adds that criticism of his autobiography would be useless because it is not intended as literature, but merely as a statement of the truth. 'If, however, some writer wished to write about me for the sole purpose of wounding me, he would be wasting his time. I am peaceful by nature, I have always kept my *sang froid*; at my age I read little, and I only read entertaining books.'

The *Mémoires* were a tremendous success. The king bought fifty copies, the queen twenty-five and the courtiers seventy-two. Catherine of Russia had twenty-four sent out to her. And they have gone on delighting readers ever since. Only in Italy today are they almost totally unread, for they have suffered that worst of all deaths that a masterpiece can undergo; they have been turned into a text-book, suitably bowdlerized and with all the most famous 'beauty-spots' indicated for the benefit of duller pupils.

While Goldoni was dictating the last pages of the book to Nicoletta, he had a visit from the Italian poet Vittorio Alfieri, who had come on a recommendation from Goldoni's old friend, the Marquis Albergati. One has the amusing impression that behind the dense clouds of exquisite courtesy neither man had the remotest impression of the other's genius. Goldoni wrote one of those schoolboyish little essays which say all the right things in all the wrong ways, a habit of his when faced with something that was beyond him. And Alfieri merely tells Albergati in a letter that he had visited 'that nice old gentleman'; indeed, the encounter made so little impression on him that he didn't even mention it in his own autobiography.

In spite of his love of women, Goldoni had always been something of a club-man, liking occasionally to relax in entirely masculine society, and this habit stayed with him into his extreme old age. Most of the members of that club which had been formed in his early Parisian days, for the enjoyment of good food, drink and conversation at the homes of the various members on Sundays, had fallen off their perches, but in 1790 three still continued to meet regularly. There was Goldoni himself and a certain M. de la Place who were both eighty-three and Charles Simon Favart, the famous librettist and admirer of Goldoni, who might have described himself as 'a mere youngster of eighty'.

There is in existence a little poem in which Favart invited 'his' *très-cher* Goldoni to luncheon; many better works have been lost to posterity, but few more touching ones can have been preserved for it. After a flourishing panegyric in which Favart drags out yet again that lamentable *'Molière d'Italie'*, he concludes:

> Mon coeur, d'estime pénétré,
> T'adresse aujourd'hui sa requète
> Pour venir demain vendredi,
> Quatre du mois, sur le midi.

One hopes they had a pleasant meal.

Rather than suggest that the French Revolution took Goldoni by surprise, it would be more accurate to say that he was unaware of its existence. Indeed, for three years the two went their own ways, the one peacefully, the other most bloodily. Only in 1792 did they become aware of each other, for in July of that year Goldoni's pension was stopped, and the rest of his few remaining days were spent in acute penury.

In contemplating the death of Goldoni one is forcibly reminded of the saying about old soldiers, for it is a slow fading away. After the publication of the *Mémoires*, the news and documents concerning him get fewer and fewer until they come to a stop altogether. There is a letter, dated 26th March 1791, in which he says that he didn't feel like going out as he had hoped because although he had taken a purgative the day before, he was a little nervous of the wind and hadn't altogether recovered from a previous indisposition. But he recovered and, eight months later, was most characteristically ordering from a certain Madame Fontain eight pounds of chocolate and three of *diablotins*. He continued more or less his old self well into 1792, for in August of that year there is a record of his dining with the Venetian ambassador. But some days after that he fell ill and probably never left his bed again, though in another letter written during this period he declares that the only good things left to him were 'a valorous stomach and a sensitive heart'. Appropriately enough, this is the last news we have from his own pen.

Nothing is known of the cause or manner of his death, but Nicoletta and their adopted son, Antonio, were by his bed when it overtook him at six o'clock in the evening of 6th February 1793, just two weeks after Louis XVI had gone to the guillotine. His death is recorded in the archives of the municipality of Paris. 'Du mardi dix neuf février mil sept cent quatrevingt treize, l'an second de la République. Acte de décès de Charles Goldoni, du six de ce mois, six heures de soir, agé de quatrevingt six ans, homme de loi, auteur dramatique, domicilié à Paris rue Pavèe Saint-Sauveur n. l, section de Bonconseil, et résident dans cette ville depuis environ trente ans, natif de Venise, marié à Nicole Connio, native de Gènes il y a environ cinquante ans.'

Ironically enough, on 7th February, Marie Joseph Chénier, brother of the guillotined poet, André, unaware of Goldoni's death the previous day, persuaded the authorities to restore his pension on the ground that Goldoni had never ceased to thank heaven that he was able to die 'French and Republican'. Whatever he might have felt about being French (which he wasn't), it seems improbable that Goldoni would have felt any overwhelming gratitude about being Republican.

He was buried in the little cemetery of Sainte Catherine, but when this was dug up in 1820, his bones were thrown into a common grave. He left no will for materially there was nothing to leave, and poor Nicoletta was pestered by creditors until she left the rue Pavée Saint-Sauveur for other lodgings in Paris, where she died two years after Carlo on 9th January, 1795.

Eighty-four years after Goldoni's death two enthusiastic Venetians caused a plaque to be put up on a building which they believed to be on the site of rue Pavée Saint-Sauveur n. 1 (today 22-23 rue Tiquetonne). It says 'Ici est décédé pauvre le 6 février 1793 CHARLES GOLDONI dit le Molière italien, auteur du Bourru Bienfaisant, né a Venise l'an 1707.'

The fact that the invidious comparison with Molière should thus have been perpetuated, that the *Bourru* is by no means one of his best plays, and that the plaque is almost certainly on the wrong house would scarcely have disturbed Goldoni. He was, as he said, peaceful by nature and always kept his *sang froid*. And he never cared much about accuracy anyway.

The comedies, tragedies, tragi-comedies, operatic libretti, musical intermezzi, scenarios and *opéras bouffes* of Carlo Goldoni

Comedy, without title and now lost, composed during the author's boyhood
Il buon padre, comedy of unknown date
La cantatrice, verse comedy of unknown date
Amalasunta, opera libretto, 1732
Il Gondoliere Veneziano, intermezzo, 1733
Belisario, tragi-comedy in verse, 1734
La pupilla, intermezzo, 1734
Rosmonda, verse tragedy, 1734
La birba, intermezzo, 1734
Griselda, verse tragedy, 1734
La fondazione di Venezia, opéra bouffe, c. 1734
Il quartiere fortunato, intermezzo, 1734-44
Don Giovanni Tenorio, o il dissoluto, comedy 1736
Rinaldo di Montalbano, tragi-comedy, 1736
Enrico Re di Sicilia, verse tragedy, 1736
El cortesan, o l'uomo di mondo, comedy 1738
Gustavo, opera libretto, c. 1738
Tonin Bella Grazia, o il frappatore, comedy, 1738
Il prodigo, comedy, 1739
Le trentadue disgrazie d'Arlecchino, scenario, 1739
Cento e quattro accidenti in una notte, o la notte critica, scenario, 1739

Oronte, re de' Sciti, opera libretto, 1740
La bancarotta, comedy, 1740
Statira, opera libretto, c. 1740
Il mondo della luna, comedy, c. 1741
Il figlio d'Arlecchino perduto e ritrovato, part scenario part dialogue, c. 1741
I due gemelli veneziani, comedy, 1747
L'uomo prudente, comedy, 1748
La vedova scaltra, comedy, 1748
La putta onorata, comedy, 1748
La favola dei tre gobbi, opéra bouffe, 1748
La buona moglie, comedy, 1749
Il cavaliere e la dama, o i cicisbei, comedy, 1749
Il servitore di due padroni, comedy, 1749
La famiglia dell'antiquario, o la suocera e la nuora, comedy, 1749
L'avvocato veneziano, comedy, 1749
Il padre di famiglia, comedy, c. 1749

The following sixteen comedies were produced as a result of the famous challenge and staged at the Teatro Sant'Angelo in Venice during the 1750-1 season:
Il teatro comico
Le femmine puntigliose
La bottega del caffe
Il bugiardo
L'adulatore
Il poeta fanatico
Pamela
Il cavalier di buon gusto
Il giocatore
Il vero amico
La finta ammalata
La moglie saggia
L'incognita perseguitata
L'avventuriere onorato
La donna volubile
I pettegolezzi della donne

The next four comedies, though written in 1751, belong to the season following the challenge:
L'erede fortunata
Molière
L'amante militare
La castalda

Il feudatario, comedy 1752
La figlia obbediente, comedy, 1752
La serva amorosa, comedy, 1752
Le donne gelose, comedy, 1752
I puntigli domestici, comedy, 1752
I mercatanti, comedy 1753
Le donne curiose, comedy, 1753
Il contrattempo, o il chiacchierone, comedy, 1753
La locandiera, comedy 1753
La donna vendicativa, comedy, 1753
Il geloso avaro, comedy, 1753
La donna di testa debole, comedy, 1753
La sposa persiana, comedy, 1753
La cameriera brillante, comedy, 1753
La maschera, part scenario part dialogue, 1753
Ircana in Julfa, verse comedy, 1754
Ircana in Isaphan, verse comedy, 1754
Il filosofo inglese, verse comedy, 1754
Il vecchio bizzarro, comedy, 1754
Il festino, verse comedy, 1754
Terenzio, verse comedy, 1754
L'Impostore, comedy, 1754
La peruviana, verse comedy, 1754
La madre amorosa, comedy, 1755
Le massere, verse comedy, 1755
Il cavalier giocondo, verse comedy, 1755
Le donne de casa soa, verse comedy, 1755
Torquato Tasso, verse comedy, 1755
La bella selvaggia, verse comedy, 1755
La buona famiglia, comedy, 1755
La villeggiatura, comedy, 1756
Il medico olandese, comedy, 1756
Il campiello, verse comedy, 1756
La dalmatina, verse comedy, 1756
La donna capricciosa, verse comedy, 1756
L'avaro, comedy, 1756
Il buon compatrioto, part scenario part dialogue, 1756
La pupilla, verse comedy, 1756
Il padre per amore, verse comedy, 1757
L'amante di se stesso, o l'egoista, verse comedy, 1757
La vedova spiritosa, comedy, 1757
La donna sola, verse comedy, 1757
La madre amorosa, comedy, 1757

Il cavaliere di spirito, verse comedy, 1757
La donna forte, verse comedy, 1758
Il ricco insidiato, comedy, 1758
La donna di governo, comedy, 1758
La sposa sagace, verse comedy, 1758
Lo spirito di contraddizione, verse comedy, 1758
Pamela maritata, comedy, 1758
Le morbinose, verse comedy, 1758
La donna bizzarra, verse comedy, 1758
L'apatista, o l'indifferente, verse comedy, 1758
I morbinosi, verse comedy, 1759
Gl'innamorati, comedy, 1759
La scuola di ballo, verse comedy, 1759
Gli amori di Alessandro Magno, verse tragedy, 1759
Un curioso accidente, comedy, 1760
La donna di maneggio, comedy, 1760
L'impresario delle Smirne, comedy, 1760
La guerra, comedy, 1760
I rusteghi, comedy, 1760
Enea nel Lazio, verse tragedy, 1760
Nerone, verse tragedy, 1760
Le smanie della villeggiatura, comedy, 1761
Le avventure della villeggiatura, comedy, 1761
Il ritorno dalla villegiatura, comedy, 1761
La buona madre, comedy, 1761
La casa nova, comedy, 1761
Le baruffe chiozzote, comedy, 1762
Sior Todero Brontolon, comedy, 1762
La scozzese, comedy, 1762
Una delle ultime sere di carnevale, comedy, 1762
L'osteria della posta, one-act comedy, 1762
L'amor paterno, o la serva riconoscente, comedy, 1762
I due fratelli rivali, one-act scenario, 1762
Arlecchino, erede ridicolo, scenario, 1762
La famiglia in discordia, one-act scenario, 1763
Il ventaglio, comedy, 1763
Les amours d'Arlequin et de Camille, scenario, 1763
La jalousie d'Arlequin, scenario, 1763
Les inquiétudes de Camille, scenario, 1763
L'amore paterno, comedy, 1763
Les amours de Zelinda et de Lindoro, scenario, 1764
La jalousie de Lindoro, scenario, 1764
Les inquiétudes de Zelinda, scenario, 1764

Gli amanti timidi, comedy, 1766
Il genio buono ed il genio cattivo, pantomime, 1768
Le bourru bienfaisant, comedy, 1771
L'avare fastueux, comedy, 1776
Le due italiane, comedy, never performed
La schiava generosa, comedy, never performed
La guerra de' Bergamaschi, five-act spectacle, never performed
Artemisia, verse tragedy, never performed
Tal padrona, tal serva, comedy, never performed
I nastri di color rosa, one-act comedy, never performed
Amor fa l'uomo cieco, intermezzo, uncertain date
Il disinganno, intermezzo, uncertain date

The following *Commedia dell'Arte* scenarios were written during Goldoni's first Parisian years:
L'inganno vendicato
Il ritratto d'Arlecchino
L'appuntamento notturno
L'inimicizia d'Arlecchino e di Scapino
Arlecchino e Camilla schiavi in Barbaria
Arlecchino carbonaio
L'anello magico
Le cinque età d'Arlecchino

Goldoni's *opéras bouffes* were performed up and down Italy and changed at the whim of actors and musicians. The published versions that exist today bear little resemblance to the originals. The *opéras bouffes* are inserted in the chronological list of works when dates of first performances are known. These are the others:
La buona figliuola
Il festino
I viaggiatori ridicoli
Vittorina
Il re alla caccia
La bouillotte
I volponi
Il filosofo di càmpagna
Gli uccellatori
Arcifanfano, Re de' matti
Il mercato di Malmantile
L'isola disabitata
La calamità de' cuori
Il negligente
La buona figliuola maritata

I bagni d'Abano
Le virtuose ridicole
L'Arcadia in Brenta
Il finto principe
L'astuzia felice
Bertoldo, Bertoldino e Cacasenno
I portentosi effetti della madre natura
Lucrezia romana
Il mondo alla rovescia
Buovo d'Antona
Il paese della cuccagna
La mascherata
Le pescatrici
Il conte Caramella
La donna di governo
Le nozze
La fiera di Sinigaglia

Bibliography

Accademia Nazionale dei Lincei, *Goldoni in Francia* (1972)

Giuseppe Baretti: *An account of the manners and customs of Italy; with observations on the mistakes of some travellers, with regard to that country* (London, 1768); *Grammatica della lingua inglese* (Leghorn, 1794); *Dizionario delle lingue italiana ed inglese* (Venice, 1795); *La Frusta Letteraria* (Venice, 1763-5)

Francesco Bartoli, *Comici italiani* (Padua, 1782)

William Beckford, *Italy* (1834)

Marino Berengo, *La società veneta alla fine del settecento* (Florence, 1956)

Charles de Brosses, *L'Italie* (Paris, 1836)

Giulio Caprini, *Carlo Goldoni, la sua vita, le sue opere* (Treves, Milan, 1907)

Mario Cevolotto, *Carlo Goldoni, avvocato veneto* (Cappelli, Bologna, 1931)

H .C. Chatfield-Taylor, *Goldoni* (New York, 1913)

Pietro Chiari, *Commedie da camera* (Venice, 1771)

Lucio D'Ambra, *L'autore delle duecento commedie (Carlo Goldoni)* (Zanichelli, Bologna, 1936)

Dizionario enciclopedico italiano, Treccani (Rome, 1955)

Luigi Ferrante, *Goldoni* (Sansoni, Milan, 1971)

Ugo Fugagnollo, *Venezia Cosi* (Mursia, Milan, 1969)

Gazzetta di Venezia (Venice, 4th October 1927)

I Giganti, Carlo Goldoni (Mondadori, Milan, 1969)

Wolfgang Goethe, *Italienische reise* (Leipzig, 1925)

Carlo Goldoni: *Mémoires de M. Goldoni, pour servir à l'histoire de sa vie, et a celle de son théatre, dédiés au Roi* (Paris, 1787); *Memorie* (Einaudi, Turin, 1967); *Opere complete di Carlo Goldoni* (Venice, 1936-8); *Opere di Carlo Goldoni* (Edizione Pasquali, Venice, 1761-78); *Commedie* (Einaudi, Turin, 1966)

Carlo Gozzi: *Memorie inutili* (1797); *Le Fiabe* (Bologna, 1884)

Gasparo Gozzi: *Opere* (Padua, 1818); *La Gazzetta Veneta* (Sansoni, Florence, 1957)

Timothy Holme, *Gondola, Gondolier* (Gentry Books, London, 1971)

Lettere italiane (Padua 1957)

Jacques Levron, *Daily life at Versailles* (George Allen and Unwin, London, 1962)

Vittorio Malamani, *Il settecento a Venezia* (Turin, 1891-2)

Miscellanea Goldoniana and *Miscellanea Maddalena* (theatrical library, Goldoni's house, Venice)

Pompeo Molmenti, *Venezia nella vita privata* (Bergamo, 1905-8)

Indro Montanelli and Roberto Gervaso, *L'Italia del settecento* (Rizzoli, Milan, 1970)

Lacy C. Morley, *Giuseppe Baretti* (John Murray, London, 1909)

Carola Oman, *David Garrick* (Hodder and Stoughton, London, 1958)

Vito Pandolfi, *Storia del teatro* (utet, turin, 1964)

Giuseppe Petronio, *Goldoni* (Palumbo, Palermo, 1962)

Guido Piovene, *Viaggio in Italia* (Mondadori, Milan, 1957)

Luigi Rasi, *I comici italiani* (Florence, 1897)

Maurice Rowdon, *The Fall of Venice* (Weidenfeld and Nicolson, 1970)

Maurice Vaussard, *Daily life in Eighteenth-century Italy* (George Allen and Unwin, London, 1962)

Index